Ellis Sharp

SHARPLY CRITICAL
SELECTED ESSAYS AND REVIEWS

London
***Jet*stone**
2017

A ***Jets*tone**paperback original.

ISBN 9781910858110

The right of Ellis Sharp to be identified as author in this work has been asserted in accordance with the Copyright, Designs and Patents Act, 1988.

© Ellis Sharp, 2017.
All rights reserved.

All unauthorised reproduction is hereby prohibited. This work is protected by law. It should not be duplicated or distributed, in whole or in part, by any means whatsoever, without the prior permission of the Publisher.

Cover design by The Ever Shifting Subject.

Contents

Part One: Novels and Novelists — 9

Part Two: At History's Edge — 40

Part Three: The Iraq War and Ian McEwan's 'Ambivalence' — 83

Part Four: Pure Wizardry: Aharon Appelfeld and Amos Oz — 129

Part Five: Shakespearean — 164

Part Six: At the Movies — 184

Part Seven: Giving Up — 196

Down with literary supermen!
      V. I. Lenin, *Novaya Zhizn*, No. 12 (November 13, 1905)

A Note on the Text

This assemblage of reviews and essays represents a selection of material from my defunct and vanished blogs *The Sharp Side* and *Barbaric Document* in the period 2003 to 2007. These were occasional pieces, usually written at speed. Quite often they referred to online material which is now no longer available. Internet publication is a fragile medium, with material deleted either by its authors or by outside forces. I have largely resisted the temptation to revise the original texts which are republished here, though I have occasionally made cuts.

Ellis Sharp, April 2017

Part One: Novels and Novelists

What is *Jane Eyre* About?

There's a silly article by Tanya Gold in today's *Guardian* (24 March 2005) about *Jane Eyre*. The gist of her piece is deeply unoriginal. It is not exactly news that Mrs Gaskell's biographical account of Charlotte Brontë is a travesty or that Haworth displays the cult of literary personality at its most fatuous. Nor is it a revelation that *Jane Eyre* projects Charlotte Brontë's fantasies about M. Heger, the headmaster of the school in Brussels where she worked. Just about everything that Tanya Gold says has already been said much more fluently and intelligently in Lucasta Miller's *The Brontë Myth*.

Tanya Gold, writing in the over-heated style that masquerades as journalism in a newspaper with a circulation that continues to plummet, calls *Jane Eyre* 'the dirtiest, darkest, most depraved fantasy of all time'. Obviously Ms Gold has never read the Marquis de Sade, let alone *Naked Lunch*. What bothers me is not her lack of originality or her attention-seeking slovenly style but her errors of fact and her failure to engage with the significance of *Jane Eyre*.

According to Gold: 'Contemporary critics had been appalled by Jane Eyre's 'coarseness', but the public was thrilled and Charlotte was a celebrity.' This simply isn't true. Although there were one or two hostile reviews the overwhelming majority were very, very favourable.

At the end of the third edition of *Jane Eyre* the 'Opinions of the press' were reprinted. They make interesting reading.

Fraser's Magazine praised the novel for the plot and 'the enchantment'. *Atlas* gushed that it was 'a book to make the pulses gallop and the heart beat, and to fill the eyes with tears'. *Critic* adored the 'riveting' plot. *The Economist* praised the fresh style, characterisation, and gripping plot. The Catholic *Tablet* liked its representation of the development of a mind, including 'the restraint, direction, and subduing' and the 'pearls of thought and sentiment' attached to the plot, concluding: 'The reading of such a book as this is a healthful exercise, and we sincerely hope may prove as attractive as it must be profitable.' *Jerrold's Newspaper* concurred in finding the novel wholesome, remarking 'it is edifying from its moral truth and beauty; and it is absorbingly interesting on account of the originality, vigour, and moral edification aforesaid'. That newspaper also liked the plot and characterisation. The *Morning Post* liked the characterisation, plot and 'thrilling interest ... in each division or department of the story'. The *Observer* thought that 'The matter and the moral of the book are good' and that it was 'truly of a most noble purpose'. The *Spectator* applauded the 'great power' of the writing and identified it as one of those novels 'where minute anatomy of the mind predominates over incidents'. The *Sun* thought that 'the characteristic which is most deserving of commendation is the very admirable delineation and nice discrimination of power'. The *Morning Advertiser* praised the intermingling of 'fact and fiction, reality and romance' which maintained the novel's 'deep and unflagging interest'. *Era* was thrilled to find 'much of trial and temptation, of fortitude and resignation, of sound sense and Christianity – but no tameness.' The *Guardian* (sic) liked the plot, the characterisation, the dialogue 'and the mystery such as would baffle the keenest scented reader'. *Howitt's Journal* thought it 'one of the freshest and most genuine books which we have read for a long time.' The *People's Journal* thought it an excellent read: 'the moral sentiments are pure and healthy; and the whole work is calculated to rivet attention, to provoke sympathy, to make the heart bound and the brain pause'. The *Sheffield Iris* applauded the novel's style, dialogue and characterisation and its demonstration that 'external beauty is inferior to loveliness of heart, and conventional accomplishments valueless contrasted with depth and originality of mind united to high moral purpose'. The *Nottingham Mercury* thought that where the modern novel was concerned, 'we have read few of a more thrilling, edifying, and purifying character than *Jane Eyre*. Without the slightest approach to cant it is eminently religious – without any strained attempts at sentimentality it is truly pathetic.' The *Church of England Journal* called it 'one of the best works of its class that has appeared for years'. The *Westminster Review* hailed it as 'decidedly the best novel of the season'.

 Jane Eyre met with the approval of the bourgeoisie, across a wide spectrum of publications. It touched a chord. It was their idea of what a really good novel should be like. Tanya Gold tries, as she puts it, 'to exhume the real Charlotte – filthy bitch, grandmother of chick-lit, and friend.' It's not a new argument that *Jane Eyre is* about sex, but it is NOT about sex as subversion. Notoriously, Mr Rochester has to be punished for flouting Victorian morality – symbolically castrated, in effect.

There is nothing subversive about Jane Eyre's attitude to sex. In Vol. III, Chapter One, Mr Rochester urges her to be his mistress and to go off and live with him in the south of France. She rejects him. Sex outside marriage is utterly unacceptable to Jane. What Charlotte Brontë succeeded in doing was effectively and dramatically to express the values of the middle class. *Jane Eyre* prizes chastity before marriage. The novel upholds religion, but it's a middle-of-the-road Christianity – nothing too extreme, like the type represented by the Calvinist, St John Rivers, or that of Mr Brocklehurst. Mr Rochester is punished – mutilated! – for his sexual waywardness and his first wife is killed off, clearing the way for his second marriage, to Jane.

Jane Eyre was a novel written and published at a moment of great crisis for the European bourgeoisie. The Chartist movement was its height, and soon revolutions broke out across Europe. *Jane Eyre* dramatised a voice that spoke of the injustice and unfairness in society – but it was a voice that sought not the overthrow of that society but assimilation within it. *Jane Eyre* is ultimately a novel about control and self-restraint. Jane appears to articulate the voice of rebellion: 'it seemed as if my tongue pronounced words without my will consenting to their utterance: something spoke out of me over which I had no control'. But that absence of restraint only occurs at the start of the novel. Later, Victorian values become her weapon against those who breach them.

Jane Eyre is about starting out as an outsider and finding your place in bourgeois nineteenth-century English society. In that sense the novel replicated the actual journey of Charlotte Brontë's own father, Patrick. He was the eldest of ten children, born to a pair of Irish peasant farmers in County Down. The children were raised as Protestants and Patrick Brontë's journey into bourgeois acceptability went from being appointed to the post of assistant school teacher at 16, then tutor to the sons of a local vicar and then acceptance into St John's College, Cambridge. It was at St John's that Patrick Prunty reinvented himself as Patrick Brontë – apparently after his hero Nelson, who was created Duke of Bronté by the King of Naples in 1799. He was, in short, seriously upwardly mobile and keen to absorb the values of the bourgeoisie. He seems to have cut himself off from all contact with his family back in Ireland. Patrick Brontë ended up as a parson – a paid servant of the ruling ideology, employed to transmit it. (Nowadays he'd be working for BBC News.)

Jane starts out as 'an uncongenial alien' but by the end of the novel she becomes a respectable, affluent married woman, with servants. A central aspect of the narrative is that it's about a plain, ordinary, poor girl who succeeds in marrying a rich property-owner – a popular fantasy template which is still around today, in modern form, in modern mass entertainments like *Notting Hill* or *Bridget Jones's Diary*.

Ideologically, it promotes the idea that to join the elite in capitalist society all you need is love – not inherited wealth, property, land or business interests. Romantic love is represented as a force that supersedes social status, education, accent, behaviour, experience, expertise, knowledge, social connections, or all the other various components of class privilege. In *Jane Eyre* a plain Jane, without substance, an airy nothing (Jane Air, in fact), becomes a woman of substance with a social identity.

The Examiner praised the novel for showing 'how intellect and unswerving integrity may win their way, although oppressed by that predominating influence in society which is a mere consequence of the accidents of birth or fortune ... in the end, the honest, kindness of heart, and perseverance of the heroine, are seen triumphant over every obstacle'.

Capitalist ideology is victorious – helped along the way by fairy tale interventions like the apparition of Jane's dead mother (who drops by to promote the importance of chastity before marriage) and the moment when Jane magically hears Rochester's voice calling out to her in the night from far, far away. There is also the matter of her magical inheritance from an uncle in Madeira, who leaves her the staggering sum of £20,000. That fortune clearly comes from the slave trade, though the novel never acknowledges this. As feminism, this is akin to *The Color Purple*, where the route out of oppression is taken via setting up a business and inheriting land and property.

Jane Eyre is an authoritarian text in the sense that there is only one point of view – Jane Eyre's. That was what so enraged Jean Rhys, who devoted the second half of her life to deconstructing the novel and rewriting it from the viewpoint of the supposedly mad wife. *Wide Sargasso Sea* challenges the iron certainties of Mrs Jane

Rochester.

The title of this novel is challenging. Something is missing: the definite article. Shouldn't it be *The Wide Sargasso Sea*? And where precisely is the Sargasso Sea? It's remote from Britain. It sounds exotic. And even when you're told where it is – 'The sea is a tract of the North Atlantic Ocean lying roughly between the West Indies and the Azores, in the Horse Latitudes' – it's still hard to get a mental hold on.

Which was the writer's point.

Jean Rhys wrote a poem which represented the Sargasso sea as a zone of destruction and entrapment: 'They say it's strewn with wrecks / And weed-infested / Few dare it, fewer still escape.' But nowhere in the novel is there any reference to the Sargasso Sea. The title is an enigma which the reader has to work out for herself.

The Sargasso Sea can mean many things. 'It is a relatively still sea but it is at the centre of a great swirl of ocean currents.' It's a zone of stasis. Columbus was becalmed in it on his first voyage. It removes (you could say) masculine power and energy. It threatens to render action inactive and mobility immobile. 'Its name derives from the tracts of floating weed on its surface.' The weed is yellow. Portuguese sailors named the sea after their native sargassum weed, found growing in wells. A popular myth held that a sailing ship which became entangled in this weed would be trapped there forever.

Jean Rhys drew attention to the Afro-Caribbean colonial sub-text of *Jane Eyre* and dramatised the point of view of the first wife. This was just one aspect of *Jane Eyre* which Charlotte Brontë excluded.

There is another, which is not one I've come across in books or articles about the novel. *Jane Eyre* was written against the background of the the Irish Famine of 1846-50, which killed as many as one million from hunger and disease. Shortly after the novel appeared, Sir Charles Trevelyan, the British civil servant in charge of Irish relief policy, published his book *The Irish Crisis*, which described the famine as 'a direct stroke of an all-wise and all-merciful Providence'. (In fact the famine was entirely bogus in so far as there was plenty of food available to feed the starving Irish; notoriously, ships were exporting food to England from a land where the poor were literally dropping dead from hunger.)

To Trevelyan, God was punishing the Irish for their inefficient ways. It was a view which slotted in neatly with the view of the English bourgeoisie that the Irish national character was defective and lacking in self-reliance.

It seems to me there are strong parallels between the ideology of individualism in *Jane Eyre* and the ideology that sustained the English bourgeoisie in their ruthless indifference to mass (and preventable) death in Ireland. In Vol. III, Chapter Two, Jane Eyre flees from Mr Rochester and wanders the countryside, hungry, outcast and desperate. Exhausted, she collapses, crying out: 'I can but die ... and I believe in God. Let me try to wait His will in silence.' Providentially, her words are overheard by a man of God, she is given food and shelter, and finds Christian charity, friendship and employment.

It's a sentimental fantasy, and it's surely no coincidence that the class which swooned with admiration over *Jane Eyre* was the same one which regarded with equanimity the deaths of hundreds of thousands of Irish peasants.

Bad Writing: *The Passion of New Eve*

Angela Carter really is a bad writer, isn't she? Stupefyingly, staggeringly bad.

I'd never read any Angela Carter before. I imagined I'd like her fiction, from the impression I'd received about her (feminist, lefty, didn't write middle-of-the-road realist sagas about adultery among the middle classes but stories of fabulation and fantasy with a satirical feminist edge).

And now I've read *The Passion of New Eve*. And not a single aspect of the book engaged me – the story, the characters, the language, zilch. The story, such as it is, concerns a British male chauvinist pig who goes off to a futuristic, collapsing USA and is there re-made as a woman.

In a desperate attempt to make sense of the novel's dreary contents, the publishers proudly cite *The Times*: 'If you can imagine Baudelaire, Blake and Kafka getting together to describe America, you are well on the way to Carter's visionary and lurid world.'

Well, in the first place, if you can imagine Baudelaire, Blake and Kafka 'getting together' I would assume you had read or understood nothing about any of those writers. I would assume, in fact, that you review books for a leading national newspaper, or occupy an important position in determining the cultural content of BBC TV transmissions, or are currently under heavy sedation in a locked room where pleasant, quietly spoken professionals come and chat to you from time to time to ask how you are getting along. (I'm feeling great, doc! Baudelaire, Blake and Kafka came to see me yesterday. They described America to me. It sure sounds a swell place!)

Carter is one of those lazy writers who think that describing something is the same as evoking it, what Wayne Booth in *The Rhetoric of Fiction* defined as the difference between *telling* and *showing*. The narrator of *The Passion of New Eve* at one point is trapped in a strange room and feels 'all the compulsion of authentic mystery'. Yet the situation is neither compelling nor powerfully mysterious. It is described, not creatively realised. A little later: 'I experienced the pure terror of Faust.' But that's just lazy cultural namechecking. No sense of terror is produced. The narrator confides that 'the unceasing restructuring of my personality under the twin stresses of so great a physical change and my programming almost unbalanced me. I felt intimations of total collapse, of absolute despair.' But these emotions aren't dramatised, they are merely listed. The whole book has a thin, impoverished quality. It's a narrative of empty gestures, not accomplishments.

The style is flashy but curiously lacklustre. A woman's skin is described as being 'rucked like a Greek peasant's goatskin bottle'. Which I suppose is evocative if you are acquainted with goat-owning Greek peasants and their quaint hand-crafted bottles. Sadly, on neither of my visits to Greece did I meet any peasants. The bottles I encountered were much like bottles anywhere else on the planet, except for the language on the label.

The Passion of New Eve is a novel in which characters talk 'with grim relish' and gaze 'with unconcealed satisfaction'. At a moment of great stress, the narrator confides: 'Then all the rest pitched in with their opinions and soon grew heated. During the discussion, I stayed still as a statue and dumb as a stone. I was out of my depths and very nervous.' Yup, totting up the clichés which litter this novel would be a seriously exhausting business. This is Dan Brown territory (but obviously Brown is a better writer – he has an imagination and he can plot). And, yes, I know it's a first person narrative and sometimes an author uses language to define the limitations of character. I know my Wayne Booth. But this is *not that sort of novel*.

When I encountered the words 'I loose my nerve in the hubbub' I generously assumed that this was just the slovenly typesetting that you'd expect from a major corporate publisher like Time Warner. But by the next page I wasn't so sure it wasn't just the consequence of a sloppy author in a rush: there, a character is described as watching 'with the prim enthusiasm of a college girl at a football ballgame'.

A *football ballgame*?

'Her writing is pyrotechnic,' gushes the *Observer* on the front cover.

I can think of other descriptions of Angela Carter's writing which also employ four syllables.

Carl Marks and Granny Trotsky

Some buttons should not be pushed.

In *Zabriskie Point*, for example, which is surely Antonioni's worst film, there's a scene in which the hero is seized during a campus demonstration. The arresting officer demands to know his name. 'Karl Marx,' our hero replies with a laconic sneer. And in the next shot we see the cop recording the name 'Carl Marks'.

I don't like this scene because I think it's trite and lazy. It invites the audience to pat itself on the back. *We are cool dudes who know who Karl Marx was and we know how to spell his name. Clever old us. And silly, silly cop.*

In reality I have a hunch that the average American cop probably *has* heard of Marx, knows how to spell his name, and also knows when a smartass college kid is taking the piss. There are lots of reasons to dislike American cops (and we James Ellroy fans know them all) but *cacography isn't one of them*.

Cut to *Memento Mori* by Muriel Spark. Among the geriatric cast of the narrative, which is about old age and death, is 'Granny Trotsky'. Priceless, eh? And if you think people's names are funny you'll be in stitches over a cast of characters which includes two Sidebottoms.

It's clear that the dotty old woman dubbed Granny Trotsky is (this will slay you) intended to satirise Trotsky the Russian revolutionary.

But the satire is grounded on nothing more than the assumption that the historical Trotsky was, well, crackers. So Granny Trotsky is represented as someone who is confused and incomprehensible:

> It was no longer possible to hear exactly what she said. Miss Taylor was the quickest in the ward at guessing what Granny Trotsky's remarks might be, but Miss Barnacle was the most inventive.

Just to add to the comedy Granny Trotsky has a 'curiously shaped head' and speaks 'with vehement nods of this head'. Even Granny Trotsky's death – 'the result of the bursting of a small blood-vessel in her brain' – mocks that of the revolutionary.

It's lazy comedy because it flatters the insular prejudices of a provincial British readership. Trotsky – he was so confused, so foolish, *you just have to laugh.*

At moments like these Antonioni and Spark press buttons which should not be pushed. They pander to their audiences. They invite an easy, complacent response. And only bad art does that.

Ford Fiesta

Richard Ford's novel *The Lay of the Land* is a warm, friendly comfortable book, full of interesting stories and characters. It's very readable, just as blockbuster Hollywood movies are very watchable. It's physically big (485 hardback pages). It's a condition-of-America novel, capturing the state of the nation – or a significant, representative slice of it – in autumn 2000. Its production values are high; Richard Ford is a writer on top form, writing what he writes as well as he'll ever write it. The writing often crackles ('I testified that I needed her the way hydrogen needs oxygen'). *The Lay of the Land*, like a lot of modern literary fiction, is written as if modernism and post-modernism had never existed. Or for that matter Borges' view that 'The composition of vast books is a laborious and impoverishing extravagance. To go on for five hundred pages developing an idea whose perfect oral exposition is possible in a few minutes!' (10 November 1941).

Like many of the reviewers, *The Lay of the Land* struck me as a derivative book. I was, like them, reminded both of Updike (for the world of the characters and their relationship issues) and of Bellow (the flow of an inner life). But I was also reminded of Dickens. *The Lay of the Land* is a narrative of people stories – its range of characters is expansive, encyclopaedic. Often, as in Dickens, they are grotesque or comical or both – Frank Bascombe's appalling next door neighbours, for example. His Tibetan business partner. His daughter's creepy New Age boyfriend. And the telling is engaging and often very funny. Bascombe's neighbours for example – monstrously plausible. You relish their end. I had a hunch there would be a satisfyingly violent Hollywood-style righteous conclusion and there is (if not exactly how I anticipated it – I guessed the wife would shoot her husband for his adultery).

Why is Ford ventriloquising these characters and concerns through the consciousness of Frank Bascombe? Because, I would guess, like Updike in *Toward the End of Time*, he seeks to address both the theme of ageing and death and the American condition. But I found *Toward the End of Time* a much more interesting read than *The Lay of the Land*. Partly because it acknowledges its own making in a way that Ford's novel never seems to. It stretches the genre of the novel; it moves out of its central story into some strange places, before (disappointingly) returning to a safe neighbourhood. Whereas *The Lay of the Land* is a reality-sodden, fact-sodden tale. It's a novel which, in the absence of tangible artefacts, would prove useful to a future archaeologist or historian seeking to reconstruct an image of American society at the end of the twentieth century. And, as in a Dickens novel, the ending is a warm, comfortable one. Good stuff happens to good people. The bad folk get their come-uppance. Decent people evade dreadful situations. *The Lay of the Land* can be consumed, perhaps, as satisfyingly and sequentially as a delightful three-course meal. The desert does not disappoint. And yet, and yet ... In the end, like that second bowl of Christmas pudding, *The Lay of the Land* was a struggle to finish. I felt full up. I started to grow bored and restless with Frank Bascombe's interminable musings about his women and his children.

The Updike influence seems strong. Updike also entices the reader with tales of marriages gone awry and the complex aftermaths of separations and reproductions. But whereas Updike infuses his narrative with figurative language – language sweet and golden as syrup – Ford has more of an historical bent. But like Updike he has the itch to make his telling bear weight. Thus his narrator is not simply hungry but 'hungry as a leopard'. A limp handshake between the narrator and his wife's first husband is not simply 'We shook hands limply' but 'We shook hands limply, in the manner of a cold prisoner exchange on the Potsdam bridge.'

The American academic critic Wayne Booth once made a famous distinction between telling and showing, with the argument that writers who show are better than ones who tell (i.e. good writers make the reader judge character for themselves by judging their dialogue and perceptions; bad writers do all the work for the reader, letting them know who to like and who to dislike). That notion came back to me reading *The Lay of the Land*, where everything is processed by Frank Bascombe. But what wasn't clear to me was what we are supposed to feel about Frank Bascombe or what the distance is between him and his creator. His insights into other people always seem persuasive. He never seems wrong about anything. He's an easygoing, likeable guy.

But what (to adopt the pointed angle of my own coarse-textured blog) of the politics of the novel? This is a book which is about a pivotal political moment in modern American history – chicanery is about to let Bush steal the presidency from Gore. Bascombe, a Democrat, is unhappy. He comments of his daughter Clarissa:

> She loathes Democrats for being prissy and isn't truly sure what party she fits in with. My secret fear is she's pissed away her vote on sad-sack, know-it-all Nader, who's responsible for this smirking Texas frat boy stealing a march into the power vacuum.

Now undoubtedly many Democrats felt that way, so this passage could reasonably be defended as realism. But not everybody felt that way and in naturalistic fiction I'd like to hear an alternative point of view. That is denied the reader. We never get inside Clarissa's head. And Bascombe's questionable politics are never challenged. There is no critique of sad-sack Gore or his equivocations. No defence of Nader or demolition of the claim (in my view absurd) that he cost the Democrats their victory. It's a pleasant, charming Democratic novel. But not a liberal one. George Eliot, for example, could give a voice in her fiction to opinions which she herself strongly opposed;

Muriel Spark, a Catholic, was able to cast Catholics as repellent and extreme.

Nor is the narrative, though inward-turning, as textured and complex and knotty as one by Bellow. Ford's narrator namechecks global warming as a topic but it remains emptier than the lurid signs which dot the landscape Bascombe inhabits. In that sense I was reminded of Ian McEwan's *Saturday*, which references Israel/Palestine but positions itself in safe, inoffensive, neutral territory.

When Ford has his narrator mention 'the refugees' sad plight in Gaza' what are we to make of this? Frank Bascombe is ignorant, for there are no refugees in Gaza; just the original population. Is his ignorance simply an expression of his creator's ignorance? I know nothing of the life and opinions of Richard Ford but I have a strong hunch it probably is. It is, I think, an unintentional historical error – not an error deliberately inserted to establish critical space between the reader and the character/narrator. This moment is not in itself of enormous significance but it serves, for me, as a symptom of larger difficulties.

Gregor Samsa's Wings

Steven Mitchelmore considers the appeal of Kafka's 'Metamorphosis':

> Blanchot says Gregor's story 'carries the reader off in a whirl where hope and despair answer each other endlessly'. This might explain the extraordinary longevity of the story, of all great modern stories. We can never choose between hope or despair.
> (http://this-space.blogspot.co.uk/2007/06/torturing-hope-kafkas-metamorphosis.html)

It's not a reading I recognise. Even 'whirl' is wrong, with its intimations of rapidity and dizzying motion. 'Metamorphosis' is a cool, slow story. A hideous condition is dealt with bit by bit. Blanchot, I suspect, was unconsciously thinking of that final scene with the charwoman, who is last seen 'whirling off violently'. That

Blanchot should substitute abstraction for her presence in the text is really quite revealing, I think.

In 'Metamorphosis' concealment is of the essence. Compartmentalisation is involved – thematically and structurally. 'Metamorphosis' is not a single fast-flowing river of prose but, like the body of an insect, divided into segments – three chapters. Gregor dies on the stroke of three. There are three doors to Gregor's room: three ways in, three ways out. Not one way. There is no single way in and out of this story. You cannot exclusively capture it for a metaphysical reading. It slips free. In its multiplicity – in its totality – it resists the net of exegesis. The jacket cover on my edition calls it a 'haunting parable on human reaction to suffering and disease', which is both true and horribly limiting.

The reaction of everyone in the story to Gregor's transformation is, surely, the exact opposite to despair. There is no despair. On the contrary, the story gives us characters learning to cope with an extreme situation, as humans do. One or two of the characters shun Gregor and depart; most stay. Their responses range from disgust, fear and irritation, to compassion, curiosity and breezy acceptance. Nobody finally gives up on Gregor; nobody sinks into paralysis. Everyone grudgingly accepts his presence. No one despairs, not even Gregor. Everyone bravely, absurdly, comically, maintains the rigmarole of everyday life.

Kafka's stories 'are among the darkest in literature, the most rooted in absolute disaster' because they 'torture hope the most tragically, not because hope is condemned but because it does not succeed in being condemned.' Again, I don't recognise Blanchot's formulation. Though the story measures life against the reality of death, it's not a dark narrative. Everyday life becomes a series of stiffly unfolding comic mishaps as the struggle to maintain appearances goes on. I'm reminded of the farcical misadventures that crop up in silent comedies. 'Metamorphosis' is not a lugubrious tale of sorrow. To say it 'tortures hope' is far too forceful and singular. The power of 'Metamorphosis', I think, resides not in something as abstract as a dialogue between hope and despair but elsewhere. Its continuing resonance as a narrative is surely because Gregor Samsa's awful family is instantly recognisable. Those philistines, those bourgeois values, those absurd efforts to muffle what is going on – family life as a grotesque farce is a theme which surely strikes a chord with many, many readers. The clash between children and their parents is a guerrilla war which never ends.

In representing a sensitive individual as a giant insect Kafka puts flesh on a metaphor. Those who are persecuted, whether by individuals, societies or states, are sometimes identified as vermin. Dehumanising the Other licenses inhuman treatment. Kafka makes it real. The image of a person turned into a giant insect is a very hard one to get out of your mind. That hideous and unforgettable image of the apple embedded in Gregor is definitely the stuff of nightmares. The world is turned upside down: normality is brilliantly represented as repellent. Such everyday items as milk and an apple become objects of disgust. Kafka reproduces that revulsion in the reader while rendering Gregor sympathetically. We get the vermin's point of view.

Kafka brilliantly roots his nightmarish narrative in a tangible reality. Patent leather boots creak. It rains. The characters are recognisable types. The dialogue is as banal, revealing and ironic as in a Jane Austen novel. Even Gregor's new identity becomes monstrously plausible. And there is even joy in his grotesque transfiguration: 'He especially enjoyed hanging suspended from the ceiling'. But the real always looks back toward nightmare. The unidentified city resembles 'a desert waste'.

Mitchelmore says: 'It is, as we know still today, a world of fierce taboos resisting the forces of change, of decay, illness and death. Gregor has, in effect, died but not left the building. His death stains the parents' starched clothing, stinks out the flat. This is how he might be read from a Marxist perspective: Gregor is the harbinger of the social problems inherent to early modern capitalism. But change also afflicts Marxists. The hope of political redemption is soon also faced by despair.'

But that kind of vulgar sociological criticism is surely long dead. There was a God that died but his first name was Joseph, not Karl or Vladimir. 'Redemption' is a religious, not a Marxist, category. Mitchelmore's description better fits the disappointed generation of 1968, whose retreat from engagement spun off in numerous directions – everything from despairing quietism to the ardent embrace of neo-liberalism. The French intelligentsia's despair after 1968 and the intellectual shapes it took (indeed Blanchot's own complicated political trajectory) is a large story. And long before the publication of *Saturday*, Alex Callinicos dryly observed that in less theoretically inclined Britain the favoured substitute for political engagement was ... cookery. That said, it's worth noting that specific and recurring material anxieties – the word 'capital' even appears – are part of that tangible world in which Kafka's nightmare is grounded. And I think I'm right in saying that Kafka uses the word 'despair' only once in the story, with reference to the past – the collapse of the family business.

I agree with Steven Mitchelmore that 'cockroach' is quite wrong. And it's an error which has been around for a long time. In the second volume of his Nabokov biography, Brian Boyd describes a day in 1954:

> In his next lecture Nabokov announced that a new translation of the book had arrived in the morning mail. He shuddered and grimaced as he held up the expensive new illustrated edition 'whose translator had substituted "cockroach" for "giant insect" in the famous opening sentence. "Cockroach!" Nabokov repeated . . . "Even the Samsa maid knows enough to call Gregor a dung beetle!"'

Nabokov's discussion of what kind of insect Gregor was appears in his *Lectures on Literature*. These are unrevised, unpolished lecture notes published posthumously (I'm not sure he would have been pleased). They are notes to a performance. His discussion of Gregor's beetlehood is whimsical, hootingly funny and brief. Nabokov ends by noting that such efforts are pointless: Gregor 'is merely a big beetle. (I must add that neither Gregor not Kafka saw that beetle any too clearly.)' Nabokov also wrote:

> *Beauty plus pity* – that is the closest we can get to a definition of art. Where there is beauty there is pity for the simple reason that beauty must die: beauty always dies, the manner dies with the matter, the world dies with the individual. If Kafka's 'The Metamorphosis' strikes anyone as something more than an entomological fantasy, then I congratulate him on having joined the ranks of good and great readers.

Is even identifying Gregor as a beetle an identification too far? I think not. There is one character in the story whose 'strong bony frame' is suggestive of an insect (the other characters, those who scuttle and scurry, are more like rodents). But whereas Gregor passively accepts his condition, this other character – the old charwoman – represents resistance. She is the only character who isn't revolted by Gregor. She is not afraid of him, either. She is on the side of life – garrulous, comical, a force of nature. The last we see of her she has a story to tell but nobody wants to hear it (another surrogate for the author, perhaps). Gregor fades away in 'vacant and peaceful meditation', whereas the charwoman departs with convulsive force, shouting her farewell, angrily slamming doors. She does not go gentle into the night.

And then that last sunlit tram ride. What does that final sentence mean? One possibility is obvious. This is that the daughter will be crushed by the bourgeois existence her parents are keen to impose upon her. We can all understand what 'a good husband' means in their terms. That desirable young body will be traded for wealth. At a darker level, there is a faint hint that she will share the fate of her brother. When you stretch your body you change your shape: perhaps one morning the daughter will also wake up as a giant insect. But is that the only metamorphosis that is possible? Is hope pathetic? Do dreams never come true? Is another shape possible?

Vladimir Nabokov, Ithaca, 1954:

> Curiously enough, Gregor the beetle never found out that he had wings under the hard covering of his back. (This is a very nice observation on my part to be treasured all your lives. Some Gregors, some Joes and Janes, do not know that they have wings.)

Flow My Tears, The Policeman Said

As titles go, they don't come much more idiosyncratic, unwieldy and comically absurd than this. Philip K. Dick was having *fun*. Into a trashy genre (with a much lower status when Dick was writing than nowadays) he introduced his obsessions, including his favourite music. Dick's weird title – policemen don't say things like that, ever – incorporates that of a lute song by John Dowland (1563-1626).

Flow My Tears, The Policeman Said (1974) is Dick in his prime. The prose is tough and edgy and as good as you get in genre writing.

And the story, residually Kafkaesque, resonates. It's about rejection and loss of self. Jason Taverner is a top TV chat-show celebrity, with millions of fans. Then an embittered old girlfriend throws a Callisto cuddle sponge at him. Its fifty feeding tubes bore into him. He manages to get the brute off him but some of the tubes remain alive inside him and he faints.

When he wakes up he finds himself in a cheap hotel. To his horror, he discovers that no one has ever heard of him. His previous identity has vanished completely. His closest associates and even his mistress have no knowledge of anyone called Jason Taverner. Worse still, to have no ID is to be a renegade. He risks being picked up by the police whom, he fears, will assume he's 'a student or teacher escaped from one of the campuses'.

From an affluent primary reality Taverner finds himself in a seedy low-life secondary reality which is identical to the first one, except that he has never existed in it. His aberrant status calls him to the attention of police chief Felix Buckman. Taverner is drawn into the world of Buckman and his strange sister. And then his original reality begins to leak back.

At the level of story it's a bizarre and compelling read, where nothing is quite what it seems and levels of reality blur in a vertiginous manner at times reminiscent of late David Lynch. But above all this novel is a satire and very, very funny. Set mostly in Los Angeles, it's a mocking imaginative version of Richard Nixon's USA. Students are forcibly kept underground ('effete, pale, clammy students living beneath the campus areas'), there are forced-labour camps for dissidents, and it's not unusual for a woman to marry more than fifty times. There is rubbish music by groups like 'the Purple People Strings' and rubbish Book-of-the-Month fiction – 'those endless dull novels about sexual misdeeds in weird, small, but apparently normal Midwestern towns'. And Police General Felix Buckman uses a special means of transport at work: 'With his rank key he opened the building's express descent sphincter'. Because after all, when you think about it, a cop is just *a piece of shit.*

Bernhard's 'Piccadilly Circus'

The story is just under a page long, in my edition: Thomas Bernhard, *The Voice Imitator* (translated by Kenneth J. Northcott; University of Chicago Press, 1997); a collection of stories originally published as *Der Stimmenimitator* in 1978.

It tells why an un-named man (specified by an unidentified narrator simply as 'a colleague of my cousin's') no longer travels on the London Underground. The reason is that at Piccadilly Circus station he once encountered a tube train in which all the passengers were dead. Some were standing, some were sitting, some fell out when the doors opened. But all were dead.

The story invites an obvious interpretation. The man is mad. The experience he describes never happened – or if it did, it happened inside his mind, not in the real world.

That the man is deranged is suggested by other details. For example, 'the Paris Métro ... had so disappointed him the first time he had travelled on it that he had decided never to set foot in the city of Paris again'. This might reasonably be considered an extreme reaction, even if the nature of the disappointment was spelled out, which it isn't. In the real world it is difficult to see why anyone should feel strongly that the Paris Métro is massively inferior to the London Underground or why the London Underground should be considered superior to 'any other underground railway in the whole world'. It patently isn't.

We learn that in the past the protagonist has enjoyed travelling on the London Underground so much that he's frequently travelled to the end of the line just for the pleasure of it. This is clearly obsessive and abnormal behaviour. From a naturalistic point of view it could be taken as a symptom of, say, an individual with Asperger's Syndrome.

But a naturalistic reading perhaps doesn't take us very far. At Piccadilly Circus the protagonist had the option of two lines: the Piccadilly or the Bakerloo. Travelling north on the Piccadilly line, and going to the end of the line, he would have arrived at Cockfosters. On the Bakerloo line he would have ended up at Harrow & Wealdstone. Travelling south on the Piccadilly line he would (at the time the story was published) have travelled as far as Hounslow or Uxbridge (the line splits at Acton Town). On the Bakerloo line he would have ended up at Elephant & Castle. Only one conclusion can be drawn from these options, and I shall draw it at the end of my analysis.

Another possibility is that the intention of the story is satirical. London's tube trains contain commuters who resemble the dead. The idea of Londoners as corpses is not new. It can be found in T. S. Eliot's *The Waste Land* and, more recently, in the fiction of Will Self.

But I don't think Bernard's intentions are particularly satirical. The thrust of the story is more to do with communicating a sense of a fictional world characterised by estrangement, isolation and absurdity. What is most striking about the story, I think, is the tone of the narrative. The narrator speaks in a cool, rational manner of what is grotesque, ridiculous and bizarre. But he never bats an eyelid. There is the mildest expression of doubt in the assertion that the protagonist *claimed* the Underground officials ignored his remarkable story of a tube train filled with corpses. It is as if the derangement of the protagonist is shared by the narrator, who resists a conventional 'common sense' response to the strange story he unfolds. The narrator, perhaps, is the true madman.

A circus is, in one sense, a place of entertainment; in another, it is an open space where a number of streets converge. Both senses might be thought relevant to this story as a space in which various lines of narrative meet. But as a space it is circular and self-contained: it leads nowhere but back to its beginning.

However, I resist the notion of art as self-contained. A text should always be judged first on its own terms, this I accept. But then the search for a sub-text may, if the circumstances are propitious and if the project can be shown to be relevant to some wider significance, properly begin. Bernhard's story is a fiction but it is one which is rooted in an actually existing material reality (and one which I know far better than Bernhard's madman). Let me therefore conclude by asserting that it is my firm belief that when the protagonist underwent his crisis at Piccadilly Circus he was on a Piccadilly Line platform and not the Bakerloo Line, because the length of the journey ahead of him would have been considerably longer and the pleasure far more intense.

An Updike Glitter

It's good to see an author of John Updike's stature reviving one of V.I. Lenin's favourite nouns, as in this complaint about the modernisation of Boston's North Station:

> A sickening smell of hot cheese wafts everywhere from a pizzeria that has been installed at the end where the cretins who attend sporting events in Fleet Center might be tempted to coat their guts with fat and gluten.

Worse, this is an age in which young women blow bubble gum:

> In this place, for decades a daily station of my pilgrimage, the young woman unthinkingly showed me her pink bubble, and then wolfed it back, seething with bacteria, into her oral cavity.

There's a lot about corporeality and disgust in *Toward the End of Time* (1997), which combines a vision of the USA in decline with the physical disintegration of its male narrator. I think it's one of Updike's more interesting novels. The materials of the book are familiar Updike territory – the world of white professional affluence, big house, eleven acres, an attractive wife, an unfaithful husband – but it's a world which is falling apart from every angle.

The novel is set in 2020, after a war with China. Swathes of the USA have been wiped out. Mexico has put up barriers to Americans trying to flee south. This vision of the USA fraying at the edges is mixed in with the elderly narrator's sense that things aren't what they used to be. Modern life has become graceless and coarse. There's a hard satirical edge to all this and the book is often very funny in conveying its main character's loathing of modern life.

In many ways it's a very traditional Updike novel – in others it explodes those familiarities. The narrative goes off in different directions. The wife vanishes. A whore takes her place. The whore goes away. Without explanation, the wife returns. What's going on?

Updike invites us to read his book in different ways. We discover that the first-person narrator is, in fact, Ben Turnbull, the character whose consciousness we are inside. He isn't thinking these events but *writing* them. The novel is a journal – but a remarkably fluent one, less like an ordinary journal or diary than, well, a novel by John

Updike. So why is he writing it? An explanation is offered at the moment when Turnbull observes the care with which his wife attends to her teeth and her fingernails (not incidental details – her teeth and fangs grow sharper as Turnbull physically dwindles):

> All these rites, I see, are her way of trying to freeze and defeat time, as mine is the writing of these scattered sad paragraphs. Futile, both exercises, but only in the long run.

But if Turnbull is the recorder of the novel's events, perhaps they do not all happen. There is a metaphysics driving the narrative on – the theory of parallel universes. Our lives arrive at defining moments and split in different directions. In one life we do this, in another we do that. Our parallel selves inhabit different worlds, simultaneously in time. This is Turnbull's condition. In one world a whore moves in to replace his wife, and the teenagers who invade his estate are murdered. In the other world his wife never leaves and there are no teenagers.

Perhaps Turnbull is not, after all, plunging in and out of time, in and out of different realities. Perhaps these are just the consoling fantasies of an ageing, libidinous male – a not particularly attractive individual – whose body is beginning to fail him. Or perhaps we really *are* in 2020 and there really *has* been a war with China. Or perhaps this is just the bitter, satirical, exaggerated vision of an elderly, dying man sickened by the vulgarity of modern American life.

As a satire, *Toward the End of Time* is frequently very funny and very entertaining. As an account of the drifting apart of a selfish, hard-nosed couple complacently immersed in their affluence and their self-satisfactions the novel is engaging and very readable. And, as so often with Updike, the book is a rich plum pudding of figurative language. There are frequent moments of dazzling brilliance – descriptions such as 'the fuzzy Rothko that insomnia painted on the ceiling'. But there is *too much of it*. The book is surfeited with style, glutted with self-consciously fine writing. And it seems to me that this goes against the grain of the novel. This is a book about the last year in the life of a man. Just beyond the last sentence of the last page is the fact of his death.

But Ben Turnbull never really confronts that void. The book processes his perceptions and insights but he never really achieves any kind of genuine self-knowledge. Updike, a prodigiously well-read author, uses Turnbull to unload quantities of fact and information upon the reader. The novel is like reading a superior kind of magazine, full of data designed to make you respond: *How interesting – I never knew that.* Often it is scientific knowledge that is dumped on the reader – astronomical, biological, geographical, anthropological. It's a novel studded with exquisite imagery, interesting knowledge, beautifully processed accounts of American society and geography and relationships. That rich surfeit becomes a wall, shutting out the consciousness of death. Death's imminence becomes the occasion for another fancy outbreak of style:

> The weather is so warm a multitude of small pale moths have mistakenly hatched. In the early dark they flip and flutter a foot or two above the asphalt, as if trapped in a narrow wedge of space-time beneath the obliterating imminence of winter.

It is, as every good student of literature at once perceives, *symbolic.*

And so, with those two sentences, *Toward the End of Time* finishes. The hero physically disintegrates in the course of the novel, losing that aspect of his physicality which most matters to him, his sexual potency. But though the narrative wavers in the direction of other possibilities, other worlds, in the end it pulls itself together and terminates with the familiar comforts of a rounded conclusion, the underwriting of the lives of solid and interesting characters, the self-conscious shine of a finely written conclusion. The deer which annoys the wife by eating plants in her garden is killed, its corpse graphically attended to, but human death is not addressed – more drowned out by noise, by wordiness, blanked and evaded by an omnipresent glitter.

The Cry of the Owl

To my mind, the three great strengths of Patricia Highsmith's writing are her prose style, her characterisation and her unconventional but powerfully compelling narratives. She was a genre writer but her novels are every bit as good as many of those books which are recommended as literary fiction. Her prose is plain and to the point. When she does use figurative language it seems organic, consistent with her fictional universe; there are no encrustations of fine style intended to impress the reader. Her characters always seem entirely plausible and her skill is to show how easily the ordinary and the banal can slide into derangement and obsession. Sometimes the slide is into violence and murder; sometimes her plots fizzle out and in the end nothing happens.

In one telling moment in *The Cry of the Owl*, one of the leading characters reflects on an incident which now seems

> less real than a scene in a story of violence on television. Had he been one of the real characters? Robert wanted to smile.

Orthodox representations of crime are, Highsmith implies, misleading. Crime is a much messier matter, which fails to conform to culturally induced expectation. Highsmith gives us amoral characters but they are never evil in the simplistic sense of tabloid journalism. She shows how human weakness and the right set of circumstances can have unexpected consequences. And the world she creates is a bleak and cheerless one. There isn't a lot of happiness at the end of a Highsmith novel. In *The Cry of the Owl* one of the characters, it turns out, is Death – but in a very subtle, understated way.

The Cry of the Owl is a stalker novel, first published in 1962. It is Highsmith at her very best (which sets me at odds with Barry Forshaw, whose list of 'The top five Highsmith books' in *The Rough Guide to Crime Fiction* doesn't include it). As such, it is interesting to compare it with *Enduring Love*. Highsmith's prose and compulsive-readability seems to me every bit as good as McEwan's. Her world is a drab American working-class world rather than that of affluent English professionals. However, the key difference is what happens. In McEwan's novel the book's sympathies are with the hero who is stalked. The crisis is finally resolved with the incarceration of the stalker and acknowledgement that the protagonist was correct all along in perceiving himself under threat. It is a deeply conservative text. At the end, civilised values and knowledge are restored; the threat to those values is placed under restraint.

Highsmith is on the other side. *The Cry of the Owl* begins with the stalker and encourages the reader to sympathise with him. We are invited to understand stalking. From this unconventional opening the story moves in a series of quite unexpected directions, which are hard to discuss without spoiling the surprises. In the end, though, 'plot' doesn't really matter for Highsmith. What interests her is human psychology in all its perversity. The stalker emerges as by far the most humane person in the story. This makes *The Cry of the Owl* a disturbing and surprising work of fiction.

Anna Kavan's 'One of the Liberated?'

Nineteenth century fiction has a tendency to resolve stories with a marriage. Once that is accomplished, all life's problems are over. Twentieth century fiction didn't agree. Anna Kavan's 'One of the Liberated?' (1975) is a short story rooted in a new marriage, told from the point of view of the husband. The couple live in the countryside. Each morning the wife drives off to the station in the husband's old Vauxhall car.

> Five days a week, she works in a publisher's office. The firm prints books on Hydraulics, the Function of Method Analysis, Kinky Kars – that sort of thing. She's a very intelligent girl.

The husband is a painter, whose work nobody wants to buy. He stays at home and paints. He does the housework. But something is not quite right:

> A compulsion seemed to be forcing her to inspect my work closely, in every detail. She even looked inside the oven, ran her finger along high window sills, normally out of reach – and she's not exactly what you'd call domesticated herself, in the ordinary

way. I became nervous, suspecting her disapproval. But she said nothing, either in criticism or praise.

Two things in particular disturb the husband. Firstly, the wife's car shaves fifteen minutes off the daily journey to the station by flying most of the way. Each morning he watches as she drives up into the air and over a nearby beech wood.

Secondly, she keeps white mice under her dress, by her breasts.

When the husband sees the mice on his wife's body he shouts at her 'idiotically' and yells 'like a lunatic'.

Small clues. We are in the realm of the unreliable first-person narrator. The husband who tells us this story is clearly having a breakdown. His wife perhaps hasn't entirely grasped the situation: she has her doubts about him but so far has retreated into a frightened silence. When she goes to work she escapes from his claustrophobic presence and feels liberated. He senses this, and perceives it as her literally taking flight.

He may be a paranoid schizophrenic. Evidently he experiences hallucinations. Violence hangs in the air. The narrator considers suicide and refers to the means available to him: 'A bottle three-quarters full of barbiturates up in the bathroom. My shotgun. The car exhaust. Razor blades.'

But it is not hard to imagine that the narrator might end up killing not himself but his wife. The story ends with a test of whether or not she is normal, 'no different from other nice girls':

I watched her drive away in the old Vauxhall, reach the bend in the road. Would she ... ? Or wouldn't she? I held my breath. As usual, she turned there to wave to me; and then went soaring up, northwards, over the hill tops, and away out of sight.

She fails the test. She is still, in the narrator's eyes, determined to liberate herself from him.

The title seems to refer primarily to the wife, who temporarily liberates herself from her husband's oppressive presence by going to work each day. But it may also allude to the husband, who is cutting loose from sanity and the restraints of normal behaviour.

The question mark in the title is sinister. What will happen the next time the wife returns home? Murder? And what are 'Kinky Kars'? Evidently, from the husband's crazy perspective, the wife owns one. But the only kinks are in the narrator's mind. And he sees himself as someone calmly rational, who tells his story in cool, unemotional prose. Which makes his madness all the more chilling and threatening.

Our Lady of the Flowers

Jean Genet, *Our Lady of the Flowers* (*Notre Dame des Fleurs*, 1943; revised 1951; trans. Bernard Frechtman).

The narrative is generated by 'Jean Genet', a man alone in a prison cell. At the beginning, he states that he is writing a book and that it is written in honour of the crimes committed by some notorious murderers. He mixes his image of these murderers with others drawn from the illustrations and content of some unidentified adventure novels. At night he reconfigures them into handsome men and masturbates while dreaming of a sexual encounter. 'So, with the help of my unknown lovers, I am going to write a story.'

What follows is a narrative which is ceaselessly aware of its own provisional, made-up quality. It focuses on four individuals: a gay transvestite prostitute named Divine, 'her' male lover Darling, a young murderer known as Our Lady of the Flowers and the narrator himself. Jean makes it clear that these three characters are creatures of his imagination. Joyously he creates them from numerous sources – newspaper reports, trashy novels, personal experience. But none of those is enough: Jean is always explaining to the reader that his knowledge is sketchy and his stories are inventions. 'Don't complain about probability,' he says to the reader on one occasion. 'Truth is not my strong point.'

What animates the novel is the telling: the conscious pleasure of creation. In her twenties, we are told, Divine cruised the Mediterranean (in both senses):

> the yacht touched at Venice, where a film director took a fancy to her. They lived for few months through the huge rooms, fit for giant guards and horsemen astride their mounts, of a dilapidated palace.

After a number of further romantic involvements Divine returns to 'her' origins in Jean's prison cell. Those romantic interludes never existed. They were written 'to console' the solitary narrator in his squalid prison cell: 'I invent for Divine the cosiest apartments where I myself wallow.' The floral imagery which runs through the book seems expressive of this urge to make a lonely existence in a prison cell blossom with colourful possibility.

Jean maintains an exuberant dialogue with the reader as he writes his story. And it's a collage narrative, with an equivocal attitude to fiction. It mocks the formulae and language of genre fiction but is also uses them. Darling, for example, is unaware that he is Our Lady of the Flowers' father. But the revelation is casually incorporated, as if Jean had just thought of it, rather than being worked towards.

Through much of its history the novel has been a bourgeois art form which speaks to a leisured class about their lives. *Our Lady of the Flowers* reclaims it for those at the margins of society. It exuberantly celebrates a *lumpenproletarian* gay sensibility, not simply in its accounts of sexual activity but also in the way it imagines its fictional world. When Our Lady, on trial for his life, uses the word 'erection' the jury is embarrassed. Genet mocks them in cartoon-like imagery:

> the twelve old men, all together, very quickly put their hands over their ears to prevent the entry of the word that was big as an organ, which, finding no other orifice, entered all stiff and hot into their gaping mouths.

The novel is also infused with a Catholic sensibility. But it's one which absorbs the lush, sensuous rites and iconography of the Church, strips them of religion, and reapplies them to the secular world of the gay *demimonde*. Genet insists on the divinity and holiness of his characters; no coincidence that the central character is named Divine. And why, it might be asked, is the novel entitled *Our Lady of the Flowers*, when this character is not the central one? Could it be that *Notre dame des Fleurs* is in part a shrine and a structure set up in opposition to that other Notre Dame? Genet's narrative seems determined both to transgress and to thumb its nose at those who might be outraged by its transgressions. It joyously investigates areas of narrative possibility normally excluded from the novel – wanking, farting and shitting, to name but three. Another prominent seam of imagery emphasizes that the book's low-life characters are regal, aristocratic and full of grace and style. And the disjunction between conventional narrative and Genet's is perhaps nowhere more obvious than in the way in which Divine, a man, is throughout referred to as 'she'. But ultimately Genet's most profound engagement with the form of the novel lies in the way he fractures his narrative, scrambles chronology and buoyantly and jauntily insists on his story's fictionality. The voice of 'Jean' energizes his endeavours.

The book itself runs backwards. It starts with Divine's death and then retraces the course of 'her' life. Genet has no interest in creating suspense: we no sooner meet Our Lady than we are told he will be executed for the murder he commits. The novel moves towards a conclusion: a hearing at which Jean might be set free. But he also considers the possibility that he will remain a prisoner, in which case he plans to 'refashion lovely new lives' for his characters. We never learn what happens. And the novel ends not with a climax but with frustrated desire. It closes with the image of the outline of an erect penis – a dotted line which is a representation of virility, of Divine's lover and of the contours of an absence.

On the Mountain

Thomas Bernhard, *On the Mountain* (translated by Russell Stockman).

The novel begins with the word 'Fatherland' – a word that resonates in all kinds of ways, with a particular historical weight for an author writing in the German language. Here its primary reference seems to be to a place: Austria.

And then a comma. This is a novel of commas. The entire novel consists of a single sentence. Commas break up the flow of the narrative. A comma divides. Commas allow a quick pause for breath, a moment to appreciate the difference between scraps of language. But a comma simultaneously connects: it insists on the maintenance of a flow of meaning. It denies a conclusion.

A comma is a language device for making a collage. And this is a collage novel. It slams dissimilar things together. The repetitious words of a lover and waking up in a bathtub. Filthy anthems beneath a filthy sky. Tassels, edgings, manure, scum.

A fiction of friction: the grinding together of a consciousness and everything that impinges upon it.

The narrative has a vexed relationship with commas. It cannot do without them but it is not happy with them:

> Everything is a lie, every comma is a lie, all of it nothing but an appalling babble, trivial, degrading, humiliating, yet I cling to these few thoughts, and every letter matters, it comes down to every last letter, and to recognizing the stupidity of it all, a storm comes and drives me into a building,

Language like a river, flowing, unstoppable. A babble alert to its own condition (in a way that soporific *comfort fiction* never knows that it is drugged and easy-dreaming). Every letter matters. A storm of consciousness, of language. It drives the narrator into society – into an Austrian condition – from which he (the gender is not in doubt) recoils.

The second word of the novel is '*nonsense*'. Italicised. Emphatic. What is it that is nonsensical? Clearly the word and the concept 'Fatherland' and all it denotes. This is a novel that mocks the state, its forms, its functions and functionaries. The final paragraph of the book begins, 'senseless seasons, formalities, slanders', referring, I think, to the Austrian judicial system. We learn that the narrator is employed as a courtroom reporter, hence his disgust with 'these infernal piles of documents against everything'. But the narrative also identifies itself as nonsense. It babbles. It refuses to participate in common sense, in good sense. It is disgusted with everything, including itself.

The novel is subtitled, 'Rescue attempt, nonsense' which replicates (precedes) that opening strategy. What is it that someone is attempting to rescue? The Fatherland, from its own absurdities? The narrator, whose condition seems perilous? The genre of the novel? Whatever it may be, that object and that effort are immediately cancelled out, identified as nonsense.

Back to that opening page.

After nonsense a comma. After the comma: a void. A break. The line snaps, as if it were the beginning of a poem. The second line begins: 'traditions keep using the same words'.

And this is a novel which detests traditions and their stale, second-hand language. The traditions of the state; the traditions of bourgeois society. But also, by implication, the conventions and language of what we might call, perhaps, the traditional novel.

On the Mountain denies the comforts of the well-rounded novel. Geography and setting are identified in the most perfunctory of ways: Paris-Lodron Street, the mountains, Vienna, Salzburg, the courthouse, the Gasthaus, the asylum, the market place.

The characters, too, are sketchy. The teacher. The teacher's wife. The innkeeper. The carnival owner. The Fräulein. Not forgetting the dog. The narrator's smelly mongrel dog is as important as any of the human characters in the book. It is an outcast, in this sense resembling the narrator.

There are stories which enlarge upon the presence of the various characters in the narrative but these stories too are sketchy, incomplete, inconclusive. There are gaps. And this is the other major formal device of the novel: spaces between the fractured, choppy paragraphs. Voids.

A kind of vertigo ensues. When the narrative rages against 'a gigantic wave of price increases, a colossal wave of price increases' is this the narrator's anger or is he mocking the peevish complaints of the bourgeoisie? I don't find it at all easy to decide.

The novel ends as abruptly as it started with a throwaway remark about the narrator's dog.

Written almost fifty years ago, this novel is as fresh as if it had been completed yesterday. It has a terrific narrative energy and force. And it has nothing at all in common with the artful constructions of contemporary *literary fiction*.

Malcolm Lowry

In Saturday's *Guardian* (8 December 2007) the poet and translator Michael Hofmann wrote about Malcolm Lowry, in the context of his Lowry anthology *The Voyage That Never Ends*.

I've no idea how good the anthology is but I'm dismayed by

Hofmann's carelessness in his *Guardian* piece. Far from having no financial support, Lowry's entire writing career was financed by his wealthy father, who gave him a regular and lifelong allowance. This meant that Lowry neither had to seek regular salaried employment nor needed to live off the proceeds of his writing (lucky for him; as sales dropped off, the U.K. royalties from *Under the Volcano* amounted to just under two pounds and twenty pence for the second half of 1950). Any wannabe writer would dream of a parent like that.

And Lowry did not leave the manuscript of his first novel in a taxi. It was in a briefcase stolen from the car of a publisher's editor. Rather oddly, Hofmann cites the 1973 biography of Lowry by Douglas Day and makes no mention of the far more impressive, accurate and comprehensive one by Gordon Bowker, published in 1993.

Hofmann's book received a lengthy review from Elizabeth Lowry (no relation) in the *London Review of Books*, 1 November 2007 (unfortunately not available on-line except to subscribers). It was not an over-enthusiastic review. In Elizabeth Lowry's opinion Lowry's later writings 'hold little appeal for the ordinary reader'. She describes Lowry's agent and editor as 'long suffering'. But when she says that 'much of Lowry's surviving fiction is unreadable' this is only true in a sense she doesn't mean. It is unreadable because most of it has not been published in the form in which Lowry wrote it; it can literally be read only by scholars who have access to the manuscripts of his unedited writing. But in the sense that she *does* mean, this begs the question of what we mean by 'readability'.

You don't often see *Under the Volcano* in British bookshops these days. But then Lowry was a modernist. Writing was a self-questioning activity; a struggle. His narrative perspective was never monocular; his first novel, *Ultramarine*, is a collage text – soliloquy in conflict with demotic conversation.

His fiction is not for those readers who require suspense, clever plotting, the drip-feed of big event, controlled self-explaining prose and the consolation of an omniscient, upbeat ending. The texts reverberate with the possibility of making sense out of a blizzard of tiny happenings – daily contingency, under the pressure both of comic absurdities and the weight of memory. The texts invite us to discover meaning, then finally deny that possibility. Lowry always sought to challenge a conventional response: the published correspondence reveals his wish to defamiliarize the text of *Under the Volcano* by using *Tristram Shandy*-style typographical devices; it's plain that his publishers were baffled by this and implemented his aspiration inadequately.

Under the Volcano begins with an absence – its first chapter is focused on a man who isn't there – and then there is an attempt to fill that void with the narrative of a long, disintegrating day. It's a day where nothing much seems to be happening; where the trivia of the everyday bears the crushing weight of turbulent memory. That turbulence is expressed stylistically: sentences are sometimes congested with accumulating materials, dragged out to the length of a page or more, overwhelming the reader. Or, just as often, they are starved of conclusion and fizzle out, terminating in dashes or ellipses. A sentence like 'Hullo, good morning' lands from nowhere: perhaps spoken by a real person, perhaps some echo in the mind. It is a style fit for a world where 'Nobody seemed to be doing anything important, yet everything seemed of the utmost hectic importance.'

Lowry's writing after *Volcano* is one of crisis and hesitation. He had written a novel which he described as 'a machine'. But having accomplished this great work of fiction he then, one might say, set out to challenge the spurious meanings it had secreted. His next novel *Dark as the Grave Wherein My Friend is Laid* deconstructs *Under the Volcano* in a profound way. It rewrites Mexico, demythologising it. In place of transcendence there is now only shabby, comic frustration. But it is also a novel about a writer who feels creatively exhausted. From that exhaustion emerges the narrative. But, crucially, the narrative was never completed in conventional terms. It exists in three parallel versions: process not product. Unfortunately the only published version is a dubious collation, put together in a very questionable way.

The key to Lowry's output in the final decade of his life is perhaps contained in his letter to his editor Albert Erskine, 14 October 1953. Referring to Hofmannsthal's 'Lord Chandos letter' (*Ein Brief*, 1902), Lowry wrote (with reference to his final novel *October Ferry to Gabriola*), 'it is this aspect of it that has made it so hard to write'. Isolated from any avant-garde, Lowry had stumbled on a key modernist text which made sense of his own writing crisis and sense of exhaustion. His writing had become an accumulation of fragments and variations. He had lost all confidence in 'character' and 'plot'. His narratives became variations on the same theme: the writer in motion, on a bus or a boat or just wandering around a city.

To express this movement required an unstable text. Narrative possibility overlapped; deepened; went nowhere and fizzled out. Narrative form accepted improvisation, jottings, diary entries, alternative versions, reflexive material about writers and writing.

On 6 January 1954, Erskine wrote terminating Lowry's contract. He was unenthusiastic about his work-in-progress; it 'lacked the surface drama and pure narrative to draw the reader in.' Plot, he meant. Dramatic events, rounded characters, the trajectory of suspense, mystery and ultimate revelation. The stuff of 'readability'.

Lowry's problem was that those he had professional dealings with in the world of publishing *couldn't read*. His theme was that of a writer who no longer believes that fiction communicates a truth. Out of that perception emerged his writing, in a form which shattered orthodox narrative: the drama of a writer's struggle. And what purer narrative could there be than writing about writing?

Martin Amis, *Yellow Dog*

Yellow Dog is cartoon thin. London-based actor and writer Xan Meo is married to a gorgeous American named Russia but after he gets beaten up and suffers a head injury his personality changes for the worse.The story of the disintegration and then recovery of Xan's marriage is interwoven with the tale of sexually-inadequate tabloid journalist Clint Smoker, retired East End gangster Joseph Andrews, King Henry IX and his royal household, and the crew of a jumbo jet which is doomed to crash. The Xan Meo story is foregrounded; the back stories mostly connect with each other, eventually.

I found it a disappointing read. The twin engines of this narrative are plot and character but neither engaged my interest. The satire on the House of Windsor – Henry IX is a replica of Prince Charles – is laboured. Clint Smoker is too much of a caricature to be remotely engaging, and the fact that his text-messaging dream woman turns out to be other than she seems is drearily predictable. Amis also takes the reader into the murky realm of child abuse and recycles his own journalistic foray into the Californian porn industry. The book is chic, glittery, disposable.

Literally so in this latter aspect. I donated my copy to Oxfam.

Part Two: At History's Edge

The Bloody British Empire

John Newsinger, *The Blood Never Dried: A People's History of the British Empire* (Bookmarks Publications, 2006). 286 pages, paperback, £11.99, ISBN 1905192126.

Newsinger has three basic propositions:
Firstly, he identifies the history of the British Empire in these terms:

> Whereas Britain after 1918 was a 'satisfied' empire, concerned to hold what it had rather than seize more, in the 19th century the British Empire, despite the liberalism of its metropolitan rulers, was a predatory empire engaged in continuous warfare.

Secondly, he diagnoses extreme violence as an inherent component of imperialism. Colonialism always requires police officers and soldiers, whose brutality towards the colonised is a fundamental condition of governance. There is no imperialism without repression and violence.

Thirdly, politicians and journalists have, historically, generally failed to confront the barbarism which formed an essential feature of British imperial rule, and this has been replicated by academics. Historians shy away from acknowledging the stupendous brutality of empire; often they ignore it completely. In so doing they fail to provide an adequate or reasonably objective account of Britain's past. Newsinger's book corrects this blind spot with a revisionist history of the British empire which focuses on native resistance to it and the extreme violence used by a supposedly civilised state to suppress it. His title echoes the words of the Chartist and socialist Ernest Jones, who in 1851 wrote of Britain, 'On its colonies the sun never sets, but the blood never dries.'

Newsinger develops these three arguments over twelve chapters which analyze, in chronological order, key episodes in the history of the British Empire. These are (1) slavery in the Caribbean (2) the

Irish famine (3) China and the opium wars (4) the Indian mutiny (5) the invasion of Egypt (6) global insurgencies against the Empire in the wake of the First World War (7) the Palestinian uprising 1936-9 (8) the struggle for Indian independence (9) Suez (10) insurgency in Kenya (11) insurgency in the Far East (12) the subordination of the British Empire to US imperialism.

I think it's a brilliant book. Newsinger is prodigiously well read and writes with absolute lucidity and clarity. His book is full of shocking examples of terror and atrocity. It's a great resource and my copy will go on the same shelf as Mark Curtis's *Web of Deceit* and Robert Fisk's *The Great War for Civilisation*. I'll probably return to this book in a future post, but for the moment let me just briefly mention Newsinger's account of the great Indian rebellion 1857-8, an insurrection which is memorialised in Trafalgar Square by the monument to Major General Sir Henry Havelock, who was in charge of the army which suppressed it.

Newsinger argues that torture was a fundamental aspect of the financial operations of British colonialism in India. Having cited the evidence for this he remarks,

> What is remarkable is how little this regime of torture has figured in accounts of British rule in India. It is a hidden history that has been unremarked on and almost completely unexplored. Book after book remains silent on the subject. This most surely calls into question the whole historiography of the Raj.

The revolt which erupted in 1857 against British rule was, he asserts, 'without doubt, one of the largest revolutionary outbreaks of the 19th century'. And it was put down with massive force and extreme violence. The mass media of the day played a crucial role in mobilising British public opinion in support of the repression. Firstly, it ran bogus horror stories, which cast the rebels as barbarians: 'It was widely reported that British women had been cooked alive, forced to eat their children, horribly mutilated with noses and ears cut off and eyes put out, and stripped naked and publicly raped. These stories were untrue.'

Conversely, the barbarism and atrocities carried out by the British army went unreported. The horrors matched those perpetrated by the Third Reich when it rampaged through eastern Europe. Sergeant William Forbes recorded witnessing 130 men hanged from a giant banyan tree. And the intelligentsia played its part, too. Charles Dickens raged that he desired 'to exterminate the race upon whom the stain of the late cruelties rested ... to blot it out of mankind and raze it off the face of the earth'.

The great rebellion was crushed. But it led to the termination of the power of the East India Company and marked the beginning of the long struggle for Indian independence, proving an inspiration to later generations.

A Few Words about *Slaughterhouse-Five*

By common consent the two great English language anti-war novels of the past 50 years are Joseph Heller's *Catch-22* (1961) and Kurt Vonnegut's *Slaughterhouse-Five* (1969). These novels were both written by men who were young servicemen in the Second World War. Heller, born in 1923, enlisted in the Army Air Corps and was trained as a bombardier (i.e. the man who aims and drops bombs from a bomber). In 1944 he was sent in combat, flying out of Corsica with B-25 crews of 488 squadron. He flew 60 missions. His nerve cracked after what one obituary writer called 'an awful experience on a bombing raid near Avignon' and for his last 25 missions he was 'terrified'. In later years, as a successful writer, Heller played down the darker side of those missions, saying that for the most part he had 'a very good time in the war'. But his sister Sylvia claimed he had a wartime diary which contained details of appalling events. Heller died in 1999 and a biography has yet to appear.

Heller experienced war from a bomber; his compatriot Kurt Vonnegut from that of one of the bombed. Vonnegut (born in 1922) served in the US infantry, was captured in December 1944, and as a prisoner of war was present in the German city of Dresden on 13 February 1945 when an Allied bombing raid laid waste the centre of the city, killing vast numbers of civilians in a firestorm. It was one of the defining moments of Vonnegut's life and the experience which he later converted into fiction in what is arguably his greatest novel.

There are big differences between the two novels. Heller's book is a lengthy comedy about the absurdity of war. It moves at a terrific pace and pays little attention to the conventions of standard realist fiction. There is no mannered fine writing and no in-depth description of characters or landscapes. The characters sometimes have absurd names, and a slightly cartoon quality. The novel is not a psychological drama and the plot is not suspenseful, setting up mysteries and then resolving them. It satirises the business of war from the perspective of the disgruntled, humane, ordinary fighting man of World War Two. General Peckem, for example, invents the term 'bomb pattern', cheerfully explaining that 'It means nothing, but you'd be surprised how rapidly it's caught on.' It results in bomber pilots not worrying whether or not they hit the target as long they can get their bombs to explode together 'and make a neat aerial photograph'. This leads on to plans for 'bombing a tiny undefended village, reducing the whole community to rubble' – a mission which is, in military terms, 'entirely unnecessary'. It's probably no coincidence that Heller started writing the book while working for an advertising agency. *Catch-22* is an anti-army and anti-organisation book as much as an anti-war book, and a major theme is the jarring friction between image and reality, and language and reality. But underlying all this is the central theme of war's stupidity and cruelty, and its irrational logic.

Slaughterhouse-Five is a much shorter novel and much more radical in its narrative form. The title refers to that part of a Dresden abattoir where Vonnegut and other prisoners of war were held captive, and where they had the good fortune to survive the massive bombing raid on the city and the firestorm that followed. Like *Catch-22*, Vonnegut's novel is an absurdist satire on war, but its defining temper is whimsical – whimsical in its strictest sense: changeful, multi-formed, capricious, unconventional, crazy, unexpected, imaginative, witty, ridiculous. Its whimsicality is signalled by the eccentric title page:

> Slaughterhouse-Five OR THE CHILDREN'S CRUSADE, A Duty Dance with Death, by Kurt Vonnegut, Jr. A fourth-generation German-American now living in easy circumstances on Cape Cod [and smoking too much] who, as an American infantry scout hors de combat, as a prisoner of war, witnessed the fire bombing of Dresden, Germany, 'the Florence of the Elbe,' a long time ago, and survived to tell the tale. This is a novel somewhat in the telegraphic schizophrenic manner of tales of the planet Tralfamdore, where the flying saucers come from. Peace.

The first sentence of the novel is: 'All this happened, more or less.' Vonnegut stands in the doorway of his story asserting that the wartime experiences described in the novel are all true, but that 'I've changed all the names'. He also describes how he went back to Dresden in 1967. He goes on to say how he has struggled over many years to write a book about the destruction of the city. He complains that in the post-war years 'There hadn't been much publicity' about what happened at Dresden and when he attempted to find out more from the Air Force he was told the information was classified. He goes on to explain why the narrative that follows is a fragmentary one: 'It is so short and jumbled and jangled ... because there is nothing intelligent to say about a massacre'. Everything is quiet after a massacre, asserts Vonnegut, except for the birds, and all they say is: 'Poo-tee-weet'. This meaningless bird cry turns out to be the closing sentence of the novel. After a rambling first chapter of autobiographical explanation, Vonnegut then gets on with his story.

His fictional alter ego turns out to be a man named Billy Pilgrim, who turns out to have been born the same year as Vonnegut. Pilgrim is a kind of holy fool – innocent, easygoing, placid. He is also 'unstuck in time'. The novel has a complicated chronological structure, jumping backwards and forwards in time, but gradually leading up to (and back to) that moment in 1945 when Dresden is bombed. Billy believes he has been kidnapped by a flying saucer in 1967, which takes him to the faraway planet of Tralfamadore, where he starts a relationship with an abducted movie actress named Montana Wildhack.

There are at least two possible ways of reading the story. We can accept Billy's version of reality literally, in which he really did visit the planet Tralfamadore and lead a surreal life, or we can interpret the narrative as the tale of a man broken by the wartime horrors he has witnessed, and who drifts in and out of consciousness, sometimes lapsing into fantasy as he reviews his life and reinvents it. All kinds of stories overlap in this novel, including Billy's wartime experiences, his career as an optometrist, his marriage to Valencia Merble, his experience of an air crash and his abduction by extra-terrestials. The narrative structure of *Slaughterhouse-Five* breaks all the usual conventions of fiction. Apart from the autobiographical material which begins and ends it, the book includes discussion of a trashy sixties bestseller (*Valley of the Dolls*), newspaper reports and events which occurred while Vonnegut was writing it ('Robert

Kennedy ... was shot two nights ago'). It comments on the novels of the fictional science fiction writer Kilgore Trout (who sounds at times a bit like P. K. Dick), who pops up as a character. It also refers scathingly to current US foreign policy: 'every day my Government gives me a count of corpses created by military science in Vietnam'.

That other great American master of 1960s whimsy, Richard Brautigan, saw his critical reputation, commercial success, and readership evaporate in the 1970s (Brautigan committed suicide in 1984), but *Slaughterhouse-Five* has kept its readers and earned its place as a modern classic, despite being quite unlike the average novel. This may be because it is a very, very funny book and, in spite of its complicated narrative structure, it has a chatty, laconic, whimsical narrative voice and is not a difficult book to read. As a satire on modern American life it has lost none of its edge. The writing is often startlingly fresh and inventive in a wholly original way. What other writer has described orgasm and ejaculation like this? 'Billy made a noise like a small, rusty hinge. He had just emptied his seminal vesicles into Valencia.' That the whole edifice spins on a very dark axis – the Dresden firestorm – also gives it a moral seriousness and a satirical bite which is frequently lacking in American comic writing, and which is noticeably missing in Brautigan's fiction, which all too often tips over into a kind of self-satisfied high-sugar-content cute sentimentality.

There is a problem with *Slaughterhouse-Five*, however. Vonnegut not only used his own personal experience and memories in writing the book but also drew on David Irving's *The Destruction of Dresden* (London, 1963). The 1964 American edition published by Holt, Rinehart and Winston is even brought into the hospital in Vermont where Billy Pilgrim is a patient and handed to the Harvard history professor with whom he shares the room.

Irving is now notorious and his reputation as a historian has collapsed, but his failings were far from obvious in the 1960s, when he appeared to be a reputable scholar. His book was an international bestseller, and popularised a number of central beliefs about the bombing raid on Dresden. One was that Dresden was a wholly innocent target of no significance, maliciously and scandalously flattened by the Allies; in a short, the air raid and the ensuing firestorm amounted to a war crime. In *Slaughterhouse-Five* Billy Pilgrim is told by an English prisoner of war that Dresden is supposed to be a beautiful city: 'You needn't worry about bombs, by the way. Dresden is an open city. It is undefended, and contains no war industries or troop concentrations of any importance.' Secondly, Irving claimed that at least 135,000 German civilians died in the Dresden firestorm. This is recycled by Vonnegut, who recounts how 'Nothing happened that night. It was the next night that about one hundred and thirty thousand people in Dresden would die.'

At the beginning of the novel Vonnegut mentions how, when he first started working on it, hardly anybody had ever heard of the raid on Dresden: 'Not many Americans knew how much worse it had been than Hiroshima, for instance. I didn't know that, either. There hadn't been much publicity.'

Slaughterhouse-Five also briefly recycles an atrocity story publicised by Irving in which American fighter planes machine-gunned survivors of the firestorm. Vonnegut's novel, like Irving's history book, became a bestseller, and enormously influential in promoting the idea that the bombing of Dresden was a war crime.

It now turns out that David Irving's version was utterly unreliable. A massive new history of the raid published last year by Bloomsbury – Frederick Taylor's *Dresden: Tuesday 13 February 1945* – asserts that it was a normally functioning Nazi city containing many vital sites of manufacturing, communications and services of great importance to Germany's war effort.

Taylor remarks in his Preface that 'As a student in the 1960s ... like so many others of my age, I had learned of the city's destruction principally through a work of fiction: Kurt Vonnegut's acidly surreal masterpiece, *Slaughterhouse-Five*.'

Taylor estimates that between 25,000 and 40,000 died in the raid – a lot less than the figure promoted by Irving and vastly less than the number of those who died at Hiroshima (100,000 out of a population of 400,000, rising to 140,000 from radiation sickness by the end of 1945, rising to 200,000 five years later). Taylor also rubbishes the idea that American fighter planes deliberately strafed and massacred survivors.

The question then arises: what are the implications of this new historical knowledge for *Slaughterhouse-Five*? Perhaps not as great as those of us who admire the novel might have feared. Clearly it's very unfortunate that Vonnegut inserts statistics into the narrative which now turn out to be utterly unreliable and wildly exaggerated. However, this occurs only on three or four occasions. They could be changed and I think they should be.

The strafing episode is less contentious as it's relatively perfunctory, consisting of just seven sentences. Taylor makes it clear that some survivors may indeed have been hit by bullets fired by fighter planes but insists that this would have been the consequence of a low-level dogfight involving the 356th Fighter Group and not a deliberate machine-gunning of civilians. (In the context of the crimes of the modern US army Taylor's conclusion might provoke incredulity but he appears to be right.)

There are other historical errors. Vonnegut describes soap and candles 'made from the fat of rendered Jews and Gypsies and fairies and communists, and other enemies of the State'. However, according to Anton La Guardia, this is legend, not fact (see his book *Holy Land, Unholy War* [John Murray, 2002], pp. 163-4).

Slaughterhouse-Five has dated in other ways, apart from those historical aspects highlighted by Taylor's book. No novelist would nowadays use the word 'fairies' for gay people. Vonnegut uses 'schizophrenic' as an adjective, something now regarded as offensive by mental health groups. He also uses the terms 'spastic' and 'Mongolian idiot' for sufferers from Down's syndrome – vocabulary now widely regarded as unacceptable. However, it would be foolish to insist that Vonnegut now alter that vocabulary. His novel is a snapshot of the language and attitudes of its time, just as every novel is.

The central core of the novel – Vonnegut's own experience of the aftermath of rhe raid and his account of Billy Pilgrim among the ruins – survives with its integrity intact. The much bigger question raised by Taylor's book is how justified is it to see the bombing of Dresden as a war crime.

The two most interesting discussions I've come across are by David Cesarini (in the *Independent*, 13 February 2004) and Michael Bradley (in *Socialist Review*, March 2004).

Cesarini remarks, 'Like Frederick Taylor, I grew up with a sense that the RAF's bombing of Dresden on 13-14 February 1945 was a stain on the Allies' war record. My unease owed much to Kurt Vonnegut's novelised memoir of his experience in Dresden as an American PoW, forced to disinter the corpses of German civilians who had been suffocated or baked to death in cellars beneath the ruins of their once-beautiful city. I read *Slaughterhouse-Five* in one sitting, and it has haunted me since.'

Cesarini complains that the raid has become a propaganda tool for the German right, and he asserts that Dresden was not an innocent city.

For Michael Bradley it was. (Bradley's was a lone voice; most reviewers seem to have adopted a position which parallels Cesarini's.) He argues that in spite of the evidence put forward by Taylor, the raid was still a war crime:

> This was terror bombing – no matter what spin you try to put on it. Even the US's so called 'precision' attacks would cost thousands of lives through what they described as 'spillage'.

Bradley contextualizes:

> The Second World War wasn't just a war about destroying German fascism. The Allies were out to destroy the German regime in order to control the postwar world. They were prepared to divert huge military resources into shaping that postwar world even if it meant weakening the fight against Germany. Britain sent thousands of troops into Greece to prevent the left wing resistance movement seizing power, and with the US rushed to disarm the left wing movements that had fought the Nazis in France and Italy.
>
> In such a war of revenge attacks ordinary people in enemy countries were not seen as potential allies. They were not seen as an important force that could potentially undermine totalitarian regimes from within. They were legitimate targets. And at the end of that line of logic came Hiroshima and Nagasaki.

I'm not totally persuaded persuaded by Bradley's arguments. I'm sceptical that if Dresden and other cities hadn't been bombed the civilian population would have risen up against the Nazis.

Part of the subtlety and complexity of *Slaughterhouse-Five* is that it in fact incorporates the counter-argument that the bombing was justified. Billy Pilgrim shares his hospital bed with a professional historian named Rumfoord. This allows Vonnegut to quote the words of Ira C. Eaker, Lieutenant General USAF., retired, who argues that those people who agonise about the victims of the Dresden bombing raid should remember 'that V-1's and V-2's were at that very time falling on England, killing civilian men, women, and children indiscriminately, as they were designed and launched to do. It might be well to remember Buchenwald and Coventry, too.'

Taylor puts it more subtly:

> This is perhaps the great, still-unanswered question about Germany and the German people between 1933 and 1945. With the vast material and spiritual riches of places like Dresden at your disposal, why place all that at risk by launching a ruthless, in large part genocidal attack on the rest of Europe? ... Did anyone really expect the world to fight back while wearing kid gloves, in order not to damage Germany's artistic treasures or kill German civilians?

A powerful advanced industrial nation with an impressive culture which believed it had a right to invade other nations, bringing misery and suffering to millions, and which never anticipated that one day this might have adverse consequences for its own civilian population ... Now what modern country does that make you think of?

And who would have thought back in 1969 that such heavy issues would continue to be fought over at the start of the 21st century partly as the consequence of the influence of a slim whimsical metafiction 'somewhat in the telegraphic schizophrenic manner of tales of the planet Tralfamdore, where the flying saucers come from'?

9/11 Conspiracy Theories

> *The twin towers were secretly brought down by demolition charges, not by the impact of crashing jets ... Photographs show that the plane which hit the South Tower had some kind of mysterious bulbous housing attached beneath its fuselage ... An 'X Team' secretly removed aircraft parts and the black boxes from the crash sites ...*

Ian Henshall and Rowland Morgan's *9/11 Revealed: Challenging the facts behind the War on Terror* (Constable and Robinson, 2005) sets the main conspiracy theories about 9/11 against the official conclusions of the Kean Commission report.

The book didn't convince me. It's well written and I'm sympathetic to what they say about a compliant corporate mass media but the idea that the events of 9/11 were in any way orchestrated by sections of the American military or intelligence or political establishment for their own nefarious purposes strikes me as highly implausible. They say that 'Corporate TV, and later the Kean Report, depicted the presumed hijackers as bloodthirsty religious fanatics, but from the carnage point of view the 9/11 events were unsuccessful.'

Eh? Three thousand dead is *failure?* I think not. Now it's certainly true that the hijackers might have ended up killing many more that day than they actually did, but their primary intention was not to kill the maximum number of Americans possible but to fly jets into symbolic targets of US economic, military and political hegemony. In that they were 75 per cent successful. They hit both the main towers at the WTC and they hit the Pentagon. In short, they hit major symbols and expressions of capitalism and militarism. They failed to hit the fourth target, which it seems likely was the White House.

The hijackings were surely a mixture of professionalism and amateurishness. Three planes were successfully hijacked and flown to their intended destinations. But I very much doubt that the hijackers who hit the WTC knew that the towers would subsequently collapse. Nor, I think, did they much care *where* they hit the towers. Had they flown the jets much lower into the towers they would surely have killed many thousands more. But they weren't playing a numbers game.

Conspiracy theorists point to the absence of film footage of a jet hitting the Pentagon and put forward the theory that it was a missile. And why, they say, did whatever hit the Pentagon hit it at *its strongest and least populated part?* But if it was a missile, what happened to Flight 77 and its civilian passengers? Are we really supposed to believe that they were spirited away to a top secret airforce base where the plane was destroyed and the passengers either executed or kept as prisoners to this day? That's not a scenario I find remotely plausible.

The time lapse CCTV footage of the impact on the Pentagon, says this book, shows 'the white flash explosion consistent with a small missile warhead. There is no similar white flash in the WTC collision photographs.' But this simply invites the reader to share in an expertise that neither the authors nor the average reader has. The Pentagon was a very different structure to the WTC. I'm not persuaded that the terrific boiling surges of exploding fuel are really all that different at the Washington and New York sites.

Why didn't the hijackers hit the Pentagon where it would have hurt most? The answer, I suspect, is that the hijackers didn't know anything about the structural strengths and weaknesses of the Pentagon building. Nor did they know about the internal layout. They seem to have believed, falsely, that it would be more damaging to hit the building from the side rather than from above. But the primary objective was to hit it, and this was successfully accomplished.

9/11 Revealed is a lucidly written book and the authors aren't fringe nutters. But ultimately all the major conspiracy theories assume that a section or sections of the American establishment were prepared to countenance the killing of large numbers of Americans and attacks on major sites on American soil for an ulterior, allegedly political motive. But Bush didn't *need* 9/11 to launch a war on Afghanistan, though obviously it made it easier. Ditto 'the war on terror'. Ditto the invasion and occupation of Iraq. At a bare minimum, and aided and assisted by the corporate mass media, you can certainly fool 50 per cent of the people most of the time, on just about anything.

Ultimately I just can't believe that you could get enough American professionals to agree to a conspiracy on that scale, implement it and then cover it up afterwards, whether it involved finding out about the proposed hijackings in advance and *letting them happen anyway*, or being in some way directly involved on the day. I find it much easier to believe that the order of the day was bungling, dithering, complacency, incompetence, career rivalries, disbelief and a failure to grasp that such an attack was either possible or was taking place.

The US military and political establishment has, of course, a long record of conspiracies and mass murder, but these all involve operations in foreign lands. These actual historical conspiracies – in Indonesia, Chile, Iraq, etc. etc. – were exposed years ago. But they attract no media coverage. The media would far rather concentrate on ludicrous death-of-Diana conspiracy theories than coups in foreign countries. American civilians or military personnel abroad are certainly expendable and the corporate media can be relied on to screen such events through a neutralising filter. But I simply don't believe that these elites would countenance the mass killing of civilians on American soil, especially when so many of the victims were their kind of people – white, middle class professionals.

That said, there's just one conspiracy theory that does cause me some niggling doubts. That's what happened to Flight 93, which crashed at Shanksville, PA. Was it shot down? There appears to be eyewitness evidence that a USAF A-10 Thunderbolt was present at the time the jet crashed. It's plausible that a hijacked jet heading for Washington D.C. would, in the circumstances of that morning, have been shot down, not least since the passengers would have been regarded as doomed anyway. But if so, would it really have been covered up? Would not a tearful President have told his fellow Americans that there really hadn't been any alternative? *The USAF took a tough heartbreaking decision and he recognised they had no choice.* Politically, Bush would surely have got away with it. But cover it up and you risk the end of your career and reputation. The US armed forces are leaky places – it's how Seymour Hersh gets to write his books. So on the whole, I finally go for the brought-down-by-a-fight-in-the-cockpit scenario.

The authors say that a one ton engine part from Flight 93 was found 1.2 miles from the crash site. 'The FBI's explanation that the engine bounced this distance from the impact crater seems next to impossible.'

Is it? I'm not an expert in wreckage scatter from an airliner crash impact. Neither, I suspect, are Henshall or Morgan.

Diana Conspiracy Theory

I'm with the conspiracy theorists on Diana's death, opines Independent *columnist Mary Dejevsky (12 December 2006).*

Why were none of the CCTV cameras at the Paris Ritz working that evening? What about that small white car that some saw in the tunnel? Why should the driver, drunk or sober, have been in the pay of the French secret services, and why – as we now learn –

were Diana's phone calls monitored by US intelligence? Why did it take so long to transport Diana to hospital? What about the speed with which the tunnel was cleaned, and why were Mercedes mechanics not permitted to examine the car?

It's very sloppy journalism.

Firstly, CCTV cameras were working at the Ritz – which is why we have footage of Diana entering the hotel through a revolving door, the driver stooping in the lobby to tie his shoelaces, and Diana and Dodi waiting at the rear of the hotel to get into their car. (Dejevsky doesn't mention the theory that the fact that the driver was able to tie his shoelaces proves he wasn't drunk – but as a woman from the *Daily Telegraph* explained on TV a while back, anyone who believes that doesn't know anything about being pissed and certainly knows nothing of the skills mastered by journalists on national newspapers, let alone Parisian chauffeurs.)

Nobody saw a small white car in the tunnel because there were no witnesses. The deduction that there had been a collision with a tiny Fiat came from forensic analysis of the wreckage and the discovery of flakes of white paint. The driver of the Fiat didn't stop because (i) possibly he or she was pissed too (ii) fleeing is the gut instinct of some drivers who have had a collision with another vehicle.

The driver of Diana's car seems to have been paid small retainers by various intelligence services who were interested in knowing who stayed at the Ritz. It's what intelligence services do – they have an obsessive interest in accumulating data.

Why were Diana's calls monitored by US intelligence? Because the Americans monitor everything. In Britain they use a place called Menwith Hill, outside Harrogate in Yorkshire. They monitor everybody's emails and phone calls, in the sense of recording them. But they don't bother reading the stuff – a gargantuan task. What they do is process it with super computers and analyse significant words. You only attract attention if you use certain words in clusters and fit a certain profile. Why does the US collect information in this way? Because if you know everything it makes trying to control the world easier.

Why did it take so long to transport Diana to hospital? Because medical procedures are different in France. The doctor on the scene tried to save her life in the wreckage. The idea that members of the French medical profession deliberately tried to kill Diana by delaying her effective treatment is an absurd thesis.

What about the speed with which the tunnel was cleaned? Well, after the wreckage had been analysed, recorded and taken away, why not? British police are always very keen to get the traffic moving after a fatal crash, sometimes to the detriment of an effective investigation of the collision. It's bourgeois police ideology. And cleaning street surfaces is something Parisian municipal government is damn good at – unlike filthy London.

Why were Mercedes mechanics not permitted to examine the car? Well, why should they be? There was no suggestion of a mechanical malfunction, which might have been bad commercial news. The police have their own investigators. The event had nothing at all to do with Mercedes.

Dejevsky claims that killing people in car crashes 'is a staple of security services the world over'. But she gives not a single example. Who has been murdered by MI5 in a car crash in Britain in the past fifty years, then? I'd be interested to know.

The conspiracy theorists also overlook a rather obvious point. Diana played a major role in her own death by not using her seatbelt. Her bodyguard, sitting in the front seat, wore one and survived. If she'd used hers she'd have lived.

Why would anyone want to murder Diana? Dejevsky has the answer: 'By breaking free from the Royal Family and behaving as she did, Diana was subverting the monarchy and thus the state.'

Well if you see a multi-millionaire playgirl as *a subversive force* I think you are crackers. But then Dejevsky is. She rounds off her piece by saying, 'I don't believe the Prime Minister lied about Iraq's lethal weapons; I fear he believed in every last tonne.'

Which, since Blair plainly planned for a war and then knowingly orchestrated a bogus reason for it, shows just how dim journalists like Dejevsky really are. But then she used to work for the BBC.

Of course it's true that Diana wrote a letter saying that Charles planned to have her killed in a car crash.

The Prince of Wales's face was a cruel mask as dawn broke over Highgrove. 'Tell M that my frightful wife must learn the meaning of the phrase "the big sleep". As soon as jolly possible.'

As he cavorted in the hot tub with two bulbous blondes, the tiny red light on Bond's water-resistant Rolex began winking urgently. The laughter of the girls rang in his ear like tinkling silver as he glanced at the LCD. It was the boss. He pressed the watch to his ear.

'It's Diana,' M said. 'His Royal Highness wants her liquidated. Now. For the sake of Britain.'

Half an hour later 007 was in a Lear jet screaming towards Orly. As he gazed down at the gunmetal grey fields of Normandy, M's final words rang in his ears. 'Not the Aston Martin, 007. Use the white Fiat Uno for this job ... '

What Lies Beneath

Richard Seymour, *The Meaning of David Cameron*.

This book basically does two things. Firstly, it analyses and describes the condition that Britain finds itself in politically and economically after the triumph of neoliberalism over the social democratic values of the period 1945-75. Neoliberalism, in Seymour's account, was a restorationist project, determined to restore the power of capital and break the power of organised labour which manifested itself in the turbulent 1970s. However, it was not simply an economic project but also a political one, extending market values into every aspect of political and social life.

Neoliberalism accomplished both the wholesale privatisation of public assets and the hollowing out the state, to make it resistant to democratic accountability. The deep unpopularity of both privatisation and British foreign policy matters little when all three of the main parties agree to it. The left's traditional social base has also been depleted by the decline in manufacturing industry and trade union membership, while at the same time Labour Party membership has become substantially middle class and internal party democracy has been massively reduced. In the name of modernity the social landscape has been transformed. The postal service has been wrecked in the name of 'efficiency', public libraries have had their book stock disposed of and seen their loan-figures collapse in the name of 'modernisation' and the space for resistance or modest reformism at a local level has been closed down by the Blair local government reforms, which ended the old democratically accountable committee structure and replaced it with behind-closed-doors cabinet decision-making. The priests and managers of the neoliberal project have been amply rewarded for their services, from the corporate media, the health manager and the Vice-Chancellor, all the way down to the local councillor. The liberal intelligentsia has collaborated with enthusiasm and Ian McEwan's *Saturday* supplies the outstanding monument: modernity is celebrated through the deeply conservative medium of the middle class realist novel, conveying the soothing message that consumption is good, progressive and rational, whereas resistance and protest is backward, stupid and, well, *selfish*. And in McEwan's fable the working class lurks at the edges, violent, irrational and diseased, requiring physical violence to keep its menace in check.

This first aspect of *The Meaning of David Cameron* is historical, supplying an account of the crucial transformations of the post-war era, including the Thatcher years (which recomposed the working class by smashing the manufacturing sector and moving towards a service-based economy) and the concomitant triumph of the right inside the Labour Party. It also reaches back further in time, providing a brief, potted history of the Conservative Party and the capitalist and class blocs it has cultivated to gain power. 'Cameronism' arrives as the latest formation in this evolving history. It is only perceived as centrist and moderate because of the way in which conservative policies and ideas once regarded as extreme and reactionary have moved to occupy the mainstream of political discourse.

Secondly, in diagnosing our modern neoliberal condition, Seymour interrogates its discourse, subjecting its categories and vocabulary to a sustained critique. In doing so the book goes far beyond its three foregrounded topics of 'Apathy' (that growing percentage of the alienated and unrepresented electorate which declines to participate in elections), 'Meritocracy' (the notion that society is intrinsically fair and that social success is determined by personal ability) and 'Progress' (the appropriation of the idea of modernity for globalisation and unfettered capitalism). The critique is Marxist, a classic project of demystification, which peels away the various ideological formations and reveals what lies beneath. Neoliberalism cultivates a language of efficiency, ostensibly value free, 'neutral' and objective, though in reality saturated in values and ideology. Thus 'meritocracy' obscures class privilege and substitutes for 'equality', while 'social exclusion' masks 'exploitation' in a capitalist society. Likewise, Seymour reinstates class war as the fundamental dynamic of the neoliberal project, and imperialism as the quintessence of the new humanitarianism in foreign policy.

As Seymour lucidly demonstrates, class is extirpated from mainstream political discourse or, at best, made fuzzy as a category by detaching it from matters of income and personal wealth – specifically, ownership of the means of production and the individual sale of labour – and relating it to various superficial cultural configurations. In foreign policy, the new imperialism resulted in New Labour strengthening its ties with the European right, which brought it still closer to the Tories.

The regenerated Conservative Party is, Seymour shows, the latest twist in a project which has long represented antipathy to collectivism as a defence of modernity. Cameronism is simply the re-branding of this history, coated with a cosmetic neoliberal scepticism and resting on the inchoate social philosophy of the likes of Phillip Blond. However, neoliberalism in its Cameronian form is about to become an even more ferocious project, promising a massive assault on working people. The problem for the left in Britain is that the Labour Party is an impediment to resistance (you have to be very soft left indeed to be enthused by the current crop of leadership candidates), while the hard left remains fragmented and fissiparous. Seymour's vision of the fightback is slightly perfunctory ('setting up community organisations' is one option he envisages), though it is admittedly a matter of history that mass discontent can erupt from nowhere and take on forms which even the best political theorist can't anticipate.

But these are early days. For the present, this is the phoney war and not much is happening. But David Cameron is assembling his jackals and setting out his battle plan. Yesterday's *Independent* indicated that wholesale privatisation of Royal Mail is on the cards. The first skirmishes will soon be here, and then the great battles. The analysis contained in *The Meaning of David Cameron* is likely to take on new weight in the months and years to come. The book certainly supplies a lucid diagnosis of the state we're in and what its roots are. And if David Cameron signifies neoliberalism regenerated – the logic of neoliberal accumulation in a fragile and vulnerable capitalist economy – what, then, is the meaning of Richard Seymour? Richard Seymour means *critical understanding* and *resistance*.

Sarah and the Cement Factory

John Fowles moved into Underhill Farm, Lyme Regis, in October 1965. He began writing *The French Lieutenant's Woman* in January 1967, completing the third and final draft in August 1968.

Ironically, he did not know the history of Lyme Regis very well when he wrote the novel. When Fowles wrote in the first chapter that 'the Cobb has changed very little since the year of which I write' he was wrong. He was also wrong when he described the beach to the west (known as 'Monmouth beach') as being empty and desolate in 1867 ('No house lay visibly then').

What Fowles was ignorant of when he wrote the novel was the existence of the Lyme Regis hydraulic cement factory. This was based just to the west of the Cobb and was a substantial enterprise. It probably started around 1830-40. When it closed in 1913 it employed 375 men, women and children. The Lyme Regis cement works was a significant business, run in stiff competition with another major producer in Wales. It can be seen marked on the First Series Ordnance Survey map.

The manufacturing process relied on blue lias, which the local coastline has in abundance. The cement works ruthlessly exploited the ledges exposed at low tide (and may also have removed some of the local cliffs). A narrow gauge railway line was built out across the ledges, which were blown up with explosives and the material transported back to land. There was also a railway line from the cement factory to the Cobb, for shipping the finished product. Railway tracking on the Cobb can be traced back to as early as 1853.

When Sarah Woodruff stood at the end of the Cobb, she would have heard the occasional sound of high explosive, seen the trundling of wagons carrying cement to waiting ships, and been aware of a large factory at the back of the beach to the west – all very different to the image of bleak isolation represented by both the novel and the film.

The Lyme Regis of 1867 was, in reality, significantly different to how Fowles imagined it to be. Industrialisation was at the throbbing heart of Lyme's existence. And traces of it still exist, most notably in the remains of the cement factory railway track, which can still be seen on the beach today.

Douglas Haig: A Great Military Commander?

Channel Five is running a weekly documentary series on Friday nights entitled *Great British Commanders*. It is fronted by Major Gordon Corrigan, who is straight out of central casting (toothbrush moustache, leathery battered face, a few teeth missing; this is a man who's clearly been in a scrap or two over the years). My antennae quivered at the realisation that last Friday's episode was on Douglas Haig, commander of the British Army on the western front in the First World War. I have minimal interest in Henry V, the Duke of Wellington or Lord Nelson, but I am interested in a man who played a large role in a war which left some of my ancestors listed on memorials to the dead of the Great War. So I taped the programme and have now got round to watching it.

Major Corrigan turned out to be Douglas Haig's number one fan. 'Haig was a brilliant soldier. He was a master of organisation and planning and a visionary champion of new technology ... Right from the beginning of his military career, when he went to Sandhurst, his natural ability shone through. It was clear he was destined for high command ... Haig was a fine man, not only brave and humane but also modest.'

Of course there was that spot of bother known as the Battle of the Somme – 60,000 casualties in a single day, *not good*. 'It wasn't anybody's fault', Corrigan briskly explained. The British army was largely an army of civilians and 'heavy casualties are inevitable while that army learns its trade'. What's more 'Haig learned from his mistakes and that's the making of a great commander.' (Eh? What mistakes? I thought he didn't make any.)

In support of his thesis the Major gazed at some pages of Haig's diary, in the company of Colm McLaughlin, curator of the National Library of Scotland. He also talked to an English woman who runs a bed and breakfast near the Somme, a French bloke who'd excavated the remains of a tank, and Earl Haig (born 1918), who remembers his dad as a lovely man.

'It was Haig who spearheaded the introduction of technology to the western front. He integrated tanks and aircraft with the troops on the ground to eventually drive through the German defences. By November 1918 the Germans had had enough. Faced with defeat on the battlefield and revolution at home, they pleaded for peace ... It was Haig's victory.'

So why do some base personages still persist in regarding Haig as a less than superb military leader?

Denis Winter's ground-breaking book *Haig's Command: A Reassessment* (1991) supplies the reasons. (Winter's book, by the way, has made him many enemies, not least by exposing the complacency and inaccuracy of standard histories of the war and its battles. Winter discovered that the Public Record Office was useless – if you want the truth, go to archives in Australia.)

Haig did not have natural ability as a soldier. He failed the entrance exam to Camberley Staff College. Luckily his sister was married to the Keeper of the Prince of Wales's racing yachts. With the help of influence at Court, Haig was admitted. His early military performance was undistinguished. His rapid promotion almost certainly owed something to him lending (actually giving) £2,000 to his senior officer, Sir John French. Winter concludes that Haig's rise through the ranks 'had always owed more to intrigue and patronage than to any evidence of talent as a soldier'.

Haig's mediocrity and incompetence as a military commander was evident from his very earliest involvement in the Great War. In 1914, at Mons, Le Cateau and Landrecies, he repeatedly bungled his command in the face of the enemy. At the first battle of Ypres, Haig claimed he had bravely ridden into the heart of the danger zone to rally his men; the episode turned out not to have existed, and was characteristic of his tendency retrospectively to fabricate accounts of his bravery and shrewdness which had no basis in historical fact. (Haig's much-quoted diary is an unreliable document because it was doctored after the war.)

In March 1915 Haig took charge of the first major British offensive, at Neuve Chapelle. The British force outnumbered the Germans three to one, with a field gun each five yards and heavy artillery every nineteen yards. Haig was confident of a great victory, asserting that 'We are entering on a serious offensive with the object of breaking the German line. It is very likely than an operation of considerable magnitude may result.' But the attack went horribly wrong. The British force advanced 1,000 yards, but at the cost of 12,000 casualties.

From this Haig went on to another splendid victory at Loos in September 1915, when he had the bright idea of sending his troops across a thousand yards of open downland at 11 in the morning, in full view of the German machine gunners. 'The result of all this was that the two divisions lost 8,000 men in the first hour.'

As for Haig the 'master of organisation and planning', in 1915 he had calculated that to fight a major battle you needed twenty-nine supply roads and seven broad-gauge railway lines. But at the Battle of the Somme he had neither. Both the road and railway supply lines were grossly inadequate. Haig planned for a battle which would last 14 days. In the event it lasted from 1 July 1916 through to November. During that time the British and German armies suffered one million casualties, fighting over an area of land just seven miles square. Contrary to the popular 'attrition' argument put forward by some Haig apologists, British casualties were twice those of the Germans.

On 1 July 1916 the French army at the Somme achieved all its objectives at a cost of 7,000 casualties. British troops failed to make any significant advance, at a cost of 60,000 casualties. (The supposedly 'humane' Haig, incidentally, remarked, 'We almost seem to be fighting against the laws of nature in trying to keep alive races who are obviously of an inferior kind' – by which he was referring to Italians ['a wretched people, useless as fighting men but greedy for money'] and the French ['Few realize the difference between right and wrong, between honest, straightforward dealing and low cunning'].)

So why did the shifty, slippery French succeed where the honest and decent British failed? Because the French army took its artillery seriously, whereas British gunners were poorly trained and had no experience of night-firing, counter-battery work or long range indirect fire. When Noel Birch was appointed Haig's chief artillery officer he was stunned to discover that there was a complete organisational shambles. There wasn't even a list available of the artillery then in France. In Winter's words, 'The great weakness was an utter lack of concern with accuracy.' That's a point worth bearing in mind the next time you see old movie footage from the Great War. The British army not only lacked the ability accurately to neutralise the enemy's front line, it was also incapable of precision creeping barrages. The impact of shelling was often merely to plough up the ground that the attacking troops had to cross, slowing them down and making them even easier to pick off. These crucial failures in British army strategy are rarely acknowledged in accounts of the First World War. By contrast, French artillery barrages possessed great tactical sophistication.

Passchendaele was the next catastrophe. By 1917 both French and German strategists appreciated the importance of flexible barrages, infiltration and attack in small groups. Haig remained wedded to the disastrously stupid tactic of massed linear advance. British casualties at Passchendaele were around 350,000 – German losses were about two thirds of that figure. In Winter's words, 'Haig's unerring instinct for choosing the worst place to launch an attack is a matter of record.'

In fact, far from being a superb organiser and brilliant strategist Haig's mind was of a rigidly conservative cast. He knew nothing about infantry, engineers or artillery – and made no effort to find out. In late 1917 he still believed that you could punch a hole in the enemy's front line and send in the cavalry. But what do trifles like strategy and supply lines matter when you have God on your side? Haig wrote: 'I know quite well that I am being used as a tool in the hands of the Divine Power and that my strength is not my own.'

As for Corrigan's claim that Haig was 'a visionary champion of new technology', that is a truly preposterous assertion. Haig is on record as complacently telling senior staff, 'I hope none of you gentlemen is so foolish as to think that aeroplanes will be able to be usefully employed for reconnaissance in the air. There is only one way for a commander to get information by reconnaissance and that is by the use of cavalry.' Haig was a cavalry man, with a mindset still firmly lodged in the nineteenth century. Far from regarding planes and tanks as cutting edge machines for winning a war, as late as 1918 Haig remained firmly convinced that they were still less valuable than cavalry, to which they should always be subordinate.

In March 1918 the German army launched an attack which drove the British back forty miles. The British lost 600 guns, suffered 40,000 casualties and 25 of Haig's 60 divisions were reduced to little more than skeletons. It was the greatest defeat suffered by any army on the Western front up to that time. Haig in fact almost lost the war. By June 1918 the German army seemed poised on the brink of victory. But German commanders, disastrously, failed to follow up their advantage. By August the German army was in retreat. This owed nothing to Douglas Haig and everything to the strategy of the French commander, Foch, who had obtained precise foreknowledge (through intelligence) of German military intentions. But the German army was far from a spent force. Less than a month before the end of the war, Haig gloomily acknowledged the strength of the

German army and thought that two more years of war would be necessary: 'In 1920, the real crushing of Germany will be possible, always provided that the British Army is kept up to its present strength.'

The sudden, wholly unexpected collapse of Germany had nothing at all to do with military defeat, because the German army was never defeated. Germany collapsed because a revolution broke out. Britain did not win through military superiority, and its victory was in spite of Douglas Haig, not because of his leadership. As a military commander he was an unimaginative mediocrity.

Manuel's *A Requiem for Marx*

As it was remaindered at £2.50 I bought a copy, out of idle curiosity: Frank E. Manuel, *A Requiem for Karl Marx*. Published by Harvard University Press, paperback, 1997. The blurb asserts that it is 'a learned and elegantly written engagement with the man and his work'. No less a reviewer than Michael Ignatieff, writing in the *New Republic*, found it 'extremely powerful'.

Let the opening sentence of Chapter 6 say everything:

> The festering wounds of Marx's self-loathing might have destroyed him, had he not found salvation in the fantasy of an arena of combat in which he would lead the forces of the proletariat to victory.

Yes, it's the old story, I'm afraid. Marx had a severe personality disorder, which gave rise to all those rum ideas he had.

And as we whisper our prayers during the special mass for the soul of Marx (which is what a requiem is about), we can contemplate such devastating revelations as this:

> In the land where *Das Kapital* was born, Tony Blair, the leader of the British Labor Party, pointedly disavowed any relationship to Marx: 'A belief in society. Working together. Solidarity. Cooperation, Partnership. These are our words. This is my socialism. It is not the socialism of Marx or state control.'

(Manuel cites this speech from the *New York Times*, October 5, 1994.)

Yup, Marx gave us a theory of class war and an analysis of the capitalist state which emphasised the centrality of the forces and relations of production – writings which might be thought to bear *some* relationship to history and society, past and present. And Blair offers 'working together' and other nebulous notions.

What Manuel doesn't mention is that it would be amazing if Blair said anything different, since the Labour Party (better identified as the Capitalist Workers' Party) has always defined itself in opposition to Marxism. It has always been a reformist party which accepts the capitalist state in all its forms. Blair's style of empty rhetoric can be traced back all the way to early Fabianism, which supplied the founding ideology of the Party. For a critical analysis of that history I recommend Tony Cliff and Donny Gluckstein's *The Labour Party*.

Two Marx Myths

In his racy popular biography of Marx, Francis Wheen demolishes the common belief that Marx wrote to Darwin expressing a desire to dedicate *Das Kapital* to him.

The claim was first popularised by Isaiah Berlin and has been repeated many times since. As Wheen demonstrates, Darwin's letter declining the offer of a dedication was written not to Marx but to Edward B. Aveling, author of a simple guide to evolutionary theory, *The Students' Darwin*.

In his blog, Ken MacLeod addresses another myth, which is that *Karl Marx predicted that the first socialist revolution would be in advanced capitalist England, but instead it happened in backward feudal Russia.*

Ken comments:

A glance at the *Communist Manifesto* shows that Marx and Engels expected, in 1847, that the first proletarian revolution would take place in Germany – the bourgeois revolution in Germany is imminent, and they expect a proletarian revolution to immediately follow it. Turning back a few pages, we find them proclaim in the 1882 preface to the Russian edition that 'Russia is in the vanguard of revolutionary action in Europe' and conclude: 'If the Russian Revolution becomes the signal for a proletarian revolution in the West, so that both complement each other, the present Russian common ownership of land may serve as the starting point of a communist development.' Not quite how things worked out, of course, but a shrewd sentence for all that!

(http://kenmacleod.blogspot.com/2006_11_01_kenmacleod_archive.html#116432031013812933)

For another insight into Marx's acuity we need only consider one of the more bizarre moments of his life – his three hour lunch with Sir Mountstuart Elphinstone Grant Duff, MP, at the Devonshire Club, St James's, in 1879. The MP had been sent on a mission to quiz the infamous revolutionary by Queen Victoria's eldest daughter.

Duff discovered that Marx was not a bloodthirsty maniac but rather an agreeable sort of chap, and wrote to the Crown Princess 'praising Marx's immense learning and dry humor'.

Marx told Duff that he expected 'a great and not distant crash in Russia'. Marx forecast that the collapse of Tsarism would be followed by 'a revolt against "the existing military system" in Germany'.

Which is pretty much what happened 38 years later. Though this last aspect tends to be muffled in British historiography, which often obscures the real cause of the end of the First World War. As I've pointed out before, the sudden, wholly unexpected collapse of Germany had nothing at all to do with military defeat, because the German army was never defeated. Germany collapsed because a revolution broke out.

Marx also forecast that arms spending would go on increasing, telling Duff that, as science advances, 'The improvements in the art of destruction will keep pace with its advance and every year more and more will have to be devoted to costly engines of war.'

He wasn't exactly wrong there, either, was he?

Orde Wingate: War Criminal

A memorial stands on the embankment, across the river from the London Eye and County Hall. Not far from Big Ben, it faces the offices of the Ministry of Defence. The front portion, facing the river, is a memorial to those associated with the Burma campaign in the Second World War. The back portion is a memorial to Orde Wingate.

The conventional view of Major General Orde Wingate (1903-1944) is that he was a brilliantly unconventional soldier, a brave man who three times won the Distinguished Service Order, and a tactician whose name will be forever associated with the guerrilla unit known as the Chindits, who fought in Burma during the Second World War. Wingate died when the plane he was on crashed into the side of a mountain in India. Winston Churchill said of him: 'There was a man of genius who might well have become also a man of destiny.'

Well, forget all that. Orde Wingate was a man who, by the standards of the Second World War and the judgments passed at Nuremberg, should have been hanged as a war criminal. He wasn't all that great as a soldier either. Major General Woodburn Kirby, author of the *Official History of the Burma Campaign* (1961), wrote: 'Wingate had neither the knowledge, stability nor balance to make a great commander. Just as timing played a great part in his rise to prominence so the moment of his death may perhaps have been quite propitious for him.'

This judgment continues to outrage admirers of Orde Wingate but if anything was far too generous. It was connections, not timing or merit, which won him promotion. Wingate's military career abroad falls into four parts: (i) the Sudan 1928-1935 – a posting he characteristically obtained through his cousin, Sir Francis Reginald Wingate, a Governor General of Sudan and High Commissioner of Egypt; (ii) Palestine, 1936-1939; (iii) the Sudan, 1941; (iv) India/Burma, 1942-44.

In identifying Wingate as a war criminal I am concentrating on his activities in Palestine. To understand his crimes it's necessary to put them into two contexts – the personal and the historical.

Wingate's personality was shaped by his extreme religious upbringing: his parents belonged to a faction of the fringe fundamentalist Christian Protestant sect known as Plymouth

Brethren, and were strict disciplinarians. He seems to have had an austere, punishing childhood; he was also saturated in the Old Testament and made to memorize passages of the Bible by heart.

This deeply damaged childhood probably accounts for Wingate's weird, unstable personality as an adult: dogmatic, arrogant, averse to taking a bath or a shower, deeply unpopular with his fellow officers, keen on outlandish health fads and contemptuous of doctors, a would-be suicide, and curiously fond of exhibiting himself naked in front of other men. He kept a Bible with him at all times and fervently believed he was the instrument of God's wishes.

Wingate's arrival in the Palestine in 1936 had an electrifying impact upon him. He was now in a landscape which he knew profoundly – but through the medium of the Old Testament, not its actual social history. For Wingate it was a mythic landscape, to be shaped by theological imperatives. He had been brought up to believe in Christian prophecy and the restoration of the Jews to the Holy Land. In effect what happened in 1936 was that British imperialism in the Middle East and the increasingly powerful Zionist movement in Palestine converged to give Orde Wingate an opportunity to put his theology into action through the instruments of terrorism and murder.

Rod Quinn rightly identifies the material, imperialist motives which sanctioned Zionism and Christianity in Palestine:

> If Christian fundamentalism provided some justification for what was essentially the British colonisation of Palestine, economic fundamentalism provided the rest. Control of Palestine meant control and strategic protection of the Suez Canal and Britain's major source of oil. In encouraging the fulfilment of God's covenant with Abraham, the British Mandate prepared the foundations for a protected European outpost policing the region. With characteristic bluntness, Winston Churchill stated that: 'The Balfour Declaration must, therefore, not be regarded as a promise given from sentimental motives; it was a practical measure taken in the interests of a common cause at a moment when that cause could afford to neglect no factor of material or moral assistance.' (Rod Quinn, 'The First Palestinian Intifada', *What Next?* 24 [2002])

Wingate came to Palestine as a Captain in military intelligence, based in Nazareth. His arrival coincided with a massive national wave of protest and resistance by Palestinians, both to British military occupation and to growing Jewish immigration and sectarian land appropriation. One important form of resistance was the sabotage of the railway system and of the pipeline bringing oil from Kirkuk in Iraq to the port of Haifa.

Wingate persuaded General Wavell, Commander of British Forces in Palestine, to let him set up Special Night Squads (SNS). These were units which combined a small number of British troops with much larger numbers of armed Jewish colonists. They were located not in British army bases but in Zionist settlements. Wingate trained his squads in guerrilla warfare and night fighting.

This military alliance between the British occupiers and the Zionist colonists took other forms. Thousands of Jewish settlers enlisted in the colonial police force. Just as Wingate was unequivocal about the true purpose of the SNS ('establishing the foundations of the Army of Zion'), so the Zionist leader Moshe Shertok understood that Jews in the occupation police service would provide valuable recruits for a future Jewish fighting force against the Palestinians.

Wingate's aim was to deter Palestinian resistance to occupation by launching attacks on Arab villages. Brutality, torture and murder were employed, ostensibly to identify and punish individuals engaged in the Palestinian resistance and to seize arms. In practice the SNS were state licensed terrorists who imposed collective punishments, both in reprisal for any local acts of resistance to occupation and in the hope of deterring wider social support for the resistance.

But Wingate, though a fanatic, was not a rotten apple in a barrel of wholesome fruit. As John Rose rightly notes, 'it is difficult to separate Wingate's excesses from the wider British apparatus of repression of the revolt ... the principle of collective punishment, so beloved by the Israeli army, was pioneered by the British' (John Rose, *The Myths of Zionism* [Pluto Press, 2004], p. 130).

The evidence for Wingate's personal sponsorship of and involvement in war crimes comes from those who were accomplices in them. Quinn cites one such instance:

> Describing his own initiation into Special Night Squad tactics, Moshe Dayan said that after killing four and capturing five

Palestinians in an attack on a 'suspect' village, Wingate provided his pupils with a practical example of his military doctrines. When the captives protested ignorance of the whereabouts of an arms cache, "Wingate reached down and took some sand and grit from the ground; he thrust it into the mouth of the first Arab and pushed it down his throat until he choked and puked.' Questioned again, the Arab still denied knowledge of the arms and Wingate ordered a Jewish Squad member to shoot the still spluttering and coughing prisoner. The Jew looked at him at him questioningly and hesitated. 'Wingate said in a tense voice, 'Did you hear? Shoot him.' The Jew shot the Arab. The others stared for a moment, in stupefaction, at the body at their feet. The boys from Hamita (the 'suspect' village) were watching in silence. 'Now speak,' said Wingate. They spoke. (Dayan, quoted in Leonard Moseley, *Gideon Goes to War*, 1955)

Tzion Cohen, another member of the SNS, described how Wingate would sometimes whip Palestinian villagers on their bare backs:

As time went on, Tzion Cohen wrote, the punishments became more severe. Sometimes Wingate would make the villagers smear mud and oil on their faces. On occasion he would shoot and kill them. (Cited in Tom Segev, *One Palestine Complete* [Abacus, 2001] p. 430)

In reprisal for the killing of fifteen Jews in Tiberias, Wingate and his troops marched into a village called Hitin. Ten men were arbitrarily selected and executed.

One of Wingate's officers, Humphrey Edgar Nicholson Bredin, once ordered all the men in a village to line up. Every fifteenth man was shot dead.

'At times British soldiers went out on operations drunk; they tortured Arabs and looted the villages' (Segev, *op. cit.*, p. 431).

No figures seem to be available for the number of Palestinians murdered or ill-treated by Wingate, his officers and men. Collectively, they presumably ran into the hundreds. Even if any Palestinians kept records of these atrocities it has to be remembered that many fled in terror in the ethnic cleansing of 1948, often leaving not just their homes but all their possessions and documents behind.

It is also the case since 1948 that the Israeli state has sought to seize statistical data owned by Palestinians. The Zionist project over the past half century has been twofold: one is to extend sectarian appropriation of Palestinian land, the other is to annihilate Palestinian national identity in every possible way.

Although the great Palestinian resistance of 1936-39 was finally broken and repressed by the power of imperial Britain, the costs to Britain were enormous. By the end of 1938 the financial burden of occupation had rocketed, 63 British soldiers had been killed and one-tenth of the British regular army was tied up in Palestine. As Quinn notes:

> One achievement of the Revolt was that the current (Conservative) British government finally recognised the three main [Palestinian] demands on immigration, land sales and self-determination. The White Paper of May 1939 abandoned partition and recommended that, though remaining tied by treaty to Britain, Palestine should be self-governing within a decade, that neither Arabs nor Jews should dominate a Palestinian government, that Jewish immigration be restricted to 75,000 per year, after which there be no immigration without Arab consent, and that sales of Arab land be restricted.

Wingate was enraged by this capitulation. Previously, in October 1938, he had requested home leave and in London had had a private meeting with Colonial Secretary Malcolm MacDonald to lobby against the findings of the 1938 Woodhead Commission, which had abandoned earlier proposals to partition Palestine into Arab and Jewish states. Now he urged his Zionist allies to rise up against the British occupation. He even offered to lead a Jewish attack on the Haifa oil refinery. But his views were too extreme even for the Zionist movement, which believed in a more cautious approach.

Wingate had by this time fallen out of favour with army command and he was sent back to Britain and prohibited from re-entering Palestine. He departed, promising his Zionist allies that he would one day return and lead a Jewish army to victory. His death in an air crash prevented that possibility but it is a fact that many of those who served in the SNS later became leading figures in the Israeli army. Today, Orde Wingate is honoured as a significant figure in the creation of Israel. Appropriately, there is even a 77-acre campus, on ethnically cleansed land, named in his honour: Yemin Orde ('in the memory of Orde').

In the words of the Israeli Ministry of Defence: 'The teaching of Orde Charles Wingate, his character and leadership were a cornerstone for many of the Haganah's commanders, and his influence can be seen in the Israel Defense Force's combat doctrine.'

This is perfectly true. Orde Wingate's inspiring example helped to make Zionist terrorism and the mass murder of civilians possible for the sectarian Jewish state and its blood-spattered army.

The Complicity of Paul Celan

Two pieces of writing define the poet Paul Celan's relationship with the philosopher Martin Heidegger. One is his inscription in Heidegger's guest book, which translates as: 'Into the Hütte-book, while gazing on the well-star, with a hope for a word to come in the heart / July 25 1967'. The other is his famous poem 'Todtnauberg'. Both pieces are reasonably interpreted as obliquely alluding to Heidegger's relationship with the Nazis. Celan evidently hoped for some kind of acknowledgement of error on Heidegger's part – an acknowledgement which Celan, as a Holocaust victim, was surely entitled to expect.

Notoriously, Heidegger kept his silence. Heidegger, delighted by 'Todtnauberg', seems to have been oblivious to the poem's inner meaning and its verbal and historical resonance. At the end, Celan wrote of 'die halb- / beschrittenen Knüppel- / pfade im Hochmoor,' ['the half-trodden log-paths through the high moors']. But as John Felstiner notes in his fine critical biography, *Paul Celan: Poet, Survivor, Jew* (1995), 'in an explosive wordplay, Celan's term for 'log' (Knüppel) also means 'bludgeon.' Translating Night and Fog he had used that word for death camp prisoners '"bludgeoned awake" at 5 a.m.'

The meeting between Heidegger and Celan is both legendary and enigmatic; it is invariably defined from Celan's perspective. How could it not be? Celan (1920-1970), an East European Jew whose first language was German, is generally regarded as the major European poet of the period after 1945. His best known poem is

'Todesfuge' ('Death Fugue'), which is commonly regarded as the finest poem to emerge from the Holocaust. It originated in Celan's personal experience. During the Nazi occupation of Romania, Celan came home one morning to find that his parents had been taken away. His father died of typhus in a concentration camp; his mother was shot. Celan himself was made to do forced labour in the Romanian camps, but survived. In 1948 he settled in Paris, where he remained until his death, apparently by suicide.

And yet to my mind there is a curious absence in a book such as Felstiner's, which is Paul Celan's own complicity in oppression and injustice. It is even more curious, bearing in mind that the year in which Heidegger and Celan had their famous encounter is also the year which brings out in Celan's writing an obtuseness which surely, at some level, parallels that of Heidegger.

Felstiner notes that in 1967 Celan had started to insert Hebrew words into some of his poems. He concludes that 'Celan's poems with Hebrew in them, especially with Hebrew ending them, trace a meridian of Diaspora yearning.' He relates the enigmatic poem 'Ziw, jenes Licht' ('Ziv, that light') to the deteriorating situation in the Middle East: 'By the date of this poem, 10 May 1967, Syrian raids and shelling had been met by Israeli air attacks, terrorists had struck the Galilee, and Nasser's Egypt was threatening in the south.' (John Felstiner's lazy use of the word 'terrorists' is characteristic of an American academic attuned to multiplicity of meaning in poetic rhetoric but obtuse when it comes to the acceptance of media language.)

Celan then wrote a poem, 'Denk dir' (translated by Hamburger as 'Think of It' and by Felstiner as 'Just think'). It's a cryptic, elusive poem, like most of Celan's verse. Felstiner carefully unpicks the historical and literary threads of the poem, interpreting it as a response to the Six-Day War and to Israel's victory. The 'you' of the poem is the Jewish people. The poem is about the Jewish 'homeland' and the Jewish people. 'Now free, they go from strength to strength', as Felstiner puts it (p. 242). Felstiner notes that an early draft of the poem carried an echo of the words 'yad vashem', which is Hebrew for 'hand and name' and the name given to Israel's Holocaust memorial. Felstiner glosses the last word of the poem as follows: 'Finally, Celan's word "unburiable" fuses the two halves of one idea: Jewish victims who could not be buried and their spirit that will not.'

Felstiner supplies the background to the poem. He describes how the Six-Day War broke out, 'stirring him to an unambiguous poem. Starting on 7 June, when Jerusalem's Old City was regained, Celan worked closely on it for two days at the clinic. His title "Denk dir" registered the jolt that Jews everywhere felt.' Celan felt an urgency about this poem: it was published straightaway in Zurich and twice in Israel's German-Jewish press. Celan sent it to the German-born Israeli poet Natan Zach, who published a translation in Israel's main daily paper. Later in the year it appeared in Germany, and it was the final poem in his next collection *Fadensonnen* ('Threadsuns', 1968).

If Felstiner is right, in this poem Celan conflated Jewish identity with the Jewish state. It seems a plausible interpretation. The Jewish 'home' is Israel; it is a refuge which has now been 'inextinguishably' achieved against 'every barb in the wire' – not just Nazi genocide but also, perhaps, Arab aggression. The Jewish people have come 'through the tumult' – again, both Nazi genocide and wars with Arabs – and 'grow stronger and / stronger', in the shape of the victorious Jewish state, 'this bit of / habitable /earth'.

If Felstiner's interpretation of the poem is correct – and I see no reason to quarrel with it– it seems to me it indicates an imaginative failure on Celan's part. Paul Celan was not a Zionist, and preferred to live in Paris rather than anywhere else, but in conflating Jewish identity with Israel and telescoping the Holocaust and the Six-Day War he produced what is surely in essence a Zionist poem. Like most of Celan's output, 'Denk dir' is an oblique, elusive work. But John Felstiner's plausible reading both of the poem and its context makes it clear that 'Denk dir' is, implicitly, under its abstractions and ambiguities, on the side of Israel, and hence of imperialism and sectarian persecution – though Felstiner is incapable of perceiving it in those terms. That the author of 'Todesfuge' should be capable of such a poem is, I think, worthy of discussion.

What particularly intrigues me are the lines referring to 'this bit / of habitable / earth'.

If I have understood the poem correctly, Celan means, in one sense at least, Israel. If he does mean this, then I think the reader is entitled to feel disgust. Firstly, because this land was land stolen by brute force. In 1948, the year Israel was artificially created, no more than 7 per cent of Palestine was owned by Jews. The remaining 93 per cent was held by indigenous Palestinians. Secondly, having stolen more than half of that land the Jewish state then set about seizing the rest, using a pitiless violence steeped in racism and sectarianism – a process which has continued up to the present day. Today only 3 per cent of land in Israel is owned by Palestinians, a land theft of quite staggering proportions. That theft was not simply accomplished by force, however. An essential component was the sectarianism built into the Jewish state. By definition, it exists to promote and prioritize its Jewish citizens.

This is the corrosive legacy of Zionism and the Jewish state to the history and culture of modern Judaism: that Jewish identity must be conflated with the bellicose, blood-drenched, pitilessly sectarian state of Israel. That coarse identification is taken for granted by Felstiner, whose own Zionist bias is revealed when he speaks of the origins of 'Denk dir': 'Starting on 7 June, when Jerusalem's Old City was regained, he worked closely on it for two days in the clinic.'

Jerusalem's Old City 'regained'?

In the Zionist account of modern history, Jews in the Middle East are always the victims, never the oppressors. It's worth looking again at Felstiner's version of the origins of the 1967 war: 'By the date of this poem, 10 May 1967, Syrian raids and shelling had been met by Israeli air attacks, terrorists had struck the Galilee, and Nasser's Egypt was threatening in the south.'

In reality, Felstiner's account of what was happening in the Middle East at this time is a meretricious, self-serving one. Israel had signed up to a demilitarised zone (DMZ) between itself and Syria. In the words of Ahron Bregman, in his book *Israel's Wars: A History Since 1947* (Routledge, 2003), 'The Israelis – who had signed up to this arrangement voluntarily rather than under a Diktat – later regretted this, and attempted to regain control over these lands by provoking the Syrians and then taking advantage of military clashes to expand control over the DMZ' (pp. 65-66). Israel was the bellicose aggressor, not Syria. What Felstiner is referring to by 'terrorists had struck the Galilee' is puzzling. None of the standard histories mentions guerrilla activities in early 1967; perhaps he is alluding to attacks by Fatah on Israeli water pipes in 1965. If so, the word 'terrorist' is fairly meaningless in this context, as Fatah guerrillas were legitimately resisting the colonisation of their land by an army of occupation, and their actions were no different to those of the French resistance in the Second World War. The theft of Palestinian water resources by Israel has always been a central aspect of the conflict, though rarely if ever mentioned by the media.

What caused the 1967 war? In his book *The Iron Wall: Israel and the Arab World* (Penguin, 2001), Avi Shlaim concludes: 'Israel's strategy of escalation on the Syrian front was probably the single most important factor in dragging the Middle East to war in June 1967' (p. 235).

Finally, Felstiner says that 'Nasser's Egypt was threatening in the south.' But this again plays down the reality of Israeli aggression. In 1967 Egypt was in the sphere of Soviet influence. Nasser was firmly told by the Russian prime minister Alexei Kosygin not to attack Israel: 'Should you be the first to attack you will be the aggressor ... we are against aggression ... we cannot support you' (cited Bregman, p. 82). The USA was not so scrupulous. Israel was informed by the CIA that the Americans would welcome it if Egypt was attacked. When the Israeli delegate to Washington, Meir Amit, told the Secretary of Defense that he would recommend to the Israeli government that an attack be launched, Robert McNamara replied: 'I read you loud and clear.'

The surprise Israeli attack on Egypt, Jordan and Syria which occurred on 5 June 1967 happened with the advance knowledge and enthusiastic support of the USA and Britain. The extent of British complicity is revealed in Jeremy Bowen's book *Six Days* (2003). Shiploads of armoured vehicles, munitions and other weaponry sailed from Felixstowe in Suffolk, where US military police guarded an arms dump. Israeli transport planes ran a shuttle service out of RAF Waddington in Lincolnshire. The Labour Prime Minister, Harold Wilson, had agreed to help Israel, but insisted that 'the utmost secrecy should be maintained'. Arms for Israel poured in from the USA. In the surprise attack that followed Israel duly wiped out the air forces of Egypt, Syria and Jordan. With complete air superiority, Israel had no difficulty in defeating the land armies of those states. 12,000 Egyptians died in the Israeli offensive. The result was the occupation of the entire Sinai peninsula, the West Bank and the Golan Heights.

In short, Felstiner's book is both classically orientalist and Zionist in its attitudes. His complacency becomes particularly acute when he describes how in 1969 Paul Celan visited Israel for the first time. Celan made a speech to the Hebrew Writers Association in Tel Aviv on 14 October, in which he said (among other things):

I think I have a notion of what Jewish loneliness can be, and I recognize as well, amongst so many things, a thankful pride in every green thing planted here that stands ready to refresh anyone who comes by ...

And I find here, in this outward and inward landscape, much of the force for truth, the self-evidentness, and the world-open uniqueness of great poetry. And I believe I've been conversing with those who are calmly, confidently determined to stand firm in what is human.

Celan enjoyed himself in Israel. He said he was 'happy to have lived so intensively, more intensively than for a long time ... I'm already thinking of coming back'.

Felstiner comments, 'Celan was also struck by the memoir a veteran Israeli writer had given him and by how, during Arab attacks on Jews in pre-state Jerusalem, Christians put crosses on their doors for immunity.' He adds: 'Celan wrote to this writer of his "anxiety for Israel".'

And that's the only way in which Arabs are, very briefly, registered in this book. Aggressive Arab nations make trouble for the Jewish state, which is obliged to defend itself. Arabs attacked Jews in pre-state Jerusalem – for reasons not given. In the index of Felstiner's book you will find 36 references under 'anti-Semitism' (together with the recommendation to 'See also Nazism; Neo-Nazism'). But 'Palestinians' are not listed; nor is 'Arab' or 'Arabs'.

As far as I can tell (though there is a vast commentary on Celan in German which has not been translated into English) Paul Celan seems to have had no perception at all of Israel as a chauvinist sectarian state founded on the violent persecution of the indigenous population.

The dogged anti-Zionist Mark Elf (who blogs at http://jewssansfrontieres.blogspot.co.uk/ and tweets at: https://twitter.com/jewssf) recently defined the basic problem of the Jewish state:

Israel exists on the basis of three things: colonial settlement, ethnic cleansing and racist laws. As far as I know it is the only state that exists on that basis. Now recognising Israel's right to exist recognises its right to those three things.

As far as I can tell, Paul Celan lacked the insight of Marek Edelman, recently cited by Elf:

Why did Marek Edelman remain in Poland [after the Second World War] as a doctor when almost all his Jewish political colleagues and people close to him personally left? Edelman used to come, now and then, to Israel, to see old friends, but no one had ever publicly asked him this question, though he had a very good answer: he didn't like the idea of the 'new nation'. In fact, Edelman was always very critical not only of Israelis' attitude to the Holocaust, but also of more sensitive issues – such as our racist laws of citizenship. In a late interview he told a Polish journalist: 'Israel is a chauvinist, religious state, where a Christian is a second-class citizen and a Muslim is third-class. It is a disaster, after three million were murdered in Poland, they want to dominate everything and not to consider non-Jews!'

Celan is the great poet of the Holocaust and one of his central themes is that of loss – one of his greatest poems is 'Aspen tree', about his dead mother. But as far as I'm aware Celan seems to have had no perception that the invention of a Jewish state involved the ruthless sectarian persecution of a people, who also suffered and who also experienced loss. Paul Celan happily accepted the privilege of travelling to Israel, because of his identity as a privileged member of the master religion.

Celan's complacency needs to be contrasted with what happened to to the Palestinian poet Mourid Barghouti. After Israel invaded and occupied that rump of Palestine known as the West Bank in 1967 it forbade native Palestinians abroad the right of return to their homeland. It did so for no other reason than racism and the basic ambition of the sectarian Jewish state of combating democracy by artificially maintaining a Jewish majority. The demographic problem was initially dealt with in 1948 by expelling the Arab majority; it was perpetuated in 1967 by the simple device of refusing to re-admit Arabs who lived in the newly occupied territories and who happened to be outside them when the Israeli army took control.

As he describes in his memoir *I Saw Ramallah* (2004), Barghouti found himself stranded in Cairo. He was not alone. In his words, Israel forbade 'hundreds of thousands of young people to return. And the world finds us a name for us. They called us zaiheen, the displaced ones. Displacement is like death. One thinks it happens only to other people. From the summer of '67 I became that displaced stranger whom I had always thought was someone else.'

And Paul Celan? His personal knowledge of sectarian persecution and displacement was as bitter as anyone's can be. But he could perceive Jews only as victims, not as racists and persecutors. There was, apparently, not a glimmer of knowledge or understanding of the plight of someone like Mourid Barghouti, who, like Celan, became a poet out of his experience of persecution.

Visiting Israel, Celan enjoyed his sectarian privileges as a Jew. Though a total stranger to the Middle East, he was a welcome guest in Israel. While Celan read his poems to admiring audiences, Barghouti was exiled. Barghouti, a native, was banned from his homeland. Barghouti was prevented from going to the places where a foreign Jew like Paul Celan could travel freely. And Barghouti, after 29 years of being excluded, found himself, on his return visit, still persecuted: 'The others are still masters of the place. They give you a permit. They check your papers. They start your files on you. They make you wait.'

Mourid Barghouti was born in 1944. In 1996, briefly, he was permitted to return to the land from which he had been excluded in 1967. He was able once again to view the room in which he was born, 'four years before the birth of the State of Israel'. He revisited the sites of his younger days. The wood at al-Nabi Saleh, for example. But now everything was changed. 'Israel seized the wood and large tracts of the lands surrounding it. It built houses and brought in settlers. The road leading to the wood – like all roads leading to the settlements – is closed to Palestinians and for the use of the Israelis alone.'

On his visit to Israel in 1969, Paul Celan gushed about his 'thankful pride in every green thing planted here that stands ready to refresh anyone who comes by'. *Anyone?* No, not anyone. Celan's complacency and ignorance is stupefying. Here, he reminds me of nothing so much as a gullible West European Communist in the 1930s, visiting Stalinist Russia and discovering there a workers' paradise.

Mourid Barghouti's experience was rather different. On his return to Ramallah he saw that 'There is less green now since Israel has been stealing the water since 1967'. The pitiless theft of Arab land and Arab water has always been a central feature of Zionism and the sectarian state it gave birth to. So, too, has the denial of access to water to Israeli Arabs. Even today, 80,000 Israeli Arabs are deliberately denied access to clean drinking water and sanitation. They are forced to rely on contaminated water. Children contract hepatitis and die. And yet Paul Celan, blind to the chauvinism and racism of the Jewish state, could see only delightful and refreshing greenery.

The issues of land and water, touched on by Celan in his poem and in his speech, remain every bit as relevant today as they did in the late 1960s. Referring to the withdrawal of Jewish colonialists from Gaza, Mustafa Barghouti (no relation to the poet) noted:

> Israel had already exhausted the water resources in Gaza by tapping the flow of underground water east of Gaza resulting in the seepage of seawater into Gaza's coastal aquifer and through the over-pumping of the existing aquifer by Israeli settlements. As such, Gazans have been left with brackish water resources that cause high rates of kidney failure. The maximum accepted level of chloride in drinking water, as set by World Health Organisation standards, is 250 mg per litre. In most areas of Gaza, the level stands between 1,200 and 2,500 mg per litre. ('The Truth You Don't Hear', 9 January 2006, AL-AHRAM Weekly Online)

To Paul Celan, Israel's victory in 1967 was a cause for celebration – a free people, the Jews, going 'from strength to strength'. Mourid Barghouti saw it differently:

> Our calendars are broken, overlaid with pain, with bitter jokes and the smell of extinction. There are numbers now that can never again be neutral: they will always mean one thing. Since the defeat of June 1967 it is not possible for me to see the number '67' without it being tied to that defeat. I see it in part of a telephone number, on the door of a hotel room, on the license plate of a car, in any street in the world, on a cinema or theatre ticket, on a page in a book, in the address of an office or a house, at the front of a train, or a flight number on an electronic board in any airport in the world. A number frozen in its frame.

John Felstiner's book on Celan no longer seems to me as admirable as it once did. And neither does Paul Celan. It is dispiriting to perceive how the great poet of loss and suffering was silent about Israel's victims. And Celan's silence about Jews as persecutors and their victims appears to be reciprocated by everyone who writes about him.

Celan's 'Denk dir'

My last post provoked responses regarding the meaning of Celan's poem 'Denk dir', a title translated by Michael Hamburger as 'Think of it' and by John Felstiner as 'Just Think'.

Steve Mitchelmore (*This Space*) cites Ian Fairley:

> Ian Fairley, in his knotty introduction to **Fathomsuns**, reads the abstraction and ambiguity of the same poem as essential to its meaning rather than obstacles to it. He suggests – though my understanding is fraught with uncertainty – that the poem is an implicit warning to Zionism and, more generally, the yearning for a homeland; a similar yearning – for clarity, for certainty, for an impossible homecoming – that we experience in reading poetry.
>
> Instead (i.e. instead of a homestead), he writes that we must live in 'the conflicted liminality of ... an unhousing which demands that we live ... with, or in, what is without.' This seems to locate the brutalism inherent in patriotic utopianisn and enacts, instead, an imaginative engagement with a meridian – 'the connective which, like the poem, leads to encounters'. **Denk dir**; think of it.

I find it hard to recognise the poem in this reading. I perceive 'Denk dir' as celebratory; expressing exultation – a tone of delight, a gasp of surprise, a momentary texture of feeling not normally found in Celan's verse. Steve refers to 'the abstraction and ambiguity of the poem'; John Felstiner by contrast finds it 'an unambiguous poem' (*Paul Celan: Poet, Survivor, Jew*, p. 241). Felstiner may be guilty of an over simplistic reading, but his interpretation makes sense of each line and word, fits the context in which the poem was written, and seems consistent with the significance of its publishing history.

What does the title 'Denk dir' refer to? Felstiner describes how the writing of the poem was triggered by Israel's success in the Six Day war of 1967. That context, which he describes, is surely an inescapable biographical fact. He says that the title 'registered the jolt that Jews everywhere felt'. My reading of Celan's title is that it means 'Just think – Jews who were once persecuted and weak and threatened with extinction now have a homeland and grow ever stronger.' Or: 'Think of it! Thirty years ago Jews were in death camps. But now they have come through that suffering and found a home.' So the title evokes, in a familiar sense, the contrast between past and present. The title is, in this reading, charged with amazement, perhaps even pride.

As a reading it seems consistent with the huge cultural shift in Jewish attitudes both to Israel and to the Holocaust outlined in Norman G. Finkelstein's *The Holocaust Industry* (2001). Finkelstein identifies 1967 as the key year when everything changed. The June war resulted in a comprehensive reconstruction of Jewish identity and of attitudes both to the Holocaust and Israel. Finkelstein and Noam Chomsky (in *Fateful Triangle* [1983]), identify the discovery of Israel's utility to US foreign policy as the driving force behind that massive transformation. They make a convincing case. Yet 'Denk dir' suggests that a European poet, isolated in Paris, remote from US society, also registered that massive shift in sensibility. In Finkelstein's account, the Holocaust was for decades a topic to be shunned; it was, for most Jews, a source of shame, an index of weakness, of massive suffering and genocide, endured passively, with relatively little resistance. Then, in June 1967, everything changed. Suddenly Jews weren't to be kicked around any more; they could hit back against overwhelming odds and put their oppressors in their place. The shameful image of the weak Jew was replaced by the proud, strong Jew; suddenly, there were heroes – brave warriors like Moshe Dayan. The tradition of Jewish resistance to Zionism ebbed; Jewish identity became merged with the muscular Jewish state, and anti-Zionists were marginalised as self-haters and collaborators with anti-Semites.

Is Felstiner's interpretation of the poem reductive and over-simplistic? I don't think Felstiner has a particular hidden agenda in his book. His orientalism is of a rather gentle kind, unconscious rather than bellicose. He is not out to score propaganda points and stresses that the war 'had not swept [the poet] up on a wave of enthusiasm. Celan was, after all, a sick man, sometimes violent and even suicidal' (p. 243). Felstiner's account of 'Denk dir' seems to me perfectly lucid and plausible, and supported by his privileged reading of manuscript variants. I don't find Felstiner a reductive biographer, in the way that some critics are, such as James Atlas, writing on Bellow, or Stephen Greenblatt, writing on Shakespeare. My biggest grouch with his book is that there is too little biography, which may be something to do with Celan's often solitary existence and ultimate elusiveness, and something to do with market forces. The English speaking world is perhaps not yet ready for an 850-page blockbuster biography.

'Denk dir' seems to have been written at some speed, and Felstiner's interpretation, appears consistent with the publishing history of the poem. Celan rushed to publish the poem 'right away in Zurich' (Felstiner, p. 242). He also sent it to the German-born Israeli poet Natan Zach, who translated it (presumably into Hebrew) and published it in Israel's main daily paper. The significance of this, it seems to me, is that Celan saw the poem as *an act of solidarity*.

It also appeared in Germany. And the following year Celan situated it as the final poem in his collection *Fadensonnen*. Why would he want to do that? Not, I think, because it just happened to be the last poem he happened to write before putting the collection together. Its privileged position is there for a reason.

Part Three: The Iraq War and Ian McEwan's 'Ambivalence'

The Sense of a Sell-Out

I'm apprehensive about Ian McEwan's forthcoming novel, *Saturday*.

The Saturday in question is Saturday February 15th 2003, when somewhere between one and two million people marched through central London to a rally in Hyde Park to protest against the impending war on Iraq by the Bush and Blair governments. It was the biggest demonstration in London's history. Around the world an estimated 35 million people marched against the impending war that day. The Indian novelist and activist Arundhati Roy called it 'The most spectacular display of public morality the world has ever seen.'

But it looks as if that display is about to be mocked by one of Britain's leading and most highly regarded writers, if an extract from Ian McEwan's forthcoming novel *Saturday* published recently in *The New Yorker* is anything to go by.

The main protagonist's views on the Iraq war in 'The Diagnosis' – an extract from an early section of *Saturday* – appear to parallel those of Ian McEwan.

Two years ago McEwan set out his views on the impending war in an essay 'Ambivalence on the Brink of War' (12 January 2003) on the *Open Democracy* website. (This essay is no longer available online.) They were reprinted in a longer version as 'Strong Cases For and Against War – But We Don't Hear Them', *Daily Telegraph*, 10 February 2003.

Back at the start of 2003, McEwan's basic posture was that the arguments for and against the war were almost evenly balanced and that there was nothing to be done anyway as the war was inevitable. He concluded that, 'the hawks have my head, the doves my heart. At a push, I count myself – just – in the camp of the latter. And yet my ambivalence remains. I defend it by reference to the fact that nothing any of us say will make any difference: ambivalence is no less effective than passionate conviction.' (My quotations are all from the *Open Democracy* essay.)

McEwan's assertion that 'the hawks have my head, the doves my heart' implies that reason and logic dictated a strong case for war. This was an odd position to take over a looming war which at the time clearly had a pre-set timetable for action, a desperately flimsy rationale, and which was obviously being initiated for reasons which had nothing to do with the threat of weapons of mass destruction, liberating a people from tyranny or for democracy but, primarily, to secure Iraq and its oil reserves for the USA, while taking out an Arab dictator who had impertinently shed his client status.

Equally strange was McEwan's claim that his own ambivalence was 'no less effective than passionate conviction'. This was simply not true. Ambivalence offered nothing, other than the comfort of sitting on the fence offending no one. Passionate conviction AGAINST the war offered the possibility of bringing about the downfall of Blair and the loss of the USA's only credible military ally. Blair was in desperate trouble, having boxed himself into a situation in which Britain would apparently go to war only if the UN passed a resolution legitimising military action. But at a time when millions of people were actively campaigning against the war, all McEwan had to recommend was paralysis and inaction. By contrast, even the leader of the Liberal Democrats, Charles Kennedy, was a raging radical, supporting the war only if the United Nations passed that resolution. McEwan's ambivalence certainly wasn't 'effective' in mustering opposition to the war, but it was certainly 'effective' in attempting to damp down protest. McEwan's message was simple: do nothing because the case both for and against war is awfully complex and anyway it's going to happen whatever. A couch potato politics.

The war was *inevitable*, wrote McEwan. True, nothing would have stopped the US from invading Iraq. But British military participation was by no means incvitable. Wars, like governments, depend on the consent and complicity of individuals. Blair needed the support of a majority of Labour MPs and, scandalously, he got it. On the same day as London's absolutely massive anti-war march, Saturday 15 February 2003, Blair addressed a big meeting of Labour Party members in Scotland. Not a single person in that audience had the guts or the inclination to heckle. It is Labour MPs and members of the Labour Party like that who allow Blair to get away with his agenda, time and time again.

Looking ahead to the war and its aftermath, McEwan wrote that he hoped that 'the regime, like all dictatorships, rootless in the affections of its people, will crumble like a rotten tooth' – which indeed it did. But he also hoped that a 'federal, democratic Iraq that the INC committed itself to at its conference can be helped into existence by the UN'. McEwan had a touchingly naïve faith in the Iraqi National Congress as the voice of the Iraqi people. But of course the United Nations declined to involve itself with either the war or its bloody, chaotic aftermath. His belief that this war had anything at all to do with bringing democracy to the oppressed people of Iraq provides just one more dismal example of the endless naïvety of those liberal intellectuals who shut their eyes to the massively documented history of American 'interventions' around the world.

McEwan also fell for the Blair line that support for the war would be rewarded by a settlement elsewhere, hoping that 'the US, in the flush of victory, will find in its oilman's heart the energy and optimism to begin to address the Palestinian issue'. Fat chance. Why should any informed person believe that US foreign policy is dictated by niceness or decency? Hasn't McEwan read William Blum's *Rogue State*? Presumably not.

The small print of McEwan's 'ambivalence' contained cop-out qualifications. McEwan finished: 'These are fragile hopes. As things stand, it is easier to conceive of innumerable darker possibilities.' The problem is that they were never 'fragile hopes' in the first place. They were delusions. And those 'darker possibilities' – the foul consequences of an American invasion and occupation – were predictable certainties.

Let's backtrack a little and check out those heavy intellectual arguments for the war that McEwan subscribed to. (To avoid the charge that I'm quoting him out of context I recommend a reading of his complete essay.)

Firstly, he went along with – on grounds of LOGIC! – the unsubstantiated thesis that Saddam had links with al-Qaeda, writing that it did not seem 'outlandish, the possibility of Saddam Hussein passing on weapons of mass destruction to the enemy of his enemies'.

Secondly, McEwan accepted the likelihood that Saddam had weapons of mass destruction. Which was, of course, the blatantly spurious pretext for the war. (As Martin Amis wittily remarked at the time, 'we are going to war with Iraq because it DOESN'T have weapons of mass destruction').

Thirdly, McEwan fell for the Blair line that the ousting of Saddam would be followed by a settlement of the Palestine-Israel conflict: 'In the right context, with the right ambitions, it could be a moral act to remove Saddam and his hideous entourage by force and restore Iraq to its people. By the right context, I refer to an attempt to begin the process of a focussed, creative and inclusive settlement to the Palestinian problem.'

McEwan's language betrays him here, I think. It is not 'the Palestinian problem' which is at issue but *the Israel problem*. Israel is a violent, sectarian, fundamentalist state which has successfully ethnically cleansed much of the indigenous Arab population, stolen most of its land, its property and its water and forced it into miserable ghettos. It has used the most savage repression to achieve its aims, which have been achieved only with the complicity or active support of Britain, the USA and other superpowers. This has been accomplished with the help of an ideology which downplays the long history of sectarianism and terrorist violence inherent in the Zionist project, perceives the Holocaust as primarily a valuable propaganda tool in casting Israelis as victims, and defines criticism of Israel as anti-semitic. So much Palestinian land has now been stolen that the two state option is no longer a realistic solution if justice and equality are to be achieved. (The vision behind Blair's 'road map' is of a pair of shrivelled Bantusans with a quiescent client Palestinian leadership which accepts the losses of the past half century and the abandonment of the 5 million Palestinian refugees scattered in squalid camps around the Middle East.) The only reasonable future in that geographically tiny part of the world is a single state where Jews, Christians and Muslims live side by side as equals, but that option requires dismantling a Zionist state in which the essence of citizenship is to be Jewish and where anyone who is not Jewish has second-class status (change 'Jewish' to 'Protestant' and you'd have Ian Paisley's paradise on earth).

There are no rational grounds for believing that the US is committed to such a goal, and McEwan's belief that support for the Iraq war might be rewarded by a settlement in Palestine was yet more wishful thinking. His language is also very vague and slippery at this point, because what does he *mean* by 'a focussed, creative and inclusive settlement to the Palestinian problem'? Fine sentiments which the most militant supporter of either Israelis or the

Palestinians could support but utterly meaningless unless tied to specifics. And one of the most intractable of those specifics is the question of the 5 million or more Palestian refugees who are leftover outcasts from the ethnic cleansing of 1948. Even most Israeli liberals (people like Amos Oz) have made it clear that in the final analysis they are committed to a sectarian Jewish state and are not prepared to see the return of Arabs to the land and the houses which were stolen from them by terror. Israel, we are endlessly reminded by its apologists, is the only democracy in the Middle East. Apart from being not true (they hold elections in Iran), the basis of Israel's pseudo-democracy is the exclusion of the majority of its electorate. Israel is a democracy for Jews only.

McEwan wrote that 'I can't say I've been much impressed by the integrity of the anti-war movement in Britain. Peace movements are of their nature incapable of choosing lesser evils. The failure to take an interest in, or engage with, Iraqi exiles, or the Iraqi National Congress meeting in London recently, was a moral evasion. All the more shameful when a large part of the INC embraces the liberal or libertarian and secular values that much of the anti-war movement professes.'

I've no idea what INC meeting McEwan is referring to, though it is fair to say that the Iraqi National Congress was perceived on the left as a collection of people who were American stooges, some of whom had links with the CIA and were involved in supplying the thoroughly bogus 'evidence' that Saddam had weapons of mass destruction. The history of events since 2003 indicates that that perception was entirely accurate.

Secondly, it is perfectly true that there were some Iraqis who appeared on TV urging us to support the war (though there were also those who spoke against it). The question is, how representative were they? At the 2004 Labour Party annual conference an Iraqi woman passionately denounced those who had dared to oppose the liberation of her country. Powerful stuff. It later emerged that she wasn't a constituency delegate but the Surrey-based wife of a member of the current Vichy regime in Iraq. (Until an anti-democrat like Blair came along, of course, no one who wasn't either a Labour MP or a trade union or constituency delegate could have spoken at the Labour conference – now dissent has been quelled and it's all about manipulation, spin and sound-bites. Not that Labour Party delegates these days seem to care, judging by the rapturous reception given at a previous conference to that criminal sleazebag Bill Clinton.) Anyone is entitled to be sceptical of unelected individuals who claim to be the voice of millions of Iraqis.

McEwan wasn't 'much impressed by the integrity of the anti-war movement in Britain'. On the insult-trading front one might say the same thing about him. Back in the 1980s McEwan was perceived as a man of the left, participating in the European Nuclear Disaramament Group, visiting the Soviet Union to campaign against the persecution of dissidents, writing the libretto for an anti-nuke oratorio 'Or Shall We Die?' (which called for 'womanly times'), and involving himself with the pressure group Charter 88. But as his fame and wealth grew, and as left-wing ideas fell out of fashion, McEwan started to move away from his younger radicalism. In an interview with Rosa Gonzalez Casademont published in 1992 (but given a year or so earlier) McEwan remarked, 'When you are young, you've got infinite time. We were happy to see that revolution on the street; as you get older you begin to doubt what will come of it, and also you might own a bit of the street by then, and you don't want it broken.' A 'bit of the street' is a modestly homely metaphor for someone who by then was probably a millionaire and by now must surely be a multi-millionaire.

McEwan's personal trajectory from left to right is a common one in our culture (it goes back at least to Wordsworth) but it hardly qualifies him to accuse others of 'a moral evasion'. In those of his generation it is seen at its starkest in the numerous former fiery young lefties who are now Blairite MPs, transformed almost overnight into enthusiasts for nuclear weapons and American imperialism. McEwan's own personal journey from left to right led him to Number 10 Downing Street on 20 November 2003. While 100,000 people marched through central London protesting against the visit of the warmonger Bush (among them John le Carré, Peter Capaldi and Ellis Sharp), Ian McEwan was enjoying the reception at Number 10 for the President and his wife. The only other two celebrities that Blair was able to persuade to come were Nigella Lawson and that old Thatcher-supporter, Tom Stoppard.

Praising Tony Blair, and denouncing those who called him Bush's poodle, McEwan was thrilled that 'It was the Blair-Powell axis of compromise that brought the US to the UN.' Sadly for McEwan his comment was written in January 2003. When the UN wouldn't play ball, the US – after trying every trick in the book, from economic blackmail to telephone tapping – contemptuously disregarded it.

McEwan wrote: 'Another empty argument I keep hearing is that it is inconsistent to attack Iraq because we are not attacking North Korea, Saudi Arabia and China. To which I say, three dictatorships are better than four.' To which anyone with any knowledge of the history of US foreign policy might reply: why should Britain involve itself in toppling foreign dictatorships which were formerly creatures of the West?

Leaving aside such trifles as international law and the invasion of sovereign states, why should Britain involve itself in the bloody, endless machinations of US foreign policy? It's not as if we haven't been here before, time and time again. The agenda which McEwan subscribes to here requires absolute silence about dictatorship and repression when it serves the agenda of US foreign policy, but enthusiastic support for human rights when the client dictator steps out of line and needs to be overthrown. Silence about terror in those client torture-state dictatorships Jordan, Egypt and Saudia Arabia, but bottomless wells of liberal concern for those poor suffering Iraqis. (Well, at least until the invasion. As far as I'm aware McEwan has had nothing at all to say about what has happened in Iraq under the US occupation.)

McEwan continued: 'To the waverer, some of the reasoning from the doves seems to emerge from a warm fug of illogic: that the US has been friendly to dictators before, that it cynically supported Saddam in his war against Iran, that there are vast oil reserves in the region – none of this helps us decide what specifically we are to do about Saddam now. The peace movement needs to come up with concrete proposals for containing him if he is not to be forcefully disarmed. He has obsessively produced chemical and biological weapons on an industrial scale, and has a history of bloody territorial ambition. What to do?'

The only 'warm fug of illogic' here is McEwan's. To say that 'the US has been friendly to dictators before' is an understatement of staggering proportions. Without recycling the material in William Blum's *Rogue State* or a lifetime of scholarship by Noam Chomsy, let's just say that US foreign policy is largely motivated by the demands of US capital, embraces human rights abuses and slaughter on an industrial scale in the pursuit of that end, and has a venomous disregard for representative democracy which resists client status.

In any case, Saddam was the creature of the United States.

McEwan's demand that *we* must do something about Saddam *now* simply mimicked the spurious urgency of the weapons of mass destruction argument. *Lawks, if we don't invade NOW those missiles will be raining down on Cyprus in just 45 minutes!*

As for the demand that 'the peace movement' come up with 'concrete proposals for containing him'. Well, really! In the first place Britain and the USA were containing Saddam, albeit in a particularly brutal manner, the price of which was paid by the children of Iraq. Secondly, no one seriously believes Saddam intended either to invade another country, or had WMDs which he intended to launch against anyone. Thirdly, why should 'the peace movement' (whatever that is) be held responsible for dealing with a petty tyrant who had always been a creature of the West's?

There is a curious rhetorical sleight-of-hand about McEwan's essay. On the one hand he was committed to inertia. He made it clear he was not supporting the anti-war movement and was opting out of doing anything practical. But on the other hand he ticked off those people who were campaigning actively against the war and denounced them for not acting in other ways he recommended. Attend meetings of the so-called Iraqi National Congress! Engage with Iraqi exiles! Contain Saddam! But why should activists take instruction and advice from someone whose position was one of armchair-bound passivity and complete immobility?

In fact McEwan's demand that something must be done about Saddam NOW was answered by his old friend Martin Amis, who showed much greater scepticism towards the war and a far sharper grasp of the realities of US foreign policy. Amis wrote: 'common sense calmly states that an expanded version of the present arrangement (inspectors, monitors, full exposure to world opinion) is sufficient to contain and emasculate Saddam until pressure builds for a coup; and that the "war on terror" can start only with the dismantling of the settlements in the territories occupied by Israel.' (Martin Amis, 'The Palace of the End', *Guardian*, 4 March 2003.)

Amis's simple insights eluded McEwan. McEwan described life under Saddam: 'No one seriously disagrees about his record of genocide – perhaps a quarter of a million Kurds slaughtered, thousands of their villages destroyed, the ruthless persecution of the Shi'ites in the south, the cruel suppression of dissent, the widespread use of torture and summary imprisonment and execution, with the ubiquitous security services penetrating every level of Iraqi society. It is an insult to those who have suffered to suggest, as some do, that the US administration is the greater evil.'

A bit of a warm fug of illogic about that paragraph, I think. Leaving aside McEwan's sloppy use of the word 'genocide', the US bears a heavy responsibility for those atrocities because it tacitly accepted and even subsidised them in the years that Saddam was a friend of the West. And events since the invasion and occupation of Iraq haven't exactly suggested that the USA has a passionate concern for human rights there. As for 'evil' – you don't exactly have to look too far in the history of US foreign policy to find barbarism and atrocities sponsored by the United States which are every bit equal to those carried out under Saddam, in Latin America especially.

McEwan's fence-sitting equivocations were in stark contrast to those of other prominent writers. John le Carré rightly denounced it as 'A predatory and dishonest war', remarking, 'There is a stink of religious self-righteousness in the air that reminds me of the British Empire at its worst. I cringe when I hear my Prime Minister lend his head prefect's sophistries to this patently self-interested adventure to secure our oil supplies.'

The dramatist David Hare wrote, 'No exponent of American foreign policy has been able to explain why one UN resolution – that voted through recently against Iraq – should be made a matter of military urgency, while another, far more pressing resolution – the one which demands the withdrawal of Israeli troops to pre-1967 borders – has been allowed to stand for thirty years, unenforced, mocking Western claims of impartiality and justice ... An unsanctioned invasion of Iraq has no legitimacy.'

The poet Edwin Morgan wrote, 'How about regime change in Jerusalem? In Riyadh? In quite a few other places it would not be hard to name? What looks like the arrogance of American selectivity is of course no more than the reality of power, and it is not new in the world. But there is all the more reason to out it, to question it, to satirise it, since the stakes today are so high. The so-called Gulf War was not really a war but a one-sided massacre. Is British public opinion happy to underwrite what President Bush clearly regards as the finishing of unfinished business? Perhaps it is. If so, these are bad times!'

The German novelist Gunter Grass wrote that 'everyone knows, or at least has an inkling, that the real issue is oil. Or, to be precise: once again, the issue is oil. The web of pretences which usually conceals the interests of the world's last remaining superpower and her chorus of allies has been worn away to expose the true interests of power.'

The Palestinian author Ghada Karmi wrote: 'For Arabs, the tolerance shown to Israel's brutality against the Palestinians and its known possession of nuclear and other weapons of mass destruction while castigating Iraq in the harshest and most bellicose of ways is nauseating.'

The novelist Julian Barnes angrily wrote that the war wasn't worth a child's finger. The novelist Iain Banks disgustedly cut up his passport and mailed it to Blair. Writers were either passionately for or against the war. Only McEwan was sort of for it but also sort of against it but also for sort of doing, er, nothing.

Two years ago Ian McEwan wrote, 'It is an insult to those who have suffered [under Saddam] to suggest, as some do, that the US administration is the greater evil.' But where, one wonders, is McEwan's tender concern for suffering Iraqis *now*?

Saturday apparently involves a fictional medical man and a fictional Iraqi intellectual. Today's *Guardian* carries a report by a real Iraqi doctor, Ali Fadhil. He has managed to get inside Fallujah, to report on the aftermath of the November assault on the city by US military forces, backed by British soldiers from the Black Watch. In the words of the paper, 'He discovered people had been shot in their beds, rabid dogs were feeding on corpses, and there was little to no water, electricity or sewage. A city of over 300,000 people had been destroyed and its inhabitants were homeless. With just two weeks until the Iraqi elections, not a single voter in Fallujah has received a ballot paper. Far from stabilising the region in preparation for the election, it seems the US military's decision to use the Iraqi National Guard against this Sunni city has fanned the flames of civil war in the entire country.'

When Fadhil reached Fallujah he found 'It was completely devastated, destruction everywhere. It looked like a city of ghosts. Falluja used to be a modern city; now there was nothing. We spent the day going through the rubble that had been the centre of the city; I didn't see a single building that was functioning.'

He encountered one local woman: 'Fallujans are suspicious of outsiders, so I found it surprising when Nihida Kadhim, a housewife, beckoned me into her home. She had just arrived back in the city to check out her house; the government had told the people three days earlier that they should start going home. She called me into her living room. On her mirror she pointed to a message that had been written in her lipstick. She couldn't read English. It said: *Fuck Iraq and every Iraqi in it!* "They are insulting me, aren't they?" she asked.'

This is where the timid and self-serving sophistication and equivocations of Ian McEwan's 'ambivalence' end.

In a coarse, brutish, murderous occupation.

In rubble and ruins, war crimes, massacred civilians, grief, squalor and humiliation.

A story which has been told many, many times before in the long, bloody history of American foreign policy.

The Meaning of Ambivalence: Some Reflections on *Saturday* and the Iraq War

Apparently the novel's main character is Henry Perowne, an affluent middle-aged neurosurgeon with two grown-up children who lives in central London with a wife who works for a newspaper.

McEwan seems teasingly to be inviting us to half-identify him with Perowne, as he also has a wife who works for a newspaper, and has two grown-up children. You could also argue that a novelist is a bit like a neurosurgeon by working with the inside of people's heads, in the sense of creating characters.

The extract published in *The New Yorker* supplies a flavour of Perowne's disdain for the anti-war movement, with arguments which replicate McEwan's published views.

Henry Perowne witnesses the marchers gathering for the great anti-war rally and finds their 'general cheerfulness ... baffling'. He thinks, 'The scene has an air of innocence and English dottiness.'

Maybe McEwan is being ironic here. Maybe we are supposed to perceive Perowne as complacent and self-satisfied. But I suspect not entirely. I think these are probably Mcewan's own views. Why are the protesters cheerful in the face of an impending war? What shallow hypocrites they are!

Answer: demonstrations often have a carnival aspect, full of creative and witty forms of protest. But one of my most enduring memories of that march is trudging slowly along Piccadilly, crushed by the biggest, slowest-moving crowd I'd ever been in in my life, *in total silence*. On the approach to Hyde Park the mood wasn't jolly, but sombre. But maybe McEwan wasn't there to witness it. (*It turns out he wasn't. He skulked at a distance, observing it but refusing to participate. A classic fence-sitting Liberal who functions in the service of imperialism.*)

Secondly, in the description of the 'air of innocence' and 'English dottiness' I think the reader is invited to perceive the anti-war marchers as a bit scatty, gullible, daft, naïve people who know nothing about the horrors of Iraq under Saddam. Perowne soon after 'imagines himself as Saddam, surveying the crowd with satisfaction from some Baghdad ministry balcony: the good-hearted electorates of the Western democracies will never allow their governments to attack his country.' The sub-text being: the anti-war movement is complicit with the Saddam regime and is working to perpetuate it.

Ah, but Perowne knows better than these gullible peaceniks. You see, he's treated an Iraqi torture victim, and as a result that makes him 'ambivalent' – that word again! – about the coming war:

> Ever since he treated an Iraqi professor of ancient history for an aneurysm, saw his torture scars and listened to his stories, Perowne has had ambivalent or confused and shifting ideas about this coming invasion. Miri Taleb is in his late sixties, a man of slight, almost girlish build, with a nervous laugh, a whinnying giggle that could have something to do with his time in prison. He did his Ph.D. at University College, London, and speaks excellent English. His field is Sumerian civilisation, and for more than twenty years he taught at the university in Baghdad and was involved in various archeological surveys in the Euphrates area. His arrest came one winter afternoon in 1994, outside a lecture room where he was about to teach. His students were waiting for him inside and did not see what happened. Three men showed their security accreditations, and asked him to go with them to their car. There they handcuffed him, and it was at that point that his torture began.

Miri Taleb seems in part to be a fictionalisation of McEwan's old mentor, the late Malcolm Bradury (whose distinguishing characteristic was indeed 'a whinnying giggle'). This is apt in two ways. I'm quite sure (because he was a right-wing liberal who voted Conservative) that Bradbury's position on the war would have been every bit as equivocal as McEwan's. Secondly, Bradbury's novel *The History Man* supplies a kind of model for *Saturday* in so far as it is narrated in the present tense and is a novel about anxiety – the anxiety of a liberal who feels his values are under threat by dark and sinister forces.

The History Man achieved a certain notoriety as a novel which projected its author's paranoia about the Marxist threat to the integrity of the modern university, based on Bradbury's personal experience of a sit-in at the University of East Anglia in 1971. (One of the students who blockaded the Arts Block there was, ironically, Ian McEwan.) *The History Man* has been described as the novel which won Margaret Thatcher the 1979 election – a risible exaggeration but one which possessed an inner truth. By creating a right-wing caricature of a Marxist virus inside the liberal new university Bradbury assisted an ideology which led eventually to the annihilation of that institution and its replacement by a new ethos of business sponsorship, tuition fees, loans and profit-orientated utilitarian education. Out with unprofitable knowledge-for-its-own-sake and departments like music, geography and classics! In with business sponsorship, targets and the requirements of capitalism! Malcolm Bradbury was instrumental in helping to destroy all that he cherished, which is always the fate of liberals.

Perowne's convenient acquaintanceship with Miri Taleb supplies him with details of the horrors under Saddam: 'The torture was routine—Miri and his cellmates heard the screaming from their cells, and waited to be called. Beatings, electrocution, anal rape, near-drowning, thrashing the soles of the feet. Everyone, from top officials to street-sweepers, lived in a state of anxiety, constant fear.'

A little later on in the narrative:

'Everyone hates it,' Miri told Perowne. 'You see, it's only terror that holds the nation together. The whole system runs on fear, and no one knows how to stop it. Now the Americans are coming, perhaps for bad reasons. But Saddam and the Baathists will go. And then, my doctor friend, I will buy you a meal in a good Iraqi restaurant in London.'

This replicates McEwan's arguments, of course. One less dictatorship in the world is a good thing.

From these insights into the horrors of life under Saddam, Perowne's attention returns to the marchers: '"Not in My Name" goes past a dozen times. Its cloying self-regard suggests a bright new world of protest, with the fussy consumers of shampoos and soft drinks demanding to feel good, or nice.'

Does it? What is wrong with an individual asserting that what the British government does in the name of Britain does not enjoy the support of that individual? To call individual protest 'cloying self-regard' is a cheap smear worthy of a tabloid newspaper.

Next: 'A placard of one of the organizing groups goes by—the British Association of Muslims. Henry remembers that outfit well. It explained recently in its newspaper that apostasy from Islam was an offence punishable by death.'

Factually, it's MAB, not BAM. It's hard to say if this McEwan's carelessness or the result of a lawyer's intervention in the manuscript. Whatever, it recycles a favourite argument of that dreary apostate Christopher Hitchens, that the left is in league with Islamic fascism.

Then next 'comes a banner proclaiming the Swaffham Women's Choir, and then Jews Against the War'.

By now the reader has got the picture. What a muddle-headed and contradictory collection of do-gooders we have assembled here!

Then Perowne releases his killer insight: 'He might have been with them—in spirit at least, for nothing now will keep him from his game—if Professor Taleb hadn't needed that aneurysm clipped on his middle cerebral artery. In the months after those conversations with the Professor, Perowne drifted into some compulsive reading up on the regime. He read about the inspirational example of Stalin, and the network of family and tribal loyalties that sustained Saddam, and the palaces handed out as rewards. Henry became acquainted with the details of genocides in the north and south of the country, the ethnic cleansing, the vast system of informers, the bizarre tortures and Saddam's taste for getting personally involved, and the strange punishments passed into law—the brandings and amputations. Naturally, Henry followed closely the accounts of measures taken against surgeons who refused to carry out these mutilations. He concluded that viciousness had rarely been more inventive or systematic or widespread. Miri was right: it was indeed a republic of fear. Henry read Makiya's famous book of that name. It was clear, Saddam's organizing principle was terror.'

What is missing from this account of the history of Iraq is, of course, the complicity of the USA and Britain in this state of affairs.

McEwan greasily gives us history wiped clean of American imperialism. The impending invasion of Iraq is simplified into A Good Thing, because it means the destruction of a vile regime. But Perowne, like McEwan, is allowed the luxury of having it both ways: 'He also worries that the invasion or the occupation will be a mess. The marchers could be right. And he acknowledges the accidental nature of opinions; if he hadn't met and admired the Professor, he might have thought differently, less ambivalently, about the coming war.'

Ah, that word ambivalence again! And the sub-text is that these foolish marchers simply have no idea of the nature of the regime that the invading armies will topple. They are ignorant.

Perowne continues: 'Opinions are a roll of the dice; by definition, none of the people now milling around the Warren Street tube station happen to have been tortured by the regime, or know and love anyone who has, or even know much about the place at all. It's likely most of them barely registered the massacres in Kurdish Iraq, or in the Shiite south, and now they find they care with a passion for Iraqi lives.'

Not only ignorant, you see, but hypocrites! Worse still, self-interested hypocrites:

'They have good reasons for their views, among which are concerns for their own safety. Al Qaeda, it's said, which loathes both godless Saddam and the Shiite opposition, will be provoked by an attack on Iraq into revenge on the soft cities of the West. Self-interest is a decent enough cause, but Perowne can't feel, as the marchers themselves probably can, that they have an exclusive hold on moral discernment. There are people around the planet, well connected and organised, who would like to kill him and his family and friends, just to make a point. The scale of death contemplated is no longer at issue; there'll be more deaths on a similar scale, probably in this city.'

Bloodcurdling stuff, eh? By now we are deep in Hitchens-land. We must all rally round Bush and the US army to protect us from these fanatical Islamic fascists!

Shortly afterwards Perowne is involved in a minor car crash, which brings him face to face with three menacing, thuggish men who appear to be criminals. He is assaulted by their leader. (Incidentally, I have a sneaky suspicion that McEwan has nicked from Iain Banks's novel *Dead Air* the plot device of a road crash resulting in involvement with criminal thugs.)

Here the extract in the *New Yorker* ends, leaving the resolution of this episode hanging in the air. But it's clear that at a sub-textual level Perowne has been put in this awful situation by those dreadful anti-war marchers, who have affected his route as a car driver and caused him to be stranded alone on an empty street to face three thugs. The thugs are presumably some kind of metaphor for Saddam and his regime, and Perowne is the cultured, decent representative of Western civilisation, *and a brain surgeon as well.*

It would be unfair to condemn a novel which hasn't yet been published and which I haven't yet read. But like I say, I'm apprehensive about what it will all add up to. I suspect it's going to be a very right-wing book indeed, which will be enthusiastically received in the USA and by Christopher Hitchens. I suspect it's going to be McEwan's own *History Man*, projecting its author's right-wing liberal anxieties and pointing a finger at the radical left.

In the meantime I've been taking a look at what my old friend Roget's Thesaurus has to say. Ambivalence can mean 'contrariety', 'disagreement' or 'equivocalness'. It's the last meaning that interests me.

Its associations include: newspeak, doubletalk, weasel word, prevarication, quibbling, double-tongued, facing both ways, vague, evasive, not give a straight answer, fudge, waffle, and stall.

The Politics of Ian McEwan's *Saturday*

This is a novel which is set entirely on 15 February 2003, the day of the great London anti-war march.

Not a single character in this novel goes on the march.

Although most of them live and work in central London, they are all doing something else that day. The march only exists filtered through the consciousness of Henry Perowne, the brain surgeon protagonist. He catches glimpses of it from a distance. He sees it on the TV news. From time to time he presents his critical commentary on the marchers.

Perowne is off to play squash, and, as a result of the road closures that day, gets involved in a car crash with a sinister thug named Baxter. Henry is 'ambivalent' about the war, as a result of knowing an Iraqi torture victim. And this torture victim would not approve of the anti-war march; from his perspective, 'Across Europe, and all around the world, people are gathering to express their preference for peace and torture.' Perowne thinks that 'the humanitarian reasons for war' is 'the only case worth making'. He doesn't like the anti-war marchers. He thinks they are frivolous. He complains that they are too cheerful: 'All this happiness on display is suspect. Everyone is thrilled to be together on the streets – people are hugging themselves, it seems, as well as each other. If they think – and they could be right – that continued torture and summary executions, ethnic cleansing and occasional genocide are preferable to an invasion, they should be sombre in their view.'

Nowhere in *Saturday* is there the perception that the forces pressing for war are precisely the same forces which subsidised, protected and armed the regime which carried out those atrocities. As a novel about politics, history and medicine, it suffers from its own unspoken narrative malady: amnesia.

McEwan dances away from troublesome specifics. We're told that Perowne has a great relationship with his son and that 'They've never talked so much before.' Among the topics of discussion are 'Israel and Palestine, dictators, democracy'. A bit vague, wouldn't you say? Pleasantly vague. Evasively vague.

Perowne's squash partner is pro-war and has to abandon his car south of the river and jog to the squash court. Perowne's wife is a high-flying lawyer who is absent all day, tied up at the High Court fighting for press freedom. Alas, the judge (sympathetic to her press freedom argument) is delayed by the demonstration. Perowne's father-in-law, a famous poet, is flying in from France for a Saturday night family get-together.

Perowne has two fabulously talented kids – so talented you wouldn't want to receive a Christmas round robin letter from the Perownes, and if you got one you'd want to forward it to Simon Hoggart. Perowne's daughter, a stunningly talented young poet about to be published by Faber, is flying in from Paris, where she is currently living. Perowne's son, Theo, a hugely talented 18-year old blues guitarist, is against invading Iraq, but he's not on the march either: 'His attitude is as strong and pure as his bones and skin. So strong he doesn't feel much need to go tramping through the streets to make his point.'

I'm still trying (and failing) to make sense of that fuzzy logic. And I don't find it remotely plausible that a cool young dude who was passionately against the war and lived just a few hundred metres from the start of the march would think: Nah, I'm not going on it, it's a complete waste of time.

McEwan does permit an anti-war voice to enter his narrative, on p. 185, when Perowne's daughter Daisy arrives from Paris and on the way home from the airport stops at Hyde Park to hear some of the speeches. She and her father proceed to have an argument about the war, with Perowne (sometimes almost verbatim) expressing McEwan's own published reservations.

Daisy, aged 18, is a tremendous fan of Philip Larkin, who is her favourite poet. 'Apparently, not many young women loved Philip Larkin the way she did.' True enough: 18 year old girls probably prefer Snow Patrol to Philip Larkin. But probably not many anti-war protesters were into Larkin either, one suspects, bearing in mind Larkin's racism, sexism and miserabilist verse which yearns for a fantasy pre-First World War England, mocks and stereotypes the ghastly vulgar working classes and has a gloomy fixation on the inevitability of death (written in his younger days – ironically when he grew old his poetry dried up and he retreated into booze and singing jolly racist chants with his charmless alcoholic lover). As Tom Paulin somewhere remarks, underneath the Larkin monument runs a stinking sewer. But McEwan himself evidently likes Larkin, whose verse is the only copyright material cited in *Saturday*.

The argument between father and daughter rages on, until Perowne stops it with a bet: 'My fifty pounds says three months after the invasion there'll be a free press in Iraq, and unmonitored Internet access too. The reformers in Iran will be encouraged, those Syrian and Saudi and Libyan potentates will be getting the jitters.' Daisy replies, 'Fine. And my fifty says it'll be a mess and even you will wish it never happened.'

McEwan finished writing *Saturday* in the second half of 2004. This allowed him the wisdom of hindsight. (At one point – p. 151 – there's a careless reference to 'the war in Iraq' – but of course *the war hadn't yet started*. What McEwan should have written was 'the war ON Iraq' or 'war WITH Iraq'.) By fixing Perowne's bet on the state of affairs in Iraq three months after the invasion, McEwan allows both sides to be at least partly right. Yes, there was a free press! Yes, there was unmonitored Internet access! But, yes, it was a bit of a mess too!

If he'd fixed his bet one year after the invasion, Perowne would have lost and the absurdity of his liberal humanism been glaringly exposed. Just after the fall of Baghdad, polls suggested that Iraqis were evenly divided on whether or not they felt liberated or occupied. By the time the USA pretended to hand over power in the summer of 2004, only 2 per cent of Arab Iraqis supported the occupation. As for the free press – Al Jazeera was booted out by the Vichy regime, anxious to stifle an independent Arab media outlet loathed by the US government.

It's noticeable that McEwan's position has shifted from that which he put forward in January 2003. 'I was against it,' he now asserts, when asked about the war (interview with Boyd Tonkin, the *Independent*, 28 January 2005). But of course, 'not as passionately as many friends and colleagues'. McEwan now claims that Daisy expresses his anti-war feelings just as much as Perowne embodies his own ambivalence, but Daisy's assertion that 'there's nothing linking Iraq to nine eleven, or to Al-Qaeda generally, and no really scary evidence of WMD' is completely at odds with McEwan's former belief that it did not seem 'outlandish, the possibility of Saddam Hussein passing on weapons of mass destruction to the enemy of his enemies'. McEwan is rewriting the record of his politics.

In January 2003 McEwan defended Blair from the charge that he was Bush's poodle and saw him as a committed humanitarian. Disillusionment has evidently now set in. McEwan's shift of position seems to me to parallel that of Greg Dyke, who confides, 'I understand what Gordon Brown means when he says he finds it difficult to believe a word that Blair says, which is odd because I didn't feel that a year ago when I was forced out. It was the publication last summer of the Butler report which changed everything for me' (*Independent*, 28 January 2005).

In *Saturday* McEwan twice mocks Blair. There's a reference to the science of the human smile: 'In the smile of a self-conscious liar certain muscle groups in the face are not activated' but 'the first and best unconscious move of a dedicated liar is to persuade himself he's sincere. And once he's sincere, all deception vanishes.'

Reprising that episode when the protagonist of *The Child in Time* has a surreal encounter with Margaret Thatcher, Perowne remembers a comic encounter with Blair at the opening party for the Tate Modern gallery. Blair, we learn, mistook him for a painter and, when told of his error, saved face by continuing to congratulate him on his artistry. McEwan, I think we can safely conclude, like Greg Dyke, feels very, very let down by Tony and no longer trusts him.

That sense of disappointment is transmitted in the scene where Perowne sees Blair on TV: 'The Prime Minister is giving his Glasgow speech. Perowne touches the control in time to hear him say that the number of marchers today has been exceeded by the number of deaths caused by Saddam. A clever point, the only case to make, but it should have been made from the start. Too late now. After Blix it looks tactical.' (It is estimated that Saddam Hussein killed around 200,000 Iraqis during his dictatorship. The number of marchers in London on on 15 February 2003 is estimated at between one and two million. Blair was [characteristically] lying through his teeth and McEwan's gullibility is once again exposed.)

It is characteristic of the narrative that those cloudy sentences of Perowne's are never subjected to irony or sceptical enquiry. In what sense is it 'a clever point' or 'the only case to make'? Far from being 'clever' isn't it just meaningless? No mention, either, of the fact that Blair brought forward his speech by several hours, in order to dodge thousands of Scottish demonstrators who were going to march on the venue where he was due to speak. McEwan's version of 15 February 2003 is devious in all kinds of way.

There is nothing in *Saturday* that seems likely seriously to damage McEwan's popularity with his American readership. The novel is prefaced by a quotation from Saul Bellow's *Herzog*. Bellow is another liberal novelist whose trajectory over the years has been from fiery young lefty to elderly reactionary. But ironically, the language of the Bellow epigraph is far more sparky, animated and stylistically daring than anything in the buttoned-up, over-wrought, mannered prose of *Saturday*. At times McEwan's style is fussily Edwardian. Whereas the average realist novelist would write 'at the end of the week he was unusually tired', McEwan writes 'he finished the week in a state of unusual depletion'.

The ravages of US foreign policy never feature in Perowne's consciousness, other than in the vaguest of ways. There are harsh words for torture regimes, but Israel is not included in the list. (Six years after publication of *Saturday*, McEwan scuttled off to Israel to accept the Jerusalem Prize, underlining his unprincipled opportunism.)

The only American in the novel is Jay Strauss, a big, tough, warm-hearted consultant anaesthetist. A patient, a stroppy black 14-year old girl from Brixton, vexes the hospital staff by her difficult behaviour. She's a bully. When a nurse is reduced to tears, only tough Jay Strauss can deal with the situation. In the face of his tough, firm no-nonsense attitude the girl's hostility collapses and, by the end of the novel, her operation a success, she wants to become a brain surgeon herself. (There's a sub-text there, oh yes. But you can work it out for yourself.)

Strauss is also a brilliant anaesthetist: 'As far as Henry is concerned, Jay is the key to the success of his firm.' Perowne's 'firm' is his team. And this is a novel in part about having *a good team spirit*. Perowne and Strauss play squash (for 16 pages – a *tour de force* of narrative description or a bloody tedious read – you decide). They both get ratty about losing, but at work they rise above such petty irritability, as good professionals should. (Team spirit, I'm afraid, always makes me think of that brilliant moment at the end of the movie *I'll Never Forget Whatshisname* where surly, sarcastic, wonderful Oliver Reed screams that it was *team spirit* that gave us the Nazi death camps.)

Strauss, inevitably, is also pro-war: 'Iraq is a rotten state, a natural ally of terrorists, bound to cause mischief at some point and may as well be taken out now while the US military is feeling perky after Afghanistan. And by taken out, he insists that he means liberated and democratised. The USA has to atone for its previous disastrous policies – at the very least it owes this to the Iraqi people.'

War for the purest motives, you see – the classic apologia of liberal warmongers, whose rule is always to come out in support of imperialist aggression. It's a position not really any different to Perowne's, even though McEwan terminates this paragraph with the sentence: 'Whenever he talks to Jay, Henry finds himself tending towards the anti-war camp.'

Tending towards is a revealing way of putting it – this is a mind that seems to flutter towards one political position, then to flutter to its opposite, but in actuality stays firmly lodged in the centre right, aligning itself with the argument that the forthcoming war on Iraq has a sound humanitarian basis and will be good for the Iraqi people. And throughout this novel there is a fastidious disdain for those dimly glimpsed, marginalised 2 million marchers. It embodies McEwan's greasy, self-serving liberalism perfectly.

A minor character, Rodney Browne, a neurosurgical registrar, is also against the war, but when Jay Strauss 'has been holding forth on the necessity of the coming war' Browne is 'reluctant to voice his pacifist views for fear of being taken apart'.

But this suggestion of balance is all a sleight of hand. The argument that it might be a war for oil is mentioned only in passing. The thrust of the novel is to make the reader sympathise with Perowne, the decent, hard-working, agonised, ambivalent liberal.

The climax of the novel subverts the pacifism of Daisy and her brother. When the thuggish Baxter and an associate force their way into the house they force Daisy to strip naked before them. She is threatened with rape. In the face of violence the representatives of civilised decency are themselves forced to resort to violence, and Perowne and Theo end up fighting Baxter and throwing him down the stairs. It's a parable of sorts. At the height of the terror Perowne hears the police helicopter as it monitors the dispersal of the protesters from Hyde Park. It's a moment calculated to appeal to *Daily Mail* readers – police resources taken up by a left-wing demonstration while an affluent middle-class household is broken into by a pair of violent, terrifying working class thugs with knives.

In a twist of fate (one of the many implausible aspects of a supposedly realistic narrative), Perowne is asked to operate on Baxter, who has suffered a serious head injury. This preposterous coincidence underlines how McEwan has for many years been a populist genre writer, essentially in the same mould as a fellow practitioner such as Lee Child. Perowne operates, successfully, afterwards deciding that he will not press charges, even though Baxter has broken Perowne's father-in-law's nose, slashed Perowne's expensive Knoll sofa, held a knife to his wife's throat, and forced his daughter to strip, then threatened her with rape. Perowne represents decency and liberal humanity; Baxter has a rare genetic condition and is biologically doomed – that is punishment enough, he decides.

On his way to the hospital Perowne encounters the cleaning-up operation after the great march: 'the debris has a certain archaeological interest – a Not in My Name with a broken stalk lies among polystyrene cups and abandoned hamburgers and pristine fliers for the British Association of Muslims. On a pile he steps round are a slab of pizza with pineapple slices, beer cans in a tartan motif, a denim jacket, empty milk cartons and three unopened tins of sweetcorn.'

This is the final mention of the march in the novel (which continues for another 36 pages), and it takes us back to Perowne's encounter with the marchers in Chapter Two: '"Not in My Name" goes past a dozen times. Its cloying self-regard suggests a bright new world of protest, with the fussy consumers of shampoos and soft drinks demanding to feel good, or nice ... A placard of one of the organizing groups goes by — the British Association of Muslims. Henry remembers that outfit well. It explained recently in its newspaper that apostasy from Islam was an offence punishable by death.'

Perowne's final encounter with the detritus of the march reinforces his earlier perception of these gullible, muddle-headed peaceniks as self-centred consumers, enjoying the good life of western capitalism while cheerily aligning themselves with the dark force of Islamic extremism. *Perowne, in other words, is right all along*. And for *Daily Mail* readers there is, I suppose, the added bonus that these lefty anti-war marchers are *a scruffy lot who drop tons of litter*.

This is more sleight of hand, of course. Those who take the trouble to travel to central London and march against the war are self-centred consumers. Those who spend that Saturday doing other things like playing squash or shopping or playing their guitars are not self-centred but superior creatures possessed of a more complex inner life.

The final 34 pages of the novel describe Perowne's operation on Baxter and his return home, where he has sex with his wife for the second time that day and finally goes to sleep. The biggest protest march in British history is simply erased from existence – a non-event, really, remote from the central drama of Henry Perowne's mind and life.

In reality *Saturday* is far less about 15 February 2003 than about 11 September 2001. From his published comments, it appears that McEwan experienced that event as something of a personal trauma. He subscribes to the US-centric 'world was changed forever by 9/11' thesis. After 9/11 McEwan abandoned writing fiction for six months. No public event in his writing career had touched him so deeply. The violent death of 3000 people, mostly Americans, was a horror much greater than all those millions upon millions who died from malnutrition, disease, torture, massacre or war in the 27 years of his career as a published writer. But then they died off-camera, and almost none of them were white middle-class professionals and they were just statistics, not individuals with life stories that interested the media.

What you don't get in *Saturday* and what you'll never get in McEwan's fiction is the kind of perception of the main character in Iain Banks's novel *Dead Air*, who comments: 'every twenty-four hours about thirty-four thousand children die in the world from the effects of poverty; from malnutrition and disease, basically. Thirty-four thousand, from a world, a world-society, that could feed and clothe and treat them all, with a workably different allocation of resources. Meanwhile, the latest estimate is that two-thousand eight hundred people died in the Twin Towers, so it's like that image, that ghastly, grey-billowing, double-barrelled fall, repeated twelve times every single fucking day; twenty-four towers, one per hour, throughout each day and night. Full of children.'

McEwan's trauma was, I suspect, partly the shock of seeing something that was personally important under attack. 'From the vantage point of the Brooklyn Heights, we saw Lower Manhattan disappear into dust,' he wrote in the *Guardian* on 12 September 2001, from the viewpoint of someone familiar with New York. 'Yesterday afternoon, for a dreamlike, immeasurable period, the appearance was of total war, and of the world's mightiest empire in ruins.' There was also, perhaps, the disturbing thought that it could so easily have been *him* on one of those planes, 'crouching in the brushed-steel lavatory at the rear of the plane, whispering a final message'.

McEwan complained that the hijackers lacked empathy for their victims: 'If the hijackers had been able to imagine themselves into the thoughts and feelings of the passengers, they would have been unable to proceed. It is hard to be cruel once you permit yourself to enter the mind of your victim. Imagining what it is like to be someone other than yourself is at the core of our humanity. It is the essence of compassion, and it is the beginning of morality. (*Guardian*, 15 September 2001).

This is perfectly true. But it is a point that could also be made against members of the US army or RAF bomber pilots. But

McEwan would never dare to articulate such a perception, even assuming he was capable of it. He is a writer who serves and flatters power; he does not challenge it.

McEwan claimed that, 'The hijackers used fanatical certainty, misplaced religious faith, and dehumanising hatred to purge themselves of the human instinct for empathy. Among their crimes was a failure of the imagination.'

In one sense, he was extraordinarily wrong. The hijackers had the perceptions of literary critics. They did not lack imagination. They were interested in symbolism. The Pentagon represented the US military war machine and the twin towers represented US commerce. There was an additional cultural spin-off. What the hijackers did by demolishing the twin towers was to mock American cultural hegemony in a curiously deadly way. Suddenly all those cinematic images of New York became an ironic comment on their own complacent self-regard. The twin towers are everywhere in that hegemonic imagery. The re-make of *King Kong,* the Hollywood *Godzilla*, old episodes of *Friends,* in innumerable Hollywood movies, Spielberg's *AI*, Schwarzenegger's *End of Days*, and in early episodes of *The Sopranos*, the twin towers are always there, somewhere. And, seeing them after 9/11, you can't help thinking of what is to come. History intrudes on fiction. 9/11 *re-imagined the past*. It mocked the staple convention of the disaster movie – a good American always, at the last moment, prevents disaster. 9/11 mocked America's image of the future. Hollywood imagined the twin towers would be there forever. It was wrong. In that most visual of cultures, partly because of the accident of a fine, clear sunlit day, partly because of the arbitrary presence of a French film crew, 9/11 supplied a visual feast.

Saturday is essentially an expansion of the ideas McEwan put forward in his two *Guardian* pieces on 9/11. Perowne's day begins with him looking out of the window of his central London home and seeing a plane on fire coming in to Heathrow. He wonders if it is another 9/11 style hijacking. That possibility evaporates. Instead a worse, more personal crisis follows later in the day. The knife wielding Baxter and his accomplice who burst in and threaten Perowne, his wife, his daughter, his son, and his father-in-law, represent a version of the 9/11 hijackers. Baxter is like a suicidal terrorist: Perowne identifies him as 'a man who believes he has no future and is therefore free of consequences'.

Baxter is, metaphorically, an Arab extremist. His genetic defect is also, arguably, a displaced version of that popular reactionary concept, the criminal gene (which is paralleled by the poverty gene and the homelessness gene, and all those other bogus genes which offer a soothing pseudo-scientific explanation for the consequences of the inequalities of capitalist society).

But what stops a dangerous and dreadful situation – the impending rape of Daisy – is the benign force of the human imagination. Baxter engages in a conversation with his intended victim (a plot device straight out of James Bond – the villain unfolds his fiendish plans but the delay this involves provides a way out of an apparently hopeless situation). He orders her to read from her book of poems. In a state of shock Daisy is able only to recite an old favourite, Matthew Arnold's 'Dover Beach'. Baxter likes it so much he asks her to recite it again, then sobs, 'It's beautiful', adding, 'It makes me think of where I grew up.' So Baxter, unlike the 9/11 hijackers, does not lack imagination. He is redeemable. He loses all interest in raping Daisy. He isn't an Arab after all!

The message of the poem 'Dover Beach' (a poem written by a reactionary liberal terrified of the working classes getting the vote) is also the message of *Saturday*. The world is a truly dreadful place full of nastiness and very, very confusing. God is dead. Nothing makes sense any more. Therefore retreat into the personal and 'be true' to your lover. Or as Lennon and McCartney put it: *All you need is love*.

Saturday, is, then, a novel about anxiety. It is in the great tradition of the nineteenth century bourgeois liberal novel, in which affluent, talented writers were terrified of the idea that their whole way of life was under threat by dark, destructive forces. Back then the threat was from working-class radicalism. The image of workers gathered together for political purposes sent a shiver down the spine of novelists like George Eliot, whose vision of the proletariat was that of a terrifying mob, a 'mass of wild chaotic desires and impulses'. Dickens in *Hard Times* suggested that those who suffered under capitalism should respond with dignified restraint, in heroic isolation. Nothing as vulgar as politics should intrude. And when those ghastly natives in India rose up against the British military occupation, Charles Dickens embraced genocide and urged the killing of every Indian. Henry James in *The Princess Casamassima* proposed that the major motive of political radicals was envy and suggested that the only decent destiny of a thinking militant was to see through the sham of revolutionary politics and commit suicide. (Thanks, Henry.)

The actions of Al-Qaeda have, alas, soured the agreeable quality of suicide as an apt political destiny, and even when liberals with a capital 'L' do something so liberal as to empathise with the state of mind of Palestinians who detonate themselves beside Israelis, they quickly find, as Jenny Tonge did, that the liberal – or Liberal – imagination is suddenly a very narrow and slyly calculating one.

Perowne is an anxious man. 'He bought Fred Halliday's book,' we're told, and having read it frets that 'the New York attacks precipitated a global crisis that would, if we were lucky, take a hundred years to resolve.' Frightening stuff, eh?

Later Perowne convinces himself that the crisis will fade, like all the ones before it. But that still leaves him with lots of other anxieties. But these are the anxieties of an affluent professional enjoying a very agreeable lifestyle. He lives in a large house in central London. He drives a Mercedes which he houses in a nearby mews. He enjoys fine food and wine. What haunts him is the threat of Islamic extremism. He fears another 9/11 style hijacking. He worries about the shoe bomber. He worries that there will be a major terrorist attack on his city. And the problem is ideology, which makes fanatics do terrible things. Perowne concludes (much in the manner of George Eliot): 'No more big ideas. The world must improve, if at all, by tiny steps.' Perowne even has an example. The design of kettles has much improved over the years: 'The world should take note: not everything is getting worse.'

Perowne is not entirely McEwan. His views on literature are different, and there are various jokes for the literati. Perowne doesn't like McEwan's *The Child in Time* or Rushdie's *The Satanic Verses*. His poet father-in-law is envious of McEwan's great friend Craig Raine. He is not well up on his Matthew Arnold. If Perowne has one shortcoming it is that his grasp of literature is weak and he does not read novels with a proper sense of appreciation – a feeble irony which flatters the ego of the reader of *Saturday*.

Predictably, the reactionary BBC has treated the publication of *Saturday* as a newsworthy event. A feature on the 'Today' programme (February 1st) called it '*Ulysses*-like'. Well, yes, it's set on a single day but apart from that it is entirely unlike Joyce's novel, which is massively radical and ambitious in its language and form. *Ulysses* is a difficult, stubborn, challenging read. The reality is that

Saturday is precisely the kind of novel Joyce set out to annihilate. As literature, it is Edwardian in temper and form It has solid characters, a suspenseful plot and uses the conventions of realism to portray an affluent middle class social world. As a product it is easy reading, shiny, highly processed. It presents itself (as realism always does) as a transparent window through which to observe a real world. Its artifice and partiality goes as unacknowledged as the shared values of a BBC news team. It emanates the stale authority of omniscience, treating its readers to little nuggets of wisdom. Here's a good example of the style: 'Sex is a different medium, refracting time and sense, a biological hyperspace as remote from conscious existence as dreams, or as water is from air.' The reader is required only to nod wisely in agreement at this profundity.

Apparently McEwan wants us to think that Perowne's fence-sitting on the war is akin to 'Hamlet-like indecision' – a cultural analogy which strikes me as preposterous. Hamlet had to decide if the ghost was a demon or a truth-teller, if his father had really been murdered, and whether or not to kill the king – rather substantial personal anxieties, with potentially lethal consequences. Perowne's banal equivocations about the rights and wrongs of war on Iraq have no personal consequences at all.

Boyd Tonkin complains that books as a cultural form don't get enough attention from TV (*Independent*, 4 February 2005), but he adds: 'On the credit side, an item about Ian McEwan's *Saturday* made the principal BBC evening news this Monday. This was not because it grabbed a gong or stirred a quarrel or triggered a fatwa, but simply because a world-ranking novelist had brought out a landmark work.'

But I can't think of anything more characteristic of the news values of the craven, imperialism-promoting BBC than that it should choose to privilege the publication of *Saturday* as deserving of respectful attention as 'news'. *Saturday* is ideologically kin to those values. Just like the BBC, it pimps for the status quo and for power. It's a novel which adopts a reverent attitude to affluence. A Mercedes is a lovely car. Squash is a splendid game. It's nice to have a big house in central London. A war on Iraq will get rid of a disgusting torture regime.

Saturday is a novel for liberals who didn't go on the march (and I have yet to read a review of the novel or hear or watch a discussion of it that engages with the question of whether or not the critic participated in that march. My guess is that probably not a single one of them did.) It's a bourgeois novel in the sense that it celebrates a bourgeois life style and worries about the threats to that way of life. At the end of the novel Perowne stands at the window, back where his day began: 'A hundred years ago, a middle-aged doctor standing at this window in his silk dressing gown, less than two hours before a winter's dawn, might have pondered the new century's future. February 1903. You might envy this Edwardian gent all he didn't yet know. If he had young boys, he could lose them within a dozen years, at the Somme. And what was their body count, Hitler, Stalin, Mao? Fifty million, a hundred? If you described the hell that lay ahead, if you warned him, the good doctor – an affable product of prosperity and decades of peace – would not believe you. Beware the utopianists, zealous men certain of the path to an ideal social order. Here they are again, totalitarians in different form, still scattered and weak, but growing, and angry, and thirsty for another mass killing. A hundred years to resolve. But this may be an indulgence, an idle, overblown fantasy, a night-thought about a passing disturbance that time and good sense will settle and rearrange.'

As usual, McEwan has his cake and eats it. He equivocates. But these parallel nightmare visions are questionable on grounds other than that the second, twenty-first century one, might not come to pass. If the twentieth century was hell, what was the nineteenth century? Paradise? What was the body count of the British Empire? In February 1903 McEwan's fictitious Edwardian gentleman may have actually had the Boer War uppermost in his mind – a war in which the British utilised the mass punishment of civilians and invented the concentration camp. And if Hitler, Stalin and Mao racked up millions of dead, what about those late Victorian holocausts? What about the 17 million who die every year on our planet from disease, malnutrition, filthy water and suchlike? What's the body count resulting from US foreign policy? If it was hell in the Gulags or the death camps, was it more agreeable being a Kikuyu in Kenya in the 1950s? As for those 'zealous men' of the twenty-first century, what is it exactly that makes them 'angry'? Perowne is supposed to represent civilised values but one of the many absences from his sensitive conscience is global warming and the link with personal consumption, car driving, air travel and all those other ingredients of an agreeable middle-class lifestyle.

But that's quite enough from me. I finish this week in a state of unusual depletion. I'm off for another listen to that timeless classic, Phil Ochs singing 'Love Me, I'm a Liberal.'

Socialist Review on *Saturday*

I was hoping I wouldn't feel compelled to say anything more about *Saturday*, but there's a part of Judy Cox's review of the novel in the March issue of *Socialist Review* that set my pulse racing.

Most of what Cox has to say I wouldn't quarrel with – apart from one minor misreading. 'Amanda' and 'Josh' in her review should be 'Andrea' and 'Jay'. And Andrea isn't, as Cox says, romantically 'tamed by her instant love' for sexy medic Jay. Andrea is a teenage black bully and only Jay is prepared to stand up to her. There's a *Daily Mail* sub-text to that episode – stroppy black teenager needs a tough male response to bring her under control (a right-wing liberal parable of the Metropolitan Police and black youth?) – although it's clear that McEwan's intention is to cast Andrea as a metaphor for Saddam.

Bullies go on bullying and it's only when someone bigger and harder than them stands up to them that they collapse and become subservient and civilised – yup, it's a metaphor for McEwan's version of US foreign policy. Jay is a big, tough, no-nonsense yank and that's what THAT little lady needs to bring her into line and turn her into a decent human being again. And, Jay's views may be a bit harsh but, hey, he's just a big warm-hearted American who means well. And where Andrea is concerned, who can say he's wrong? Such are the manipulations of the liberal novel.

Judy Cox thinks the novel 'falls short of expectations, and its failure is a political as well as an artistic one'. But just before this observation she finds some REDEEMING FEATURES: 'The great strength of the book is McEwan's innovative structure. By setting all the action within a 24-hour period, everyday events are invested with deep and unexpected meaning. Sex, the squash match, shopping for dinner, a visit to his mother – all provide insights into Henry's and our lives. And it is a great read.'

Oh yeah? First of all, McEwan is not being 'innovative' in using a life-in-the-day narrative structure. Let's ignore the howlingly obvious example of *Ulysses* (which makes the use of the term 'innovative structure' for *Saturday* just a wee bit over-stated, don't you think?). How about Malcolm Lowry's *Under the Volcano*? Not a book I've seen in bookshops lately, so maybe it's out of print, or, as a dense, ambitious, troubling text, just deeply unpopular in the age of Harry Potter, Tolkien and *The Da Vinci Code*. Lowry's hero has something in common with McEwan's Henry Perowne, in so far as he is a sensitive upper-crust Englishman. There the resemblance quickly fades. Lowry's hero is turned inside out – a doomed specimen adrift in a world he can't understand and destined to be thrown on the garbage tip of history.

Secondly, I don't find anything in Henry Perowne's day that is 'invested with deep and unexpected meaning'. Let's look at Cox's list and start with the sex. Perowne's day begins with REALLY GREAT SEX which sends him off into 'a biological hyperspace as remote from conscious existence as dreams'. This reminds me of nothing so much as D. H. Lawrence's windy ramblings about sex. And this is what leads up to that hyperspace:

They kiss and she says, 'I've been half awake for a while, feeling you getting harder against my back.'

'And how was that?'

She whispers, 'It made me want you. But I don't have much time. I daren't be late.' Such effortless seduction! His wish come true, not a finger lifted, the envy of gods and despots, Henry is raised from his stupor to take her in his arms and kiss her deeply. Yes, she's ready.'

At the end of his day, Perowne has MORE REALLY GREAT SEX (somehow I feel the book's movie rights will already have been sold). This is how it's described: 'But when they've finished kissing he says, "Touch me."

As the sweet sensation spreads through him he hears her say, "Tell me that you're mine." "I'm yours. Entirely yours." "Touch my breasts. With your tongue." "Rosalind. I want you."'

After more writing in this style we get to the orgasms: 'The end comes in a sudden fall, so concentrated in its pleasure that it's excruciating to endure, so concentrated in its pleasure, like nerve ends being peeled and stripped clean.'

Is this really the finest fictional prose of our time, written by an author of world class status? Can you imagine Gunter Grass or Gabriel Garcia Marquez writing lines like those?

It's instructive to compare the passage with the sex scene at the end of *Under the Volcano*: 'The Consul's eyes focussed a calendar behind the bed. He had reached his crisis at last, a crisis without possession, almost without pleasure finally, and what he saw might have been, no, he was sure it was, a picture of Canada. Under a brilliant full moon a stag stood by a river down which a man and a woman were paddling a birch bark canoe.' This is bad sex, beautifully described. The Consul isn't even paying attention to the woman he's having sex with. He's not really enjoying sex. And what he sees on the calendar is a laughably bad romantic stereotype, which reverberates with meaning – trite ideas about a nation's identity, banal representations of a man and a woman paddling through the wilderness, banal views of nature, the clichéd masculinity of the noble stag. I don't think you'll find anything as resonant or as challenging as that in *Saturday*.

Next, the squash match. I don't myself find any deep or unexpected meanings in McEwan's 16 pages of exhaustive description of a game of squash, which seems to carry no meaning more sophisticated than that games-playing brings out aggressive instincts which civilised men can rise above.

Then there's 'shopping for dinner'. Perowne drives his Mercedes to Marylebone High Street (he never reflects on his use of a big gas-guzzling luxury car for incredibly short journeys around central London) and is soothed by the thought that 'The largest gathering of humanity in the history of the islands, less than two miles away, is not disturbing Marylebone's contentment ... It isn't rationalism that will overcome the religious zealots, but ordinary shopping and all that it entails.'

This part of the book does a number of things, I think. One is that it focuses attention on people who *aren't* marching. It privileges consumption over commitment. The marchers are 'gathering to express their preference for peace and torture', whereas the busy crowds shopping in Marylebone High Street hold the secret to the survival of secular Western culture : 'It isn't rationalism that will overcome the religious zealots, but ordinary shopping and all that it entails.'

In other words, all those people who didn't go on the march and went shopping instead were much finer people, who were defending civilisation far more effectively. Worse still, the anti-war marchers are the wrong sort of consumers: they are slobs who drop their litter and, worse, they eat stuff like hamburgers and pizza with pineapple slices. The people shopping in Marylebone are a much finer species, who buy lobsters and mussels and monkfish and know a thing or two about food and cooking (not like those lefty plebs and proles with their frightful junk food). Reading this section of the novel reminded me of an observation that Alex Callinicos once made, to the effect that a disillusioned generation of lefties who'd given up on revolution and gone on to become part of the managerial elite of modern capitalism had become foodies – fine food and cooking had become a substitute for their previous passion for social justice. And lastly, this section elides the anti-war marchers with 'the religious zealots' who are plotting dreadful acts of terror against cities like London. The gullible peaceniks just don't understand – instead of marching against war they should be down at the fishmonger's!

Ironically, about 3 weeks ago the *Independent*'s gossip columnist Pandora excitedly reported a sighting of Ian McEwan at a dinner party with the new Commissioner of the Metropolitan Police, Sir Ian Blair. The two were deep in conversation. The ideologist of liberal anxiety about Islamic terror meets a leading agent of state repression over a fine meal – how delightfully apt!

Last in Cox's list is Perowne's visit to his mother. McEwan's own late mother suffered from dementia, and this section of the novel bears all the hallmarks of being autobiographical. This, to me, was the one section of the novel that worked. It brilliantly evokes what it must be like to have a close family member who has lost all sense of self. You feel obliged to visit them, but at the same time it's a complete waste of time as they don't know who you are and will have no memory of your visit. The theme, however, isn't original, and a recent example can be found in Graham Swift's novel *Last Orders*.

Later, back home, Perowne prepares the fish he's bought earlier in the day. What interests me about this section is McEwan's use of collage. Collage is a technique associated with avant-garde artists and writers, but McEwan domesticates it for his own conservative purposes. As Perowne gets to work he keeps glancing at the TV news: 'On the big Hyde Park state, sound-bite extracts of speeches by a venerable politician of the left, a pop star, a playwright, a trade unionist. Into a stockpot he eases the skeletons of three skates. Their heads are intact, their lips girlishly full. Their eyes go cloudy on contact with the boiling water.'

The politician is obviously Tony Benn, I guess the pop star is Miss Dynamite, and the playwright Harold Pinter. I'm not sure who the trade unionist is. By juxtaposing these figures with the skates, McEwan obviously intends subliminally to mock them. 'Their heads are intact' perhaps signifies that these speakers are lucky to be alive and enjoying the fruits of free speech, not like Saddam's victims. Their 'lips girlishly full' hints that they are adolescent in their politics and their speeches. The eyes which go cloudy hint at the bogus sorrow of the anti-war movement, full of passion for a people it knows nothing about. The 'boiling water' is, I think, a metaphor for the tortures inflicted by the Saddam regime.

It's the second time in the novel that McEwan has a dig at Harold Pinter, so there may be something personal here. Back in the 1980s the two were reported to be buddies, but maybe they've fallen out over their politics. If McEwan is using his fiction to settle personal scores it wouldn't be the first time. McEwan's first marriage to Penny Allen broke up in acrimonious circumstances and there was a bitter custody battle over their children. In McEwan's novel *Amsterdam* the place where it all starts to go wrong for the sensitive composer hero is in the vicinity of Allen Crags in the Lake District. Making fun of the name of the mother of your children strikes me as being a bit, well, illiberal.

Liberal Values Revisited

'I can't say I've been much impressed by the integrity of the anti-war movement in Britain. Peace movements are of their nature incapable of choosing lesser evils. The failure to take an interest in, or engage with, Iraqi exiles, or the Iraqi National Congress meeting in London recently, was a moral evasion. All the more shameful when a large part of the INC embraces the liberal or libertarian and secular values that much of the anti-war movement professes.'

That was the novelist Ian McEwan back in January 2003, explaining why he wasn't supporting the no-war-on-Iraq campaign.

McEwan's words came rattling back into my mind this summer as I read Seymour M. Hersh's book *Chain of Command*. Hersh's book is chiefly about the Abu Ghraib scandal, which arose from the Bush administration's enthusiasm for torture, and the policy origins of the 2003 US and UK invasion of Iraq. No one reading Hersh's book can doubt that Tony Blair is a brazen liar, who knew perfectly well that the war had been planned well in advance, and that the public reasons advanced for it were entirely spurious. Seymour M. Hersh is one of that increasingly rare species known as an investigative journalist, and his sources are people within the US military and political establishment. His book ought to be on every lefty's shelf as an essential work of reference.

Remembering McEwan's glowing comments about the INC, I was interested to discover more about this outfit from Hersh's book.

The Iraqi National Congress was an opposition group devoted to the overthrow of Saddam Hussein. It was led by Ahmad Chalabi, who was born into a wealthy Shi'ite banking family. Chalabi came to England in 1958, when he was 13, and has lived outside Iraq for most of his life. In 1992 he was convicted in absentia of bank fraud in Jordan. (The conviction was recently quashed by the Jordanian regime, though it's not clear to me if this was for reasons of justice or politics.)

Chalabi's belief was that the Iraqi regime had no popular base and would collapse at the first sign of serious opposition. In November 1993 he presented the Clinton administration with a plan for overthrowing Saddam Hussein. INC supporters would organise simultaneous uprisings in Basra, Mosul and Kirkuk. When these occurred Chalabi was confident that the Iraqi army would go over to the side of the insurrection.

Chalabi's plan received American backing and CIA support. In March 1995 the insurrection was launched. It was a massive flop. The CIA agent in charge told Hersh: 'No one moved except one Kurdish leader acting on his own – three days too late. Nothing happened.' No one defected from the Iraqi army. By the end of the following year 130 INC members in Iraq had been caught and executed.

After this non-event the CIA and the US state department lost interest in Chalabi. He also faced dissent from within the ranks of his own organisation. In Hersh's words, 'Chalabi managed to maintain his hold on the I.N.C., despite repeated charges of from his coalition's members of mismanagement, self-aggrandizement, and corruption.'

The INC then became 'a rallying point for political conservatives'. Chalabi became the darling of an outfit which called itself 'the American Enterprise Institute' (i.e. right-wing Republicans). In February 1998 forty prominent Americans, including Caspar Weinberger, Frank Carlucci and Donald Rumsfeld, published an open letter to President Clinton warning him that Saddam Hussein posed an immediate threat because he had a stockpile of biological and chemical weapons. Reviving Chalabi's plan, they said 'Iraq today is ripe for a broad-based insurrection'. They recommended that (i) the INC be recognised as the provisional government of Iraq; and (ii) frozen Iraqi assets of more than $1.5 billion be released to fund the provisional government.

The Clinton administration was unimpressed, but under pressure from Congress signed the Iraq Liberation Act, which allocated $97 million for training and military equipment for the Iraqi opposition. However, by the end of 2001 the INC had received only around $10 million. A review carried out by the State Department 'found that the I.N.C.'s accounting practices and internal controls were inadequate, and raised questions about more than $2 million in expenses.'

During the 2000 presidential campaign the INC received promises of support from both the Bush and Gore camps. With Bush in power, Chalabi's old cronies were suddenly in positions of enormous influence: Donald Rumsfeld became Defense Secretary, Paul Wolfowitz became his deputy and Douglas Feith became an Undersecretary of Defense for policy. According to Hersh, 'There was a close personal bond ... between Chalabi and Wolfowitz and Perle, dating back many years.' Chalabi's personal connections included I. Lewis Libby, who was Vice President Dick Cheney's chief of staff, and James Woolsey, former head of the CIA.

After 9/11 the INC began publicising stories of Iraqi defectors who claimed they had information which connected the attacks to Saddam Hussein. One defector insisted that the September 11 operation 'was conducted by people who were trained by Saddam'. Another claimed to have seen Arab students being given lessons in hijacking on a Boeing 707 at an Iraqi training camp. These stories were without foundation.

The murky story of the links between Chalabi and the right-wing fanatics around Bush is laid out by Hersh, who notes that within the American establishment there was considerable hostility to the INC.

Rumsfeld, Wolfowitz, Perle and Cheney were all rooting for Chalabi, but many were not convinced by his credentials: 'The INC's critics noted that Chalabi, despite years of effort and millions of dollars in American aid, was intensely unpopular among many elements in Iraq.' In the 1990s the CIA funnelled millions of dollars annually to the INC. The largesse dried up around 1996 'essentially because the agency had doubts about Chalabi's integrity'.

A former station chief for the CIA in the Middle East told Hersh: 'It would be ridiculous to tie our wagon to Chalabi. He's got no credibility in the region.'

But the war-hungry Chalabi and his INC, strangely, had great credibility with Ian McEwan.

Tonkin on Banville, Banville on McEwan

I bought the *Independent* today. On page three Boyd Tonkin rages and froths furiously about the Booker Prize being awarded to John Banville for his novel *The Sea*.

I didn't bother watching coverage of the Booker, in part because I couldn't care less who won. I have no idea whether or not *The Sea* is a great novel or not, but Boyd Tonkin's anger certainly made it sound *interesting*. Giving the Booker Prize to *The Sea* was, he fizzed, 'the worst, certainly the most perverse, and perhaps the most indefensible choice in the 36-year history of the contest.' Apparently *The Sea* is 'an icy and over-controlled exercise in coterie aestheticism ... [its] prose exhibits all the chilly perfection of a waxwork model'. That sounds to me like the kind of thing the Boyd Tonkins of this world would say about Samuel Beckett's writing; it almost makes me want to rush out and buy the book.

What annoys Tonkins also annoyed the *Sunday Times* reviewer, who grumbled that 'Banville has a talent for sensuous phrasing and pungent observation of human frailty, but in other areas important for fiction – plot, character, pacing, suspense – *The Sea* is a crashing disappointment.' But Banville evidently intends to disappoint those readers who think that serious fiction should aspire to the condition of genre fiction, where suspense and characterisation in primary colours is everything. He recently remarked, 'Yes, human beings have an unflagging desire for stories, it is one of our more endearing traits. The great Modernists, with eminent exceptions, disdained this desire, as they disdained our longing for a recognizable tune, a pretty landscape, a poem that rhymes.'

Boyd Tonkin's literary values are hinted at by his reference to 'a perfect, enduring gem of a First World War story by Sebastian Barry'. *A gem of a story*. The formulation makes me wince. But what really causes Tonkin to burst a blood vessel is that the final shortlist of six titles 'unaccountably omitted Ian McEwan's *Saturday* – a novel that fell victim to a staggeringly vicious and inept review in the *New York Review of Books* by none other than John Banville'.

Inept? What Tonkins is objecting to is not, I think, Banville's ineptitude, but his set of fictional values.

Noah Cicero, *The Human War*

Noah Cicero's *The Human War* makes a very interesting contrast to Ian McEwan's *Saturday*.

Saturday is classic corporate literary fiction. By that I mean that it is an ordered narrative with carefully drawn characters, a suspenseful plot with amazing twists and a satisfying closure at the end. It is an artful novel, with a shiny surface – no contemporary British writer supplies the gloss of style better than McEwan. Most of all, McEwan's novel is set in an agreeably affluent world of shared middle class values and commodities. The nice car. Travel by car, even for very short distances. Squash at a private club. Shopping at a marvellous fishmongers. Food, cooking, a fabulous meal. Consumption at its finest. The big, agreeable home in a desirable location. And the narrative reproduces the values of this class. The villain is a working-class yob: uneducated, brimming with violence. No coincidence, I think, that he has a hereditary disease. But there are other forces out there. The yob is the local embodiment of violence which is now global, manifested as international terrorism. But the narrative is also troubled by those foolishly resisting any attempt to liberate the oppressed Iraqi people: self-indulgent marchers, Muslim extremists, intellectuals, pop singers. These people should be shopping and cooking, not marching and protesting. The values of *Saturday* embody those of a powerful managerial class which determines news values and cultural values. Interestingly, the BBC went into a collective swoon of rapture when it was published. *Saturday* is good product; good commodity. It comes packaged with the approval of powerful or prominent media figures who share those values. And it is a commodity which sells to those who want 'a good read' and whose consumer choices get the stamp of hegemonic approval. An important book. If you don't read it you are culturally incomplete.

The Human War is everything that *Saturday* isn't. That's what makes it such an exciting and invigorating read. It's also why you may have difficulty in finding a copy in a corporate bookstore and why you may not have read about it in the reviews section of the corporate press.

The Human War begins:

Two hours till war.
   It's six o'clock. Bush said at eight, people must die.
   I'm going to Kendra's. I'll hide out there. Are the terrorists coming?
   I'm standing in my living room at my parents' house. My dad is sitting on his special seat, my mom on the couch, and my brother on the reclining chair.
   They're watching the news.
   The news isn't saying much.

And this is how war is for the populations of those first world industrial states which launch wars on countries far away. It is all mediated by television.

Cicero represents a short period in the life of a disaffected white working class young American in a dead end place in the two hours before the start of the invasion of Iraq and afterwards. The start of a devastating war is registered nowhere other than in the narrator's head as he looks at the time and realizes the invasion has begun. This is, in other words, a novel in which the presence of war is dramatised through its absence.

Whereas *Saturday* secretes copious spurious meanings as it speaks for power, *The Human War* gives us the world of the powerless. Some of the characters are for the war, others are against it, but none of it matters. Their opinions are irrelevant; nothing they say will make any difference. *The Human War* doesn't come to any neat conclusions: it is a novel about confusion mixed with revulsion. Stricken by powerlessness and poverty, the characters retreat into sex, drugs, booze.

The style of the book is beautifully consistent with its subject matter. It is a spare novel (at 86 pages a novella, strictly speaking – the Snowbooks edition includes two stories as well). It is written in a bare, stripped down prose.

I think it is a beautifully crafted work but there is no flashy, artful striving for literary effect of the sort you find in prize-winning fiction. The prose is a brutal vernacular. This is how a huge American underclass talks. Reading *The Human War* I was reminded of the kind of world Kurt Cobain came from – marginalised, poor, dysfunctional. An American world far removed from Hollywood or John Updike's fiction.

There is no plot, as that term is popularly understood. There are no little mysteries which are set up for the solving; no amazing twists at the end. This is a world where nothing much happens. Mark, the narrator, goes off to see a girlfriend, Kendra. They have sex. He drives off and goes to a coffee bar. He has a conversation with a black man who lives in the woods. An acquaintance named Jimmy comes in and they go off to a strip joint. They drink. Mark ogles the lap dancers. He pays for their services. He has a perfunctory conversation with one of them. A girl named Nicole asks him to fuck her. He agrees. Mark, who is on medication, gets more and more drunk.

I won't spoil the ending, other than to say that in a novel in which not a lot happens (in corporate narrative terms), in the final pages not a lot happens.

Or rather, it does. Because *The Human War* is asserting that this fictional universe is as legitimate as any other. And its concentration is not on enormous dramatic events but on the inconsequential and everyday. The sex scene with Kendra is free of spurious meaning: it is simply sex plus conversation. Cicero's impoverished characters are light years away from the 'characters' of novelists who feed us rich, complex interior worlds of memory and symbol. Mark can contemplate huge significant events, with himself at the centre of them, but they are literally all in the mind. All he can do is fantasize.

The living pulse of this novel is thus not in mystery, suspense and revelation, but in its dramatic representation of alienation. Nothing happens, repeatedly.

Once again, let me advert to the form of the narrative. It consists almost entirely of one sentence paragraphs, most of them very short. On page after page it starts to look like poetry. This, too, is apt, because there was really only one text that came to mind while I was reading *The Human War* and that was Ginsberg's *Howl*. And this novel too is a kind of howl: a convulsion of rage and despair at those who survive on the margins of a stunted society. But though it repeatedly philosophizes and asks questions, it never supplies cute answers. It's a blizzard of questioning and doubting; in short, it's also about what it is to be young and trying to work out a personal philosophy of life.

If what you want from a novel is a fast-paced drama of big events – bank robberies! shootings! extreme emotions and sizzling confrontations! – this book is not for you. It is not remotely escapist. Rather, it leads the reader back into the real.

It would be a mistake, I think, to assume that Noah Cicero just sat down at his keyboard when he was drunk and hammered the book out. It would also be a mistake to assume that the narrative endorses Mark's position on life, the universe and everything. His attitude to women might well upset and antagonize some readers. But Mark is not exactly a role model. Best to remember, also, that his surname is Swift. He has something in common with Gulliver at the end of his travels, loathing the world around him. He also has a raw honesty about his quest for authenticity and truth. This is not a complacent book, which tries to put over a set of values on the reader.

The Human War is also, it must be said, a very funny book. It satirises American life, and I kept hooting with laughter at its deadpan wit. But it doesn't disrespect or patronise its characters. So what is *The Human War* in the end? A satirical anti-war masterpiece. A study of the condition of a contemporary underclass. A working class classic. A hugely engaging read. A novel that will be read in one hundred years time, long after all that corporate liberal fiction has long since been forgotten.

Three Years Ago Today

It's exactly three years ago today since the biggest demonstration in British history, when up to two million people marched through London to Hyde Park to register their opposition to the impending invasion and occupation of Iraq.

As you'll be aware, the British media today has been full of commemorations of that important event, with chat shows and political pundits on the news talking of nothing else. Literally hundreds of people who protested on that day have been invited into studios to talk about that experience and how they feel about it in the light of the latest prisoner-abuse scandal in Iraq and the state of that country today. BBC News executives have made a heartfelt apology for misleadingly giving the impression that Saddam really did have WMDs, and for giving so little space to anti-war voices in the run up to the invasion.

Whoops! Just a dream. I think I must have imagined that there was such a march. It's all in my head, doctor. And yet, as one of those who marched on that *invisible* protest, I am, as you can imagine, now feeling pretty foolish, because, of course:

- Saddam's vast armoury of weapons of mass destruction was subsequently exposed to the world. If we hadn't invaded when we did, missiles would have shortly afterwards rained down on London and New York. Not to mention the nerve gas ...
- The invasion was the most popular in history. Hundreds of thousands of Iraqis poured out of their homes to welcome our troops, in scenes reminiscent of France in 1944. Even today many Iraqi homes fly the Union Jack and the Stars and Stripes, in honour of their liberators.
- The absolute minimum of damage was done to Iraq, with virtually no civilian casualties or homes destroyed. Troops rushed to secure Iraq's archeological treasures from looters, and showed the benign nature of the occupation by leaving the oil ministry alone.
- The Iraqi National Congress was elected to power with an overwhelming mandate, and has since proved to be a shining example of honest, decent government. Corruption is simply unknown in today's Iraq.

- The bad old days of repression, torture and beatings are gone forever. Today all of Saddam's notorious prison centres like Abu Ghraib have been shut down. Today, people can walk freely along the street without fear, and Iraqis from around the world have poured back to their homeland to enjoy the fruits of a free society. Women enjoy a freedom that makes them the envy of their sisters across the Middle East.
- Britain and the USA, refusing to take anything from the Iraqi treasury, have poured billions into the new Iraq, ensuring a reconstruction programme unrivalled anywhere in the world. Today, Iraq is the envy of the Middle East, with its shining new hospitals, new universities, gleaming new railways, motorways and tram systems, reservoirs, sewage treatment works, and low-cost public housing.
- The behaviour of the invasion troops has become an icon of good conduct, with every soldier fluent in Arabic, each soldier evincing a profound respect for the local culture and religion, and a cheerful, friendly attitude to Iraqis which has been fully reciprocated by an appreciative population.
- Because of the previous two factors, terrorism has withered on the vine. In the face of the marvellous example set by the USA and Britain, it is quite simply not possible to recruit anyone in the Middle East for terrorism any longer.
- Blair kept his word about a settlement for the Palestinians. The US terminated its subsidies to Israel, Britain ended arms exports, the EU ended its preferential trade agreements and Ariel Sharon and many senior Israeli members of the armed forces were arrested for war crimes. The UN took a tough line with Israel, closing down its nuclear weapons sites, and insisting that Israel adhere to numerous UN resolutions it had previously chosen to flout. The Wall was demolished, settlement building frozen, Palestinian refugees were allowed to return to their land for the first time in over half a century, the sectarian Jewish 'Right to Return' was abolished, and the chauvinist racist sectarian Jewish state was dismantled and replaced by a diverse free society with no discrimination on grounds of religion, ethnicity, gender or sexuality.

To Tony Blair and George Bush, the Sharp Side says, humbly and sincerely: *thanks, guys*!

Footnotes to a Novelist's *Saturday*

I've just come across a couple of items which shed more light on a prominent British novelist's attitude to the invasion of Iraq and the massive anti-war march in London that preceded it.

I'd like to unpick Ian McEwan's arguments in stages.

First off, this argument of his: 'I never thought that in the run up to the war we were discussing simply the difference between war and peace. We were discussing the difference between war and continued torture and genocide and abuse of human rights by a fascist state. I missed any sense of that complexity in the peace camp.'

Oh yeah?

I don't see 'complexity' in that line of argument. I see vulgar simplicity. It reduces the invasion and occupation of Iraq to a human rights issue. But that was not the rationale for the war. Secondly, by a rhetorical sleight of hand it makes those who oppose military invasion and occupation complicit in 'torture and genocide and abuse of human rights by a fascist state'. But any consideration of the history of Iraq needs to take into account the reality that Saddam's human rights abuses, when at their most ferocious, were subsidised and tolerated for many years by the two states subsequently most intent on overthrowing him – the USA and Britain.

Secondly: 'I certainly had the feeling that whatever the strong moral arguments were for deposing Saddam, the Americans would not be good nation-builders. But I had a moral problem with this view among the 2 million protesters that you should leave Saddam in power in a fascist state with 27 million Iraqis under him. The problem is that they felt good about it. I thought they should have opposed the war but also felt bad about it.'

Let's set aside that first sentence's unquestioned assumption that the USA has the right to send military forces thousands of miles in order to do a spot of 'nation-building' in someone else's country.

Let's ignore the patronising stance of someone who advises anti-war protesters how they should behave, while scrupulously declining to join them. Let's not be so cruel as to remember McEwan's enthusiastic support for that sleazy, self-interested clique who called themselves the Iraq National Congress, naïvely and ignorantly viewed by him as truly representative of the Iraqi people. Let's forget his gullible belief that there might well be a connection between Saddam and al-Qaeda ('Nor does it seem outlandish, the possibility of Saddam Hussein passing on weapons of mass destruction to the enemy of his enemies' – maybe not, if you were daft enough to believe he ever had them in the first place). Let's ignore the continuation of that slippery rhetorical strategy whereby anti-war protesters are made responsible for Saddam's tyranny. No, what's really objectionable about McEwan's argument is his lazy and complacent assumption that 2 million people all felt 'good' about the Iraqi regime, and what's more that McEwan *knew* what 2 million protesters were all *collectively* thinking.

And now: 'I think if Bush and Blair could press a button and we could all fast forward backwards, rewind the tape, they'd probably do this differently. But I don't think they fully grasped, and even the anti-war (movement) could have never fully grasped the fantastic viciousness of the insurgency against its own people.'

Underneath these words lies the thesis not that the invasion and occupation of Iraq was *wrong* but that *it should have been done better*. And that the chief source of the suffering of Iraqis is ... Iraqis!

All quotations are cited from this very apt source: http://normblog.typepad.com/normblog/2005/07/ian_mcewan_inte.html.

Funnily enough, Matthias Matussek, former London correspondent of *Der Spiegel*, claimed last year that on two occasions at which he was present, the novelist 'was adamantly in favour of the Iraq war', a claim vehemently denied by McEwan.

The Whirligig of Time

As you may recall, there's a bestselling novelist who defined the great anti-war march in London, 15 February 2003, as 'marching for

[Saddam's] torture' (in Iraq). As he put it: 'I never thought that in the run up to the war we were discussing simply the difference between war and peace. We were discussing the difference between war and continued torture and genocide and abuse of human rights by a fascist state. I missed any sense of that complexity in the peace camp.'

Before the war, justifying his fence-sitting and 'ambivalence', he referred to 'the widespread use of torture and summary imprisonment and execution, with the ubiquitous security services penetrating every level of Iraqi society. It is an insult to those who have suffered to suggest, as some do, that the US administration is the greater evil.'

And so the whirlgig of time brings in its revenges ...

Torture in Iraq 'worse than under Saddam'
Thursday 21 September 2006 17.18 BST

Torture in Iraq is worse now than it was under the regime of Saddam Hussein and 'is totally out of hand', according to a United Nations investigator.

'The situation is so bad many people say it is worse than it has been in the times of Saddam Hussein,' said Manfred Nowak, a UN special investigator on torture, at a press conference in Geneva.

Mr Nowak is in Geneva to brief the UN Human Rights council – a body that addresses human rights violations – on the situation of the United States detention facility at Guantanamo Bay.

He is one of five UN human rights investigators who in February called for the closure of the camp on the grounds it was a 'torture camp'. The calls were rejected by the US.

'Corpses appear regularly in and around Baghdad and other areas. Most bear signs of torture and appear to be victims of extrajudicial executions,' said the report.

(http://www.guardian.co.uk/
world/2006/sep/21/Iraq)

Part Four: Pure Wizardry – Aharon Appelfeld and Amos Oz

The Blindness of Aharon Appelfeld

Aharon Appelfeld, *The Story of a Life* ((translated from the Hebrew by Aloma Halter, Hamish Hamilton, 2005).

The Israeli novelist Aharon Appelfeld is a writer whom journalists approach with deference and admiration. 'He is someone you immediately want to tell things to; beneath the jaunty peak of his sailor's cap, his sea-blue eyes gleam with inquiry,' gushed Hephzibah Anderson, writing about *The Story of a Life* and her meeting with its author (*Observer*, 21 August 2005), adding breathlessly: 'When he speaks of writing, he gestures like a magician pulling a rope of silk scarves from deep within himself.'

Reviewing the book in the *Guardian* (Saturday September 24, 2005), Lisa Appignanesi was similarly paralysed by admiration for the man and his memoir:

> Like a series of luminous paintings discovered in the darkness of a vaulted church after the bombs have fallen, this memoir evokes a wonder which is on the other side of language. Its scenes need to be contemplated, tasted, savoured.

In the *Independent* (23 September 2005), Carole Angier concurred, asserting: 'Primo Levi read him "with awe and admiration". So will you.'

Well, speak for yourself, Carole. I think myself that Appelfeld is at best an interesting minor novelist. When I read *Badenheim 1939* I found it a crushing disappointment – thin, one dimensional and heavy-handed in its use of irony and metaphor. Designating it a 'Modern Classic' as Penguin Books do strikes me as more a marketing ploy than an informed literary judgment. I don't think Appelfeld has ever truly freed himself from two of his dominant literary influences (Kafka and Camus) and the range of his interests and sympathies strikes me as being far too narrow to make him a great writer. However, evaluating a living writer is always a subjective exercise. My purpose here is not to rate Appelfeld's fiction but to focus on his memoir. The deference accorded to Appelfeld seems to me quite illuminating when contrasted with, say, attitudes to Peter Handke and his politics.

The critical reception of *The Story of a Life* is itself very revealing of the Orientalist impulse in Western intellectual life. In Britain, the only remotely critical note sounded anywhere came at the end of Theo Richmond's review in the *Sunday Times* (11 September 2005):

> Is this slim book of 198 pages the story of a life? In essence, yes, but there are some curious gaps. The boy escaped from 'an accursed camp'. Which camp? How did he escape? Appelfeld's mother was murdered, but what became of his father, last seen on a forced march? On one page, he refers to himself as an orphan, so it was baffling to read in a Jewish paper that his father survived the Holocaust and was reunited with his son in Israel. Of the writer's marriage, wife and family, not a word. This is a humane and moving memoir, but has the author taken reticence too far?

But if Appelfeld is indeed reticent about large areas of his life, so too are those who write about him. The first thing that struck me, even before I'd started reading the book, is the lie in the first sentence of the author blurb: 'Aharon Appelfeld has lived in Israel since 1946'.

No he hasn't.

Israel didn't exist in 1946.

Aharon Appelfeld arrived in *Palestine* in 1946. Apart from a perfunctory reference to Palestine (p. vii), it's a fiction reiterated by Appelfeld himself ('1946, the year I came to Israel', p. 107, repeated p. 109 and p. 127, together with 'the moment I arrived in Israel', p. 111).

Palestine was, of course, wiped off the map in 1948 by armed Jews. The difference between 1946 and the violent annihilation of Palestine and its majority Arab society by Jews in 1948 is a crucial one, but is not registered by two of the reviewers I've quoted. Theo Richmond carelessly loses three years when he says of Appelfeld that 'In 1949, the mentally scarred loner sailed for Haifa to start a new life'. For Carole Angier, Appelfeld's postwar existence is telescoped into 'A brief rebirth in Italy; then new life in Israel'.

What is written out of history in Carole Angier's lazy formulation is, of course, the 1948 Naqba – *the catastrophe* – the erasure of Palestine and the forcible eviction of its population. It's a very common erasure by those who are either ignorant of the twentieth century history of the Middle East or who have a vested interest in promoting the Jewish supremacist state. Thus the website of The Holocaust Teacher Resource Center states that '[Aharon Appelfeld] immigrated to pre-state Israel in 1946.'

Any formulation will do to avoid the word 'Palestine' – a rhetorical strategy designed to muffle the historical reality of Jews as ethnic cleansers and bellicose aggressors. And of course it is almost never remembered that one-third of the Zionist army in 1948 comprised Holocaust survivors. The Holocaust survivor as a racist thug, a murderer or a rapist, is not a figure you will ever encounter in Western constructions of the Jewish identity or historical experience.

In Chapter 16 of *The Story of A Life*, Appelfeld dramatises a scene on the ship in which he sailed to Haifa in 1946. It's a poignant account of a five year old Jewish girl, an orphan. One leg has been amputated. The child smiles. Asked about her past she says all she remembers is the rain. Repeatedly she mentions the rain – nothing else. It's a short, poetically charged chapter which eloquently adumbrates many of Appelfeld's central themes, both as a novelist and autobiographer – the suffering of a child, the way in which the human mind negotiates the residue of unspeakable horror, the struggle to articulate such horrors in words, and the friction existing between Jews who are survivors, who are all, literally, in the same boat. And little Helga is also clearly a kind of surrogate of Appelfeld himself, then fourteen years old, his mother murdered, his father lost. But it's an artful, polished chapter. It may be based on a real incident but it's surely a novelisation of it rather than a literal rendering. It's improbable that Appelfeld could exactly remember dialogue overheard in 1946. The girl's eloquently dramatised refusal or inability to tell a larger story is clearly a kind of metaphor for Appelfeld's own memoir.

If it weren't for the large woman who pesters the child, demanding to know her story, the chapter would risk the charge of sentimentality in its portrayal of a brave, angelic child amputee. It ends:

Helga sat on the lap of the man who had adopted her. The light returned to her face. She moved her lips, muttering softly. The man took her small hand, brought it to his lips, and kissed it. 'Soon we'll reach Palestine,' he said. 'There we'll have a house and garden.' (p. 97)

It's a perfect emblem of Appelfeld's profound moral complacency that he clearly neither intends nor is capable of perceiving even the smallest possibility of irony in those last two sentences. When the ship docked, he arrived at the Arab port of Haifa in 1946 – or as he blandly puts it, 'Israel' (p. 109). And then?

Between the years 1946 and 1948, I was in the Aliyat Hano'ar Youth Movement, and between 1948 and 1950, I was an apprentice at the agricultural school founded by Rachel Yana'it at Ein Kerem (*sic*), on the outskirts of Jerusalem. (p. 118)

The name Ein Karem probably means nothing at all to European and American readers of Appelfeld's acclaimed memoir. Palestinians have a different perspective. 'Before 1948, Ein Karem was known as the most beautiful of all the Jerusalem villages.' That year, during the Naqba, its 3,000 Arab inhabitants were forcibly evicted. The village was then repopulated 'in its entirety' by Jews, *none of Middle Eastern origin*. The Church of John the Baptist was closed down. The two mosques were closed down. None of the Arab inhabitants of Ein Karem was ever permitted to return. Today Ein Karem is a home for 'wealthy Israeli professionals seeking a relaxing life in a beautiful village' (Mariam Shain, *Palestine: A Guide* [2005], p. 342).

If we want to learn what happened in the Arab city of Haifa – Appelfeld's 'Israel' – we need only turn to Ghassan Kanafani's long story 'Returning to Haifa', with its account of how its Arab population was driven out in 1948 by Jewish terrorists. It is a reasonable speculation that Appelfeld has never read it. He has never shown the slightest interest in any perspective about his homeland other than that of Judaism. *And where exactly was Appelfeld during the height of the Naqba? He doesn't say.* Palestinian suffering has no existence for Appelfeld: his gaze is inward. 'The years 1946 to 1950 were years of verbiage; when life is full of ideology, words and clichés abound. Everyone talked' (p. 123).

But those were years of something more than just talk:

> In early 1947, Jews owned 7 per cent of the land in Palestine; three years later, they had seized 92 per cent of land within the new state, including Arab homes and buildings of every kind. ... this constituted a colonial occupation on a scale, and with a speed, without precedence in colonial history.
> (John Rose, *The Myths of Zionism* [2004], p. 149)

When the first great phase of ethnic cleansing ended in January 1949, 90% of the Palestinian population of what became Israel was living in refugee camps in the Jordanian occupied West Bank, Lebanon and Gaza.

Joel Gordon, reviewing Lawrence Davidson's *America's Palestine*, comments that Davidson describes the disregard for the indigenous inhabitants of Palestine as 'a form of ethnic cleansing on the conceptual level' (http://www.logosjournal.com/issue_5.1/gordon.htm).

Gordon regards this notion as 'provocative' but it seems to me that Appelfeld's memoir is a perfect example of that proposition. Appelfeld says, 'We had come to Israel, as the saying went, 'to build and to be rebuilt' (p. 116). That the building of the Jewish state was done on stolen property is a matter of complete indifference to Appelfeld: he completely erases Palestine and its indigenous population from his self-serving memoir. He continues with a reference to 'the ideological complacency that sought to make me into a man of narrow horizons, which I refused to be' (*ibid.*). In the context of his Orientalism the smug tone of self-congratulation is remarkable.

No one in the West would use the word 'holocaust' without an awareness that that word now carries a specific historical resonance. But Appelfeld uses the word 'catastrophe' (e.g. pp. 185, 187, 189) as if it had no resonance at all in the land in which he has spent most of his life. *The Story of a Life* is, at a foundational level, a work of Naqba denial.

The parallels between the lives and writing of Aharon Appelfeld (born in 1932) and Ghassan Kanafani (born in 1936) are loose but striking. When they were children, their societies were shattered by brutal, racist occupying forces; forced into exile, they had to reconstruct their lives and became novelists and intellectuals. Their creative impulses are drawn from a lost childhood world and societies on the brink of being extinguished forever. But Kanafani was exiled and then murdered by the Jewish state with which Appelfeld unequivocally identifies.

Heidegger has commonly and quite reasonably been charged with being blind to his own blindness, but it's a charge which should also be levelled against Appelfeld. Indeed, Aharon Appelfeld supplies a perfect example of the moral corruption of modern Judaism in its Zionist incarnation and of the reluctance in Western intellectual life to confront that corruption. The (un)critical reception of *The Story of a Life* testifies to an enduring Orientalism which is blind to Appelfeld's own pernicious and extreme brand of Orientalism.

Appelfeld is completely silent about the *Naqba*. Perhaps he played no active role in it but it seems unlikely he was unaware of it occurring. Nor can he have been unaware that his new existence in Israel was predicated on the expulsion of the majority Arab population. With a characteristic lack of irony (shared by his admiring reviewers) Appelfeld describes how in the 1950s he was a member of the New Life Club, which among other things 'arranged memorial services for small towns and remote villages that had been wiped out during the war' (p. 184). But the society which piously remembered the lost villages of Europe was itself responsible for destroying 531 Arab villages and 11 urban neighbourhoods, as well as seizing entire cities like Haifa.

Bypassing this crucial period, which saw half of Palestine's population turned into refugees, Appelfeld writes only of himself. He describes how little formal education engaged him during his years at the Hebrew University of Jerusalem, 1952-1956:

> I wanted to return to the orchard. The quiet orchard that changed with each season now seemed to me like a spring of blessing. I loved the hours I spent there alone, plowing and harrowing the soil, spraying the insects, watching for the fruit to ripen in the spring and for the leaves to fall in the autumn, and then pruning the trees in winter. (pp. 146-7)

This is the lyrical expression of a memory; it is at the same time classic Zionist propaganda. It erases from history the question: whose land, whose orchard? Such questions do not trouble Appelfeld.

In setting out the Zionist blueprint in *The Jewish State*, the slippery Theodor Herzl never once mentions Arabs, in John Roses's words 'as though they did not exist' (*op. cit.*, p. 95). But Herzl was well aware of their existence, and was also well aware that their deportation was an essential requirement of the establishment of a Jewish supremacist state.

Like Herzl, Aharon Appelfeld self-servingly blanks out the existence of Palestine and its Arab population. He mentions a friend, a fellow Holocaust survivor, who now owns a factory and 'has a house in Herzliyya and an apartment in Jerusalem' (p. 178); what's more there is 'a large library in his home. He is interested in philosophy, literature, the arts, and medicine' (p. 179). Like Amos Oz, Appelfeld gives us an image of cultured and sensitive Israelis; all that is missing is the material conditions of that culture – property and land theft, institutionalised sectarianism, state violence, massive injustice. Appelfeld is completely blind to his own position as the privileged beneficiary of sectarianism and discrimination; his conscience is unstirred by pitiless repression taking place just a short distance from his agreeable existence.

When Appelfeld does mention Palestinians at all, it is from the viewpoint of Zionism. Interviewed by the *Boston Review* (December 1982), Appelfeld asserted that 'The Zionist movement began around a hundred years ago. Then Palestine was a waste – rocks and hills and sand. Very under-populated by Arabs.'

Those last two sentences are just as much odious self-serving rubbish as the notion that the world is run behind the scenes by a secret conspiracy of Jews or that the number of Jews who died in the Shoah has been exaggerated, or that they weren't gassed but died of illness. But such is the power of Orientalism within Western culture that, while Peter Handke is demonised for his pro-Serbian sympathies, Appelfeld's extremist views attract no attention, let alone even the faintest whisper of criticism.

Appelfeld's suggestion that late nineteenth century Palestine was a 'waste' containing a handful of Arabs scratching a living in the dirt is ludicrous. By 1880, for example, more than 30 million oranges were being exported to Europe from Palestine every year. John Rose cites the case of the Jewish writer, Ahad Ha-Am, who visited Palestine in 1891 and who wrote that it was 'difficult to find fields that were not sown' by Arab peasants. The racist fiction that Palestine was 'a waste' is comprehensively debunked in Chapter Five of Rose's book.

Appelfeld's assertion, prompted by the sympathies of his interviewer, that Zionism's involvement in land struggles and territorial rights 'was not and ... is not' part of the original plan is chutzpah on a truly gargantuan scale. It is as indifferent to historical truth as it is to the central role played by sectarian land law in establishing and sustaining a Jewish state. In Israel 94.5 per cent of all land is now administered either directly by the state or by Zionist institutions, on behalf of Jewish citizens only. Appelfeld's hardline Zionist beliefs register the moral blankness at the heart of his concept of Jewish identity, or what he has blandly called 'the complex of Jewish existence'.

Appelfeld transmits the aura of the Holocaust survivor, so he is always treated very deferentially by European and American journalists. And of course in a central way his story is a remarkable one: a child surviving off his own wits after the murder of his mother and separation from his father. His reinvention of himself as an intellectual and a leading Israeli novelist who spurned the German language and learned Hebrew is a striking achievement. But it is an achievement with a dark side, which is that of his complicity in the sectarian project known as the Jewish state. Appelfeld's complicity is present in his role as a soldier involved in its wars, as an academic and intellectual, and as a prominent novelist happy to promote his views on the politics of the Middle East through the medium of newspaper and magazine interviews. He is also, in a very small way, a state asset, whose work is promoted and circulated by the Israeli Ministry of Foreign Affairs.

Appelfeld's opinions play less well to a Palestinian intelligentsia. He once remarked, 'What is happening here in Israel has to wait fifty years before becoming literature.' This drew a retort from Mourid Barghouti, the Palestinian poet excluded by the Israeli state from his homeland because of his race and his religion:

> The Holocaust has been written as a novel, as poetry, as music, as theatre – as everything – in the Fifties and Sixties. It didn't have to wait fifty years to be written. Israel has been established for fifty-six years and the West Bank has been occupied for thirty-seven years. They have been occupiers for thirty-seven years and that's not long enough to look at themselves and see what they have become? Where exactly is their human gaze directed? (Both quotations from Ahdaf Soueif, *Mezzaterra* [Bloomsbury, London, 2004], p. 332)

In the case of Aharon Appelfeld the only reply to Barghouti's question is surely: *inwards and backwards*. Appelfeld has no interest in or sympathy for Palestinians. He is pitilessly ignorant of the Other and pitilessly indifferent to their experience or their writing. Palestinians have no existence for him, other than as a threat to his beloved version of Judaism. Appelfeld, like Zionists generally, is incapable of constructing Israel as anything other than a victim, or criticism of Israel as stemming from anything other than the same kind of virulent anti-Semitism which he witnessed as a child. Everything, for Appelfeld, is simplistically framed by the Holocaust.

In 2004, pressed by an interviewer from the Israeli paper *Ha'aretz*, Appelfeld complained:

> There are not yet trains from Jenin to concentration camps in the Negev. There are no smokestacks. Yet, the *Guardian* and *Le Monde* feel the need to draw that comparison every day. To say of the Jews that they are a little like the Nazis. Not exactly Nazis, just a bit. When I see that, I say that there is something very deep in European civilization: the need to demonize us runs very deep.

But his claim that every day the *Guardian* compares Israel to Nazi Germany is preposterous. His ridiculous and paranoid notion that contemporary Europeans have an innate need to demonise Jews simply recycles the traditional Zionist line that all critics of Israeli sectarianism and human rights abuses are secret anti-Semites. Generalising about Europeans is as fatuous (and in its own way as Orientalising) as generalising about any other large, diverse body of people (Americans, say – or even Israelis). For Appelfeld, Israel is the only true representative of Judaism: in *The Story of a Life* he speaks of 'a Jewish world that had renewed itself in the Land of Israel' (p. 155) (the upper case used in 'Land' signifies, I think, Appelfeld's Messianic sense of Israel as sacred Jewish territory – another device which extinguishes the vulgar reality of stolen property).

Chapter 27 of *The Story of a Life* describes Appelfeld's IDF service in the Yom Kippur war, when, as he blandly puts it, 'I found myself stationed alongside the Suez Canal'. The chapter describes the relationship between Holocaust survivors and the younger generation. It ends:

The three days that I spent with that unit not only brought me close to the young soldiers, but also gave me a deeper insight into my own life. As in every war, there hovered above us a sense of fate hanging in the balance. Who knew what awaited us?

The voices of the soldiers became more lighthearted and jovial toward the end of my stay. The cease-fire appeared to be holding. I found it hard to part from this unit of young people on whose shoulders rested the fate of a people welcome neither in Europe nor in this part of the world. As different as the struggle was here, it was, nevertheless, the same ancient curse pursuing us.

It's amazing that Appelfeld gets away with this tosh. The origins of the Yom Kippur war lay in Israel's refusal to withdraw from land it had occupied in 1967. On the Arab side it was a war of liberation against a bellicose Zionist state which, not for the first time, had invaded and occupied land outside its own borders. Egypt and Syria hoped to 'force the superpowers to intervene and put pressure on Israel to withdraw' (Avi Shlaim, *The Iron Wall: Israel and the Arab World* [Penguin Books, 2000], p. 319).

Appelfeld's reduction of the war to the 'ancient curse' of anti-Semitism is characteristic of his attitude to all modern Middle Eastern history. As far as he is concerned the clock stopped in the early 1940s. Europe is a hotbed of anti-Semitism. The Middle East is a hotbed of anti-Semitism. Israel represents world Jewry. Israel is hated because it is a Jewish state.

As an alibi for Zionism it's so threadbare it's barely worth engaging with.

Let's also consider his cited example of Jenin. In mentioning this refugee camp of 15,000 residents, Appelfeld was clearly alluding to events there two years earlier. In the words of a fellow Israeli academic with a far more humane grasp of these events than Appelfeld:

> What did clearly happen in Jenin [in 2002] was that the Israeli forces simply ignored the fact that there were an unknown number of civilians in the areas that they attacked day and night with missiles from Cobra helicopters and demolished with bulldozers, in order to clear the way for the invading tanks. No one came to execute these people individually; they were crushed and buried under their bombed or bulldozed homes. Others died

of their wounds in alleys, or cried for days under the ruins, until their voices faded away. (Tanya Reinhart, *Israel/Palestine: How to End the War of 1948*, Seven Stories Press, New York, 2002)

Reinhart cites the case of the A Sha'abi family, crushed alive in their house by a giant Caterpillar D-9 bulldozer; their nine bodies were recovered six days later when the Israeli army withdrew. Not as bad as the Holocaust? True, obviously. But as a response, surely a coarse and inhumane one.

The crimes of the Israeli state against Palestinians, though enormous, are self-evidently not on the same scale as those of Nazi crimes against European Jews. And it's perfectly true, as Appelfeld suggests, that Zionism is not a genocidal project. Exterminating the world's Arabs has never been its dream. In that the distinction with Hitler's Germany is crystal clear.

It is however true that Zionism has always, from its origins, been quite consciously about seizing land and expelling an indigenous population to make way for a sectarian Jewish state. Its leading thinkers and activists have all been racists, with an ingrained loathing and contempt for Arabs. A genocidal impulse has always been inherent in Zionism and Israel may yet carry out an atrocity on a scale which dwarfs past massacres of Arabs by Zionist Jews. These are truths about which Appelfeld, as a man who all his adult life has benefited from his privileged existence as a member of the master religion in an ethnically cleansed land, is completely in denial.

The entire history of Israel can be understood only in the context of the Zionist desire for land, the expulsion of non-Jews, and the creation of a sectarian state in which citizenship would be defined not by birth but by religion. It is this last factor which makes Israel unique.

David Hirsh of the anti-boycott group Engage says: 'Zionism is not racism. Zionism is Jewish nationalism and it is not fundamentally different from other forms of nationalism.' But this is quite untrue. Zionism is fundamentally different to nationalism. To be Jewish is to belong to a religious group, not a national group. All nations except Israel define citizenship by birth, not religious identity. Travellers who land at an Italian airport are not divided into two queues – Catholics and Other Religions. If you are born in Italy to a non-Catholic family, the state does not discriminate against you and make you a second-class citizen who is forbidden to buy land. Therein lies a central difference with the sectarian Jewish state. Zionism is a Jewish supremacist ideology and Israel, like its founding ideology, is inherently chauvinist. Israel is institutionally sectarian and substantially, though not exclusively, racist (it imports black Jews from Africa to maintain its demographic superiority over its Arab population). Israel defines citizenship by religion with the same rigour that Hitler's Germany defined citizenship by race. Israel is a corrupt and sectarian democracy, born out of sectarian violence and terror, democratic only by virtue of expelling the majority Arab population and then maintaining an artificial Jewish demographic superiority.

No one could possibly blame Appelfeld for the way in which he ended up in Palestine as a bewildered and damaged teenager. Appelfeld's focus on the Holocaust is understandable but it completely disables his understanding of events in the land of his exile. He is a man who emigrated to the Middle East from Europe and, sixty years later, finds no discomfort at all in remarking, 'I am not familiar with the Arabs. For me they are an abstraction.' The complacency in that remark is stupefying. Appelfeld cannot rely on the Holocaust to shield him forever from the implications of his subsequent role as a soldier in the IDF, as an academic, and as a novelist and intellectual.

But Appelfeld's complacency is protected by other intellectuals of an Orientalist cast of mind. In his Introduction to the Penguin edition of *Badenheim 1939*, Gabriel Josipovici blandly writes, 'Today [Appelfeld] lives in Israel, devoting his time to writing, after spending thirty years teaching at the University of the Negev.' Let's give that educational institution its full name: Ben-Gurion University of the Negev. David Ben-Gurion was a leading Zionist and Israel's first prime minister. His history is well documented. Let's leave aside Ben-Gurion's complicity in attempting to cover up the Qibya massacre in 1953 (69 innocent Arabs, two thirds of them women and children, murdered by an Israeli army unit led by a young major called Ariel Sharon) or his central role in creating Israel's nuclear arsenal or the fact that 'Ben-Gurion had surprisingly little knowledge of Arab culture and Arab history and no empathy whatever for Arabs ... Ben-Gurion could not conceive of a multi-ethnic society, embracing Jews and Arabs' (Avi Shlaim, *op. cit.*, p. 96).

In a civilised society all of these factors might be thought something of an impediment when considering a suitable candidate after whom to name a university. Yet in one sense what could indeed be more apt than 'Ben-Gurion University of the Negev' because, as Ben-Gurion wrote in 1937, 'Negev land is reserved for Jewish citizens whenever and wherever they want. We must expel the Arabs and take their place'?

The Negev is a highland region which comprised slightly more than one third of historical Palestine. Ben-Gurion's ethnic cleansing fantasy was a knee-jerk response to the Peel Commission Partition Plan of 1937, which recommended that the Negev remain under Palestinian rule as it was an exclusively Arab region. Prior to 1948 the Negev was inhabited almost entirely by semi-Nomadic Palestinian Bedouin tribes; the major urban centre of population was the town of Birsheba.

In 1948 Ben-Gurion's racist dream came true: the entire Arab population of Birsheba was driven out by the Zionist army (one-third Holocaust survivors, let's again remember) and the Negev was almost completely emptied of its indigenous population, leaving behind just 11,000 Bedouin.

It's important to note that the ethnic cleansing continued long after the war of 1948. In the 1950s the Israeli army forcibly moved the remaining Bedouin into a restricted area outside Birsheba. This was done to steal the good agricultural land they owned and push them on to inferior land. The Bedouin were 'Confined to a space less than 10 per cent of the area of the land they had formerly possessed' (Hussein Abu Hussein and Fiona McKay, *Access Denied: Palestinian Land Rights in Israel* [Zed Books, 2003], p. 114).

As a Professor of Hebrew Literature at Ben-Gurion University of the Negev, Appelfeld enjoyed an academic career spanning three decades amid the ruins of the comprehensively annihilated Palestinian society which once existed there.

When Appelfeld says there are no concentration camps in the Negev he is wrong. There are no death camps but there are detention centres which are essentially no different to Dachau in its early years. These are political prisons where Arab prisoners are brutalised by racist Jewish guards and where children are forced to sign confessions written in Hebrew, a language they do not understand. Appelfeld's blindness to their existence is reminiscent in its own modest way of Heidegger's indifference to the death camps.

Historically, the blatant sectarian discrimination against the Bedouin in the Negev did not cease in the 1950s. The expropriation of Bedouin land in the Negev and the eviction of Bedouin homes as part of a forced relocation policy continued throughout the period of Appelfeld's tenure as an academic at Ben-Gurion University and continues to this day. And while the Bedouin were forced bit by bit into as small an area of land as possible, the land they formerly owned was seized for more and more Jews-only agricultural villages, settlements and farms.

Palestinians who have resisted moving to 'development towns' for Arabs are deemed to be living in 'unrecognised' zones and their hamlets and villages are denied electricity, running water and municipal services by the Israeli state. The Negev is a place where ethnic cleansing has been continuing over half a century and where an indigenous Arab population has been subjected to forced relocation and the denial of basic services.

Appelfeld's evident indifference to the sectarianism and ethnic cleansing underpinning his agreeable existence as an academic is reciprocated by Gabriel Jospivici, who finds it appropriate in his Introduction to allude to T. S. Eliot's anti-Semitism but whose bland reference to Appelfeld's long tenure at the University of the Negev omits to note either its history or the telling reality that this institution, with hundreds of academics, has just three Arabs on the faculty.

'The World of Aharon Appelfeld' was the title of the University of Cambridge's 2003 conference, attended by Josipovici and speakers from Ben-Gurion University, Bar-Ilan University (targeted by pro-Palestinian AUT activists because it has expanded on to Palestinian land) and The College of Jude and Samaria in Ariel, a college built unlawfully on Palestinian land. Ironically, among the subjects up for discussion were those of detachment and silence.

Aharon Appelfeld is also, famously, a citizen of Jerusalem:

I'm writing mainly about Jewish fate. Jerusalem, I would say, is the heart of Jewish history. So I cannot imagine myself being a Jewish writer and not being in Jerusalem. It is not a question of it's noisy, it's not noisy. It is not a question of politics even. I'm a Jewish writer, I'm living amongst my people, and I'm trying to understand the complex of Jewish existence. So where can a Jewish writer live?

Theodore Herzl knew full well that the Jewish state involved taking over land currently occupied by non-Jews and then expelling them, a task which he advised should be carried out 'discreetly and circumspectly' (Greg Philo and Mike Berry, *Bad News from Israel* [Pluto Press, 2004], p. 3).

Theodor Herzl visited Jerusalem in 1898 and dreamed of turning the city over to Jews. His dream was expressed in the characteristically racist language of Zionism:

> The musty deposits of two thousand years of inhumanity, intolerance, and uncleanliness lie in the foul-smelling alleys ... If we ever get Jerusalem and if I am still able to do anything actively at that time, I would begin by cleaning it up. I would clear out everything that is not something sacred, set up workers' homes outside the city, empty the nests of filth and tear them down, burn the secular ruins and transfer the bazaars elsewhere.

In other words, *get rid of the dirty Arabs*. Herzl's racist vision was duly implemented and Arabs now form only a minority of the city's population. Arab citizens, currently about one-third of the city's residents, get only 12 per cent of its welfare budget, even though their poverty rate is more than double that of Jewish residents. They get 15 per cent of the education budget. A stunning 98.8 per cent of the city's budget for culture and art goes to Jews. Overall, the Arab share of the services' budget is under 12%, meaning a four-to-one difference in spending per person between Jews and Palestinians.

When Appelfeld says, 'I'm a Jewish writer, I'm living amongst my people, and I'm trying to understand the complex of Jewish existence', what he is blind to is his own privileged status in a sectarian society. Jerusalem's Jewish population, who make up about 70% of the city's 700,000 residents, are served by 1,000 public parks, 36 public swimming pools and 26 libraries. The estimated 260,000 Arabs living in the east of the city have 45 parks, no public swimming pools and two libraries. 'Since the annexation of Jerusalem, the municipality has built almost no new school, public building or medical clinic for Palestinians,' says a B'Tselem report. 'The lion's share of investment has been dedicated to the city's Jewish areas.'

Palestinians in East Jerusalem, often the city of their birth, are not considered citizens but immigrants with 'permanent resident' status, which, some have found, is anything but permanent. In the old South Africa, a large part of the black population was treated not as citizens of the cities and townships they were born into but of a distant homeland many had never visited. 'Israel treats Palestinian residents of East Jerusalem as immigrants, who live in their homes at the beneficence of the authorities and not by right,' says B'Tselem. 'The authorities maintain this policy although these Palestinians were born in Jerusalem, lived in the city and have no other home. Treating these Palestinians as foreigners who entered Israel is astonishing, since it was Israel that entered East Jerusalem in 1967.'

Fleeing from Europe, Appelfeld regarded German as 'a language drenched in the blood of the Jews'. He blocked out the possibility of writing in German and reinvented himself as a Hebrew writer: 'You see, it would be not only a paradox, it would be tragic, to write in the language of the murderers. Just to think about it is enough to stop it.'

It's a dubious concept, I think, blaming a language for the crimes committed by those who speak it. Shakespearean English was also the language of those who committed atrocities against the Irish. American English is the language of torturers and war criminals but also the language of poets and novelists. Paul Celan's response to the Holocaust seems to me far more effective than Appelfeld's: he chose to confront the culture which destroyed his family in its own language. He became the leading post-war poet who wrote in German. He made Germans aware of his suffering through their own language and culture.

Appelfeld's differentiation between guilty German and innocent Hebrew is a deeply ironic one, in the light of the history of Israel. Who nowadays could deny that Hebrew is now also the language of racism, mass killing, atrocity and a sectarian state? Hebrew is a language drenched in the blood of Arabs.

Uniquely, Jean Genet witnessed both occupying troops who were Nazis (in Paris) and occupying troops who were Jews (in Lebanon), and what he saw was not the guilt of German and the innocence of Hebrew but *identity*. Jean Genet was in Paris in 1939-45; he was also in Lebanon during the 1982 Israeli invasion. There is a telling moment in his book *Prisoner of Love* (1986) in which he describes his shock at seeing that 'The road signs between Beirut and Baabda were in Hebrew'. It reminded Genet of that earlier occupation:

> Arriving in Beirut from Damascus and seeing those signposts at the crossroads was as painful as seeing Gothic lettering in Paris during the German occupation.

For Genet, the Hebrew language 'induced a sense of unease':

> Not only did this writing belong to the enemy – it was also an armed sentry standing over the people of Lebanon.

Worse than unease, Hebrew produced 'nausea'. Hebrew seemed to express the very essence of the bellicose Jewish state and the misery it had inflicted on the Palestinians:

> the letters were separated by immeasurable spaces filled with several layers of time – a time as dead and incalculable as the space between a corpse and a living eye looking at it. In the space between each Hebrew letter, generations have been born and spread abroad, and its silence shattered us worse than bullets and bombs. (Jean Genet, *Prisoner of Love*, [trans. from the French by Barbara Bray, New York Review Books, 2003], pp. 310-311)

Ironically, the sectarian discrimination which defines the Jewish state in which Appelfeld so fervently believes is also evident at the most basic level of language. To Edward Said, Hebrew supplied a tangible expression of the Jewish supremacism that underpinned the condition of Israel:

> It seems to me therefore absolutely crucial to achieve some kind of real normalization, where Israelis can become part of the Middle East and not an isolated sanctuary connected to the West and denying and contemptuous and ignorant of the Palestinians. One sign is that wherever you go in Israel, the road signs are written in English and Hebrew, There's no Arabic. So if you're an Arab and you can't read Hebrew or English, you're lost. That's design. That's a way to shut out 20 per cent of the population. So

it's very important for Israelis to be forced intellectually and morally to confront the realities of their own history. (David Barsamian and Edward W. Said, *Culture and Resistance: Conversations with Edward W. Said* [Pluto Press, 2003], p. 21)

Aharon Appelfeld's *The Story of a Life*, and the interviews he gives to journalists, show all too clearly that even Israel's most prominent writers and intellectuals refuse absolutely to confront their own history. Appelfeld, like the majority of Israelis, perceives Israel as a victim. He is a Naqba-denier, narrow in his sympathies, oblivious and indifferent to the Other, using phrases like 'to erect walls' (p. viii) and 'working the land' (p. ix) without a trace of understanding of what such terms mean to dispossessed Palestinians brutalised by sectarian Jews. He describes *The Story of a Life* as 'a description of a struggle' (p. viii) but he is oblivious to the material conditions which allowed his reinvention, blind to the struggle of those who have an equal right to justice.

Appelfeld is clearly as incapable of understanding his own blindness as Heidegger was, which raises the question: *what is to be done?* Well, it would be nice for once if journalists challenged this old man's complacencies, but somehow it's hard to see that happening.

At the level of culture the challenge is to those who have directly suffered at the hands of the barbaric, sectarian state with which Appelfeld has foolishly aligned himself. Hundreds, perhaps thousands, of Palestinian intellectuals are now fluent in Hebrew, as result of being incarcerated as political prisoners in the Israeli Gulags. What one of them needs to do is write a masterpiece in Hebrew which forces Zionist culture to acknowledge the Other in the way that Celan forced German culture to face up to the truth of his experience. To write in Hebrew and to write better than Appelfeld; that, at the level of culture and humanity, is one challenge for the victims of Zionism.

Philip Roth and the Two Aharon Appelfelds

Over at *The Existence Machine*, Richard Crary reflects on the writing of Philip Roth. In the course of his discussion he mentions the role played by Israel in Roth's developing career and treatment of Jewishness.

> Towards the end of the book, Portnoy recounts the events of his trip to Israel, having fled his latest *goyische* girlfriend in Greece after a nasty fight. Arriving in Israel, he notices something: 'I am in a Jewish country. In this country, everybody is Jewish.'
> (http://yolacrary.blogspot.com/2007/07/portnoys-complaint-philip-roth.html)

It perhaps goes without saying that Portnoy, or Roth, does not see – or does not notice – Arabs. This I find, well, *interesting*, to say the least. But I won't delve into what that absence represents.

This reminded me that recently on his blog *Anecdotal Evidence*, Patrick Kurp posted an appreciation of Aharon Appelfeld. Like many others, he was bowled over by the man and by his memoir. Patrick Kurp writes in glowing terms of

> *The Story of a Life*, his emblematic chronicle of 20th-century horrors narrated by a voice as quiet and oblique as the voices in his novels ... Appelfeld's aesthetic remains rooted in indirection. Even when his narrative is dry and factual, a mist clings to his words.
> ... His friend Philip Roth has written that Appelfeld possesses the 'playfully thoughtful air of a benign wizard'.
> (http://evidenceanecdotal.blogspot.com/2007/05/tiny-precious-particles.html

That phrase pops up, in a slightly differently worded paragraph, in Roth's book *Operation Shylock* (1993), which I've recently been reading. My impression is that this may be Roth's least popular title. It's a fascinating book and I was gripped by Roth's engagement with Israel, Appelfeld and those two inescapable contexts, the Holocaust and the Zionist state's treatment of the Palestinians.

Aharon, a small, bespectacled compact man with a perfectly round face and a perfectly bald head, looked to me very much like a benign wizard, as adept in the mysteries of legerdemain as his namesake, the brother of Moses.

Roth's vision of Appelfeld is of a gentle and affable magician entertaining children at a birthday party. The analogy is apt: 'legerdemain' means, among other things, 'sleight of hand' and 'trickery'. As I have suggested elsewhere, Appelfeld's craft of indirection and reticence is, in his memoir, not wholly admirable. Appelfeld's memoir is not innocent. It has a repellent and offensive Zionist sub-text. That sub-text is very clearly connected to the public pronouncements about Israel and the Middle East which Appelfeld repeatedly makes in interviews.

The Story of a Life is in fact emblematic in a way that Karp doesn't acknowledge: that's to say, emblematic of the vexed relationship which exists between the Holocaust, the sectarian Jewish state and the Palestinians it violently dispossessed in 1948 and has been brutalising and dispossessing ever since. One symptom of it is the fact that the Israeli museum dedicated to the Holocaust, Yad Vashem, stands within sight of an atrocity which the state of Israel neither recognises nor has ever shown the slightest interest in atoning for – namely, Deir Yassin, where civilians were massacred and (according to Robert Fisk) women were disembowelled: 'The mass grave is believed to lie beneath a fuel-storage depot that now stands at one end of the Jerusalem suburb' (Robert Fisk, *The Great War for Civilisation: The Conquest of the Middle East*, 2005, p.454).

In his book *The Myths of Zionism* (2004) – which has a sensitive chapter on this relationship – John Rose quotes Afif Safieh, who wrote

> The Israeli political establishment inflicted on Palestinians four types of denial. First came the denial of our very existence. Then followed the denial of our rights. All this was accomplished by the denial of our sufferings and the denial of their moral and historical responsibility for this suffering.

Philip Roth, I think, understands this very well (or came to understand it; perhaps not in his younger Portnoy days). The origins of *Operation Shylock* lie in a trip Roth made to Israel in the late 1980s to interview Appelfeld for *The New York Times*. It reveals material about Appelfeld and his past which you won't find in *The Story of a Life*. It also includes other revelations, such as this one:

> Aharon's house was in a development village some twenty minutes due west of Jerusalem, just off the road to the airport.

A *development village*. Questions, anyone?

Operation Shylock is subtitled 'A Confession' and represents itself as non-fictional in its thrust but its final words are, 'This confession is false.' It's not easy to establish whether the book is almost entirely or only partly imaginary. This is apt, because the book explores the subject of identity – Jewish identity, the condition of Israel, the various selves of Philip Roth. No coincidence, either, that another topic is the trial of John Demnjanjuk, whose case hinged on issues of memory and identity (was, or was not, Demnjanjuk really a notorious Nazi concentration camp guard known as Ivan the Terrible? – the case was unresolved when Roth wrote his book).

Operation Shylock is a raw, ramshackle book, and its criticisms of Israel produced predictable reactions. Roth was denounced by a furious Rabbi for 'self hate' and the novelist Alexander Theroux raged about 'Mr. Roth's crude and tendentious bigotry'.

Roth's central conceit is that upon arriving in Israel he discovers that there is an impostor who has taken on his name and identity. The other Philip Roth is a scandalous figure, who mocks everything that the 'real' Philip Roth believes in:

> He had picked up Aharon's *Tzili* and was showing me how far he'd got in reading it. 'This stuff is real poison,' he said, 'Everything Diasporism fights against. Why do you think highly of this guy when he is the last thing we need? He will never relinquish anti-Semitism. It's the rock he builds his whole world on. Eternal and unshakeable anti-Semitism. The man is irreparably damaged by the Holocaust – why do you want to encourage people to read this fear-ridden stuff?'

This is plainly not what the 'real' Philip Roth thinks of Appelfeld's fiction, which he has energetically promoted and applauded. But as a perception of Appelfeld the man it is stunningly accurate. Appelfeld's sensibility is lodged deep in a past and in a society which no longer exist. This supplies an exemplary source for his fiction but is disabling when he has to address why the contemporary Zionist state is widely regarded with hostility. Representing the European condition as a seething sea of anti-Semitism is the lazy trope of Zionists not prepared to scrutinise the history of their sectarian state or the priviliges it affords them as members of the master religion. Roth, I think, shrewdly understands this. He sees that there are two Aharon Appelfelds – the novelist, whose work can only ever be judged on its own terms, and the wounded, fallible man.

Operation Shylock strikes me as both a more humane book than Appelfeld's *The Story of a Life* and every bit its artistic equal. Appelfeld's book pares down his life to a collection of privileged moments; Roth, by contrast, is a putter-inner, not a taker-outer. Wild, exuberant confession, not cool reticence. And Roth's animated mixture of journalistic reportage, autobiographical confession and lurid fantasy is fascinatingly problematic. Roth gives us a Babel of competing voices (including a feverish Palestinian voice) but resists making any one authoritative. *Operation Shylock* altogether lacks the complacency and faint air of self-congratulation which, resisting the master's magic, I find in *The Story of a Life*. *Operation Shylock*, I think, understands the human condition better and represents it better. And it is alert to The Other.

As one of the impudent voices of the text says to number one Appelfeld fan 'Philip Roth':

> For what justification is Mr. Appelfeld from Csernowitz, Bukovina, for the theft from them [the Palestinians] of Haifa and Jaffa?

Pure Wizardry

There's a short story by John Updike entitled 'Ethiopia', about a young American couple on holiday in that country. An anxiety which grows through the story is the possibility that an aircraft – the kind of airliner which the couple intend to depart on – might be hijacked by Palestinian terrorists. The theme is first introduced at a party when they are introduced to a woman who is a leading presenter on state TV:

> His magical hand turned a dial, and there she was, giving news about the latest Palestinian hijacking. 'Hitler,' a swarthy but handsome gentleman was telling the young American wife, 'had the correct idea but was not permitted to complete it.'

This, of course, is the device known as collage. A woman on TV reading the news; an unrelated fragment of dialogue at a party. Distinct and apparently unconnected material is juxtaposed to create a new dimension of meaning. The juxtaposition enforces a connection between what is conventionally or rationally unconnected. Here, a symbolic or poetic significance is subliminally established. Though John Updike is far too sophisticated a writer ever to spell it out overtly, that meaning is not hard to detect. Palestinian terror is akin to the attempted Nazi genocide of European Jewry. Hitler killed six million Jews but failed to kill the rest. Palestinian terrorists are completing Hitler's work.

Updike's meretricious collage came to mind when I read the essay 'The devil's progress' by Amos Oz in last Saturday's *Guardian Review*. Amos Oz is perhaps Israel's best known and most distinguished novelist. He was awarded the Goethe prize in Frankfurt on 28 August and his *Guardian* piece is an amended version of his acceptance speech. Oz is also a non-fiction writer and a prominent commentator on Israeli-Palestinian relations.

At one point in 'The devil's progress' Oz mentions Lotte Wreschner, the mother of his son-in-law, and how her family were persecuted by the Nazis. He writes:

> She and her sister were transferred to Theresienstadt [concentration camp]. I wish I could tell you that they were liberated from Theresienstadt by peace demonstrators carrying placards saying 'make love not war'. But in fact they were set free not by pacifist idealists but by combat soldiers wearing helmets and carrying machine guns. We Israeli peace activists never forget this fact, even as we struggle against our country's attitude towards the Palestinians, even while we work for a liveable, peaceful compromise between Israel and Palestine.

As in the Updike story, Palestinians are connected to the Nazi holocaust, albeit in what is ostensibly a far more benign way. But this time the link is made up of three elements. The bridge between Nazi persecution and the Palestinians are 'pacifist idealists'. They are not concretely identified but it is obvious that Oz is referring to protest movement which developed in the 1960s in opposition to the American intervention in Vietnam.

A moment's reflection is enough to indicate the absurdity of Oz's historical analogy. Unless they'd discovered a time machine it's hard to see how protesters bearing placards with a slogan coined in the late 1960s could have turned up at the gates of a concentration camp in 1945. The lighthearted slogan 'make love not war' was no more representative of the anti-war movement than 'save water, bath with a friend' represents today's diverse Green movement. The 1960s anti-war movement was not about an abstract principle such as pacifism but about opposition to yet another imperialist war of occupation by the United States of America.

Oz's distaste for the sixties anti-war movement, I think, reflects the reality that he is a privileged child of US imperialism. He is a Zionist, though that commitment is not obvious in his *Guardian* article. Without American dollars, American armaments and American protection, the privileged life and writing career of Amos Oz would have flatlined long ago. In the USA he is a revered figure. Last year the University of Pennsylvania hosted 'The Amos Oz International Conference', focusing on his life and works, describing him as 'Israel's greatest living author and peace advocate'. A peace advocate, in fact, whose gritty realism teaches him the need for 'combat soldiers wearing helmets and carrying machine guns'.

Oz's point of view is also no doubt rooted in the fact that he himself is an ex-soldier. According to the entry on Amos Oz in Wikipedia: 'Like most Jewish Israelis, he served in the Israeli Defence Forces. In the late 1950s he served in the kibbutz-oriented Nahal unit and was involved in border skirmishes with Syria; during the Six-Day War (1967) he was with a tank unit in Sinai; during the Yom Kippur War (1973) he served in the Golan Heights.'

Much of Oz's article, perhaps not surprisingly, is centred on Goethe, Faust and German literature. This is broadened out into a discussion of morality in the modern age. Oz complains that in the modern age ideas of good and evil have been erased by social science, 'overruled by the idea that circumstances are always responsible for human decisions, human actions and especially human suffering. Society is to blame. Painful childhood is to blame. The political is to blame. Colonialism. Imperialism. Zionism. Globalisation. What not. So began the great world championship of victimhood.'

Eh? The sweeping generalisations and tangential arguments come so fast it's hard to get much of a purchase on them (but note that 'Zionism' is one of the things that isn't responsible for human suffering). Today, Oz says, 'we' have 'emerged from the evil of totalitarian rule', which may come as surprising news to that one quarter of the world's population which lives in China. Elsewhere he says, 'I know some people who are willing to kill anyone who is not a pluralist', a ludicrous exaggeration for which the only appropriate adjective is 'journalistic'.

His sensibility is deeply reactionary and his argument about morality seems to me quite wrong. His basic thesis is that some people are inherently good, others inherently bad, and that we should not excuse acts of evil by identifying the source of that evil anywhere else but in the individual. I believe this is the reverse of the truth. Good or evil is present in anyone. Acts of evil against other people usually originate in the shaping forces of an individual's background (family and parents, class, education) and depend firstly on a shutting down of human empathy (easy enough if you are uneducated or if you have been raised by racists or religious fundamentalists) and secondly on the right set of circumstances. One classic situation in which evil acts occur is when troops (usually young, male and poorly educated) occupy a foreign land, and when those troops have a different language, culture, skin colour or religion to the people of the land they are occupying, and when they have been conditioned to regard those people as inferior. American troops commit atrocities in these circumstances; so do British troops; so do Russian troops; so do Japanese troops; so do German troops; so do Israeli troops. So do the troops of any nation.

Edward Said once wearily referred to 'the ubiquitous Amos Oz'. I know exactly what he meant. Oz pops up everywhere, trumpeting himself as a caring Israeli, a liberal humanist, a peacenik. He postures as a liberal but he is is absolutely against co-existence with Palestinians, other than on Zionism's repressive terms. Zionism is a despairing, segregationist ideology, which propounds that Jews must have their own state, where Jews come first, and where Jews are not obliged to live as equals with anyone else but Jews. Zionism loathes the thought of diversity, other than among members of the master religion; it is contemptuous of equal rights, and pitilessly sectarian. Oz, like most Zionists, has a vested interest in the propaganda he spreads around the globe, the sectarianism he so surreptitiously and assiduously promotes and the substantial material privileges which sectarianism affords him.

Edward Said's disdain for Oz presumably still rankles. Hence the remark: 'Was Goethe a condescending 'orientalist', as Edward Said might have him?' Note that slippery word 'might'. In fact Said nowhere condescends to Goethe in his book *Orientalism*. He notes that German Orientalism (unlike French and British Orientalism) was rooted in books, not actual experience of the Orient, and that though Goethe supplied a key German Orientalist text it was based on the experience of a trip down the Rhine. Oz denies that Goethe was an Orientalist and asserts that 'It was not the extreme and imagined exoticism of the east that tempted him, but the strong and fresh substance that eastern cultures, eastern poetry and art may give to universal human truths and feelings.' When Oz approvingly quotes Goethe, beginning with the line 'God is of the east possess'd' he ironically and unwittingly confirms Said's thesis.

What astonishes me about Oz's *Guardian* piece is its chutzpah. 'I believe that imagining the other is a powerful antidote to fanaticism and hatred,' he concludes. This is stupefying coming from a man who keenly defends Israel's so-called 'security wall'. Oz doesn't want to live alongside or among Palestinians; like a white South African he wants to preserve his privileged existence behind a fence, while the blacks live in a slum out of sight. Oz is adamantly against allowing Palestinian refugees back to the homes and villages they were terrorised from in 1948, or into Israel at all.

If he was the kind of caring, imaginative liberal humanist he is often represented as, he would enthusiastically endorse the single state solution, in which Jews, Christians and Muslims lived alongside each other as equals. This is the only realistic and humane solution to the enduring crisis in Israeli and Palestinian relations, but Oz has no interest in it. He wants apartheid and the privileges it brings him, not equality under the law and co-existence.

Which brings me back to the linking of Palestinians and Nazis. Why is it so important to connect two historically distinct and quite unrelated sets of people? It's hardly a puzzle. The persecution of

European Jewry by Nazi Germany is used to deflect attention away from the reality of Israel as a sectarian state and its long history of repression of the Palestinians. The Holocaust is used to shut down any criticism of Israel by insinuating, or explicitly asserting, that such critics are anti-Semites. Knowledge of the Holocaust is used to silence knowledge of the *Naqba*.

Neither John Updike nor Amos Oz has any direct experience of living under the Nazis. One modern author who did was the French writer Jean Genet. When Genet was in Lebanon in 1982 during the time of the Israeli invasion he noticed that the signs on the road to Beirut were in Hebrew: 'Arriving in Beirut from Damascus and seeing those signposts at the crossroads was as painful as seeing Gothic lettering in Paris during the German occupation.' (Jean Genet, *Prisoner of Love* [translated from the French by Barbara Bray, New York, 2003], p. 310).

The Israelis reminded Genet of the Nazis. This, of course, is an unthinkable thought in hegemonic Western culture. As Genet observed, it was 'Very smart of Israel to carry the war right into the heart of vocabulary, and annex the words holocaust and genocide' (p. 374). The colonisation of this moral vocabulary by Zionism ensured that the invasion of Lebanon by Israel was not represented as an act of lawless aggression, and similarly dropping tons of bombs day and night for three months on a capital with two million inhabitants was not terrorism. How could it be when carried out by Israelis, who have a monopoly on the words holocaust and genocide? 'Words are terrible,' Genet concludes, 'and Israel is a terrifying manipulator of signs.'

The wizardry of Oz – the great 'peace advocate' vexed by 'pacifist idealists', the man who passionately believes in imagining the other but who prefers not to live among them on equal terms – also reminds me of 'Fascinating Fascism', Susan Sontag's essay on Leni Riefenstahl. Sontag notes how language is used to sanitise: Riefenstahl is described in a 1974 book as having sprung to international fame 'during Germany's blighted and momentous 1930s'. As Sontag dryly remarks, 'It takes a certain originality to describe the Nazi era as "Germany's blighted and momentous 1930s".' But that certain originality is still around. On its website the University of Pennsylvania explains that 'Amos Oz roots his writing in the tempestuous history of his homeland.'

Ah, yes, *tempestuous*. But somehow 'tempestuous' is not the first word that comes to mind when considering the first 57 years of a bellicose sectarian colonialist settler state born out of ethnic cleansing, with an impressive record of terror, land theft, human rights abuses, collective punishment, torture, extra-judicial assassinations and repression on a staggering scale.

The Amos Oz Hard Disk

Edward Said once wearily referred to 'the ubiquitous Amos Oz'. Said, of course, was perfectly positioned to get the true measure of someone like Oz.

Glancing at today's page in the weekly TV guide I spotted that The Ubiquitous One is back again – yup, at 10.40 pm tonight on BBC1 there's a one-hour documentary entitled *Amos Oz: The Conscience of Israel*.

Amos Oz is as much the conscience of Israel as Jeffrey Archer is the patron saint of truthfulness and integrity. If anyone seriously deserves that accolade it's the academic and author Ilan Pappe (whose articles about Israel appear from time to time in the *London Review of Books*), not a slippery apologist for land theft and sectarianism like Oz.

I'll be setting the VCR. According to the TV guide, in tonight's programme Oz will give 'an eye-witness account of Israel's birth through the publication of his childhood memoir *A Tale of Love and Darkness*'. As it happens I'm two-thirds of the way through this memoir, which is a deeply dishonest, manipulative piece of Zionist propaganda. Oz is not Israel's conscience – he's Israel's Leni Riefenstahl.

The British paperback edition of *A Tale of Love and Darkness* (Vintage) bears on its cover a single quotation: *'One of the funniest, most tragic and most touching books, I have ever read.* GUARDIAN'. What it doesn't say is that the unidentified *Guardian* reviewer was Linda Grant – a fanatical Zionist. Regular visitors to the blog *Lenin's Tomb* may recall she had a run-in with its proprietor, Richard Seymour. You can read the full exchange in the Tomb's archives (under 'Lenin's long 'uns'). As Seymour put it with his customary clarity:

The murder and ethnic cleansing of Palestinians in 1947-8 was a planned component of the theft of Palestinian land. The settlements, from WWI onward, were contiguous with British colonialism in Palestine, and were often co-opted into the occupation. The final success of the Zionist movement was to replace the British occupation with a European settler occupation.

Needless to say that's not the kind of historical background you'll find in *A Tale of Love and Darkness*. It's a Zionist family saga, packed with eccentrics and warm-hearted, rollicking Dickensian characters. Reviewing the book for the Israeli publication *Haaretz*, Avirama Golan put it well in describing it as an 'autobiographical novel'. All autobiography involves an element of fiction-making but Oz's is of the full-blooded variety. He purports to remember lengthy conversations he had as a child. His recall of places is crammed with improbable detail. But the book isn't an innocent memoir. His colourful yarn of Jewish family life is disturbed by bad people – Arabs. Virtually invisible in the first half of the book, they emerge from the shadows of Palestine to make trouble. It's not hard to see why this self-serving account of Zionists as a loveable, warm-hearted, cuddly people whose existence is threatened by crazy irrational Arabs has proved massively popular in Israel.

Avirama Golan notes, 'Every choice [Oz] has made – literary, historical, psychological or linguistic – reveals how bound he is to the "hard disk" of Zionism, as he calls it.' That hard core of belief which drives Oz is exposed at its rawest in his short, avuncular book *Help Us To Divorce: Israel and Palestine – Between Right and Right* (Vintage), which I've just finished reading. Let's take a peek at some of the core beliefs of Amos Oz, taken from *Help Us To Divorce*:

(i) 'The Israeli Jews are in Israel because there is no other country in the world which the Jews, as a people, as a nation, could ever call home' (p. 5).

Eh? To be Jewish is to belong to a religion. Jews live quite happily alongside other religions all over the world. Religion does not define statehood. Italy may be a Catholic country but to be Italian all that's required is that you are born there, not that you are a Catholic.

As for 'no other country in the world', the Zionist pioneers in fact considered setting up a state in Argentina and in central Africa before finally settling on Palestine.

(ii) 'Both peoples, Israeli Jews and Palestinian Arabs, have equally deep, different historical and emotional roots in the country' (p. 10).

This simply isn't true. Zionist settlers did not arrive in Palestine until the late nineteenth century. Arabs had been living in Palestine for centuries. Even when the United Nations allocated land for a sectarian Jewish state in 1947, Arabs formed the majority of the population of that state.

By 'emotional roots' I assume Oz is referring to the Bible. Apart from being a work of fiction, this cannot reasonably be said to provide an adequate mandate for a racist, colonising twentieth-century project. Ironically, modern archaeology has established that although a historical entity called Israel did briefly exist around 800-700 BCE it was not Jewish but pagan, and Jerusalem was not its spiritual centre.

(iii) 'Half the population of Israel are people who were kicked out of Arabic and Islamic countries' (p. 19).

This is false. In 1948 there were 800,000 Jews living in Arab countries – around 6% of the world's Jews. Iraq, for example, had a 2,500 year old Jewish community. The British government thought it would be a marvellous idea if the Jews got out of its puppet colony Iraq and let ethnically cleansed Palestinians take over their homes. Not surprisingly there was no great enthusiasm for the deal among those on whose behalf it was being brokered. Then, in the face of the reluctance of Iraqi Jews to leave, a 14-month terror campaign of anti-Jewish bombings began. And who was behind this terrorism? All the historical evidence points to Israel. And it worked. Jews were terrorised out of Iraq by Jews, to inflate Israel's minority Jewish population.

(iv) 'Modern Israel is not a product of a colonialist enterprise' (p. 21).

The chutzpah of Zionists like Oz really is extraordinary. The documentation on the original aspirations of Zionism and its subsequent occupation of Palestine is enormous. Both in its theory and its practice Zionism is and always has been a ruthless colonialist project. Theodor Herzl, the father of Zionism, was enormously impressed by the way Cecil Rhodes had appropriated Mashonaland and Matabeleland from its indigenous population. He thought this supplied a marvellous example for the setting up of a future Jewish state. First expropriate the land, then get rid of the natives – though as Herzl cautioned, 'the process of expropriation and the removal of the poor must be carried out discreetly and circumspectly'.

(v) 'The Jews have a right to be a majority in one small land' (p. 30).

Here we come to the sectarian core of Zionism. Why should Jews – or any religious or ethnic group – have *a natural right* to be a majority anywhere, least of all in a land they have stolen from the indigenous population by brute force?

Israel has arrived at a Jewish majority population only through ethnic cleansing, reinforced by its sectarian 'Law of Return', which allows Jews from around the world to emigrate there, despite having no connections with the Middle East whatsoever. Simultaneously, Israel denies Palestinian refugees the right to return to the homes they were driven out of in 1948 and the land that has continued to be stolen from them bit by bit over more than half a century. Israel refuses to allow these refugees within its borders. And that's fine by Amos Oz. As far as he is concerned everything will be resolved if the Palestinians are given their own state which, as he charmingly puts it, 'will be even smaller than Israel, but it will be home' (p. 30). And that's where those 5 million refugees will have to squeeze in, because there's no room for them in a state determined artificially to maintain a Jewish majority.

(vi) 'Not one of them [Israelis and Palestinians] is an island and not one of them can completely mingle with the other. Those two peninsulas should be related and at the same time left on their own' (p. 81).

Under the homely metaphors, this is the argument of a racist and a sectarian. It's hardly surprising that Oz is a keen supporter of the wall which is being built to fence the Palestinians into their open-air prisons, or that he supports a state which refuses to admit Palestinians in the West Bank who marry Israeli Arabs. Such cruelties are indeed very reminiscent of apartheid South Africa. But then Israel is a state in which racist remarks by a senior government minister attract little comment. Back in August 2003, cabinet minister Gideon Ezra urged that Arabs should be used as security guards in Israel because only they have 'the sense of smell needed to smell other Arabs'.

Gideon Levy remarked at the time ('The Scent of Racism', *Haaretz*, 25 August 2003):

Separate lines for Jews and Arabs have long since become second nature here. There is no need to go as far as the occupied territories – where apartheid roads for Jews only and curfew for Arabs only have long been the reality – in order to witness the separation. It's here, within the country. Under the aegis of the security situation the phenomenon has grown to worrisome proportions, far beyond what's necessary. Arab students find it difficult to rent apartments in Jewish cities solely because of their ethnic origin and without any security justification. The country's Arab citizens are increasingly loath to venture out of their towns and villages because of the suspiciousness and humiliation they encounter in every contact with Jewish citizens or with the authorities.

The most eloquent critics of Israel are themselves Israelis, and Jews are at the forefront of the anti-Zionist movement. Amos Oz isn't one of them. Amos Oz 'the conscience of Israel'? Don't make me bleedin' laugh, as my aunty Dot used to say.

Yet More Wizardry of Oz

Whereas today's *Independent* offers its readers Robert Fisk on the crimes of Ariel Sharon, the *Guardian* supplies more from the slippery pen of Israeli novelist and so-called 'Left Zionist', Amos Oz.

Instead of acknowledging the truth that the withdrawal from Gaza was a retreat motivated by economic and military considerations, not by the slightest wisp of concern for the Palestinians, Oz arrives at the preposterous conclusion that Ariel Sharon was no longer the old brute of yesteryear but a changed man and a gutsy proponent of peace.

This is perhaps unsurprising, since Oz's Zionist apologia *Help Us To Divorce* (Vintage, 2004) ends with the bizarre vision of Sharon as a man who can solve the conflict, 'And though Sharon is, as everyone knows, a hefty figure of a man, we will carry him shoulder-high, my friends and I.' Needless to say the blood-spattered old war criminal did not solve the conflict, and only a shallow blusterer like Oz could possibly have thought otherwise.

He is leaving us taking with him the answers to two great mysteries: why in the autumn of his life had he suddenly converted so radically; and what else was he going to do in the direction of peace and reconciliation?

... Ariel Sharon is leaving us even as he is signalling to us – I understand my mistakes. I finally tried to mend them, but life was just too short. (https://www.theguardian.com/world/2006/jan/07/comment.mainsection)

But before you reach for your hanky, pause to consider what the exciting radical new Ariel Sharon achieved in the year 2005 – something which the caring liberal Amos Oz maintained an absolute silence about (along with the compliant mass media of the USA and Britain):

(i) Israel extra-judicially murdered 286 Palestinians (more than the number of state executions in Saudi Arabia). A statistic worth remembering when you see Spielberg's *Munich* and its sanctimonious line about Israel not having the death penalty. That figure includes 68 children murdered by the Israeli army.

(ii) 4,000 Palestinians were arrested.

(iii) 1,700 Palestinians were wounded by the Israeli army.

(iv) Israeli occupation forces razed 2,115 dunums of land, uprooted some 58,700 trees and destroyed 52 wells.

(v) Israeli occupation forces confiscated 29,713 dunums of land for the separation barrier.

(vi) Israeli occupation forces destroyed 1,692 Palestinian homes.

(vii) Occupation forces established 877 military checkpoints, obliging Palestinians to queue, sometimes waiting for hours, sometimes being turned back at the whim of Jewish racists.

Even More Amazing Wizardry of Oz

The ubiquitous one, Israeli novelist Amos Oz, is back!

As I never buy the *Evening Standard* I missed it, but apparently he's been doing his very popular crocodile tears act. Indeed, Amos Oz is just the sort of Israeli intellectual that a rabidly reactionary rag like the *Standard* can do business with.

Amos Oz's heart goes out to dead Lebanese civilians, but his Left Zionist anguish (Oz is a Left Zionist in much the way that the young Goebbels was a Left Nazi) is tempered by his gritty awareness that it's all Hezbollah's fault.

And it seems like only yesterday our Amos was celebrating 'a moderate centre-left coalition, headed by Ehud Olmert.'

Oz's latest wizard solution to the problem of those pesky Arabs is

> open negotiations with an Arab League delegation (in effect Egypt and Saudi Arabia) ... Let us not forget that almost every Arab government is as concerned by the rise of Hamas – as threatened by it – as Israel.

Yes, our dear friends in the pro-Western totalitarian torture states of Egypt and Saudi Arabia know how to deal with the threat posed by Islamists. These friendly Arab regimes know that Islamists attract support because they are not corrupt, they do not lead extravagant lifestyles, and they provide welfare programmes for the poor. So *lock them up and don't allow anyone to vote for them.*

For a flavour of Amos Oz's rhetorical strategies I recommend Chapter 39 of his acclaimed memoir *A Tale of Love and Darkness*. It's in the biography section of most corporate bookstores and you can stand there and read it for yourself in a couple of minutes or so (pp. 293-5).

It begins with a lyrical landscape description, which includes 'the smell of the Land of Israel from time immemorial'. (An impressive odour, for a state which has currently existed for only 58 years.) Oz glimpses a Bedouin woman in the distance, 'a human figure standing motionlessly draped in black from head to foot'. (What this image conceals is the slow seizure of Bedouin land which has continued year after year since the great ethnic cleansing of 1948, a project which is laid bare in Abu Hussein and Fiona McKay's book *Access Denied: Palestinian Land Rights in Israel* [2003]).

Oz chats to a neighbour, Mr Shmuelevich. Mr Shmuelevich grumbles that Shimon Peres is selling out to Arafat, and says, 'It seems one holocaust wasn't enough to teach us a lesson.' Oz mentions hearing the Moonlight Sonata being played on a piano in Shmuelevich's house the night before, and compliments his daughter on her beautiful playing. Mr Shmuelevich 'smiles ... like a shy schoolboy who has suddenly been chosen as form monitor by secret ballot' and reveals that it was his granddaughter who was playing. 'She writes beautiful poems too. So sensitive.' Oz wryly promises to read them when he has the time.

Back in my study, with a mug of coffee in my hand and the morning paper spread out on the sofa, I stand at the window for another ten minutes. I hear on the news about a seventeen-year-old Arab girl who has been seriously injured by a round of bullets after she tried to stab an Israeli soldier with a knife at a roadblock outside Bethlehem. The early morning light that was blended with a grey mist has begun to glow and turned to a harsh uncompromising light.

And there you have it. Israelis are loveable folksy types who cultivate their gardens and whose granddaughters play Beethoven and write poetry. Whereas Arab girls stab soldiers. It's very sad that Arabs have to be shot but let's face it, *they bring it on themselves.*
Pure wizardry.

Part Five: Shakespearean

Essence of Genius: Shakespeare's Portrait

The so-called Chandos portrait of Shakespeare, in the National Portrait Gallery, 'has always been the favourite likeness of Shakespeare' (S. Schoenbaum, *Shakespeare's Lives* (Clarendon Press, 1991, p. 203).

Which is just one of the many problems associated with this painting. A supposed image of Shakespeare, which it is still impossible to authenticate, is preferred over the only two genuine representations of the playwright which must have had some resemblance to him. The first of these is the limestone effigy by Gheerart Janssen in the Church of the Holy Trinity at Stratford, installed no later than 1623. The second is the copper engraving by Martin Droeshout, on the title page of the 1623 First Folio.

The Janssen effigy shows Shakespeare as podgy, mostly bald and with his mouth open. The church suffered from dampness and the effigy has been repeatedly retouched over the centuries. In 1793 it was painted white.

Droeshout was too young to have known Shakespeare, so scholars have agreed that his engraving must have been based on a miniature or drawing of Shakespeare, probably made in Shakespeare's late thirties or early forties. That in itself, to my mind, throws even more doubt on the Chandos portrait. If the Chandos portrait is of Shakespeare, showing him in his prime, why didn't John Heminge and Henry Condell commission Droeshout to copy that, instead of something else? Another question involves the relative ages of Shakespeare in the Droeshout engraving and the figure in the Chandos portrait. The latter has a receding hairline but isn't yet bald. Shakespeare is unequivocally bald in Droeshout. But to my eyes the figure in Droeshout isn't any older than in Chandos; he could well be younger.

Ben Jonson's poem 'To the Reader' appears to praise the engraving, saying that 'the Grauer had a ftrife / with Nature, to out doo the life'. But it is impossible to draw any firm conclusions from Jonson's poem. He might have been speaking sincerely; he might merely have been mouthing conventional platitudes; he might even have been writing with his tongue wedged firmly in his cheek. The scholarly consensus is that the engraving is amateurish. In his *Shakespeare: A Life* (1998), Park Honan raises another possibility: Ben Jonson might not even have seen the engraving before writing his salutation. His praise was simply required as a publishing convention.

However, Honan goes on to say of Droeshout, 'That the engraving of the head is accurate is supported by the bust at Holy Trinity, which has comparable skull proportions and the same famous perpendicular forehead.'

In her book *Ungentle Shakespeare: Scenes from His Life* (Arden Shakespeare, 2001), Katherine Duncan-Jones suggests that Shakespeare was a fatty:

> It can be surmised that Shakespeare was distinctly corpulent, since both the Stratford bust and the Martin Droeshout engraving show him as plump-faced. Given that most portraits aim to flatter, he was probably in truth plumper still.

So what, then, of the National Portrait Gallery's Chandos picture? The man in the painting is no fatty. On the contrary, he's the dark, swashbuckling type. It is certainly interesting that the gold ring in the sitter's left ear and the undone drawstrings of the shirt may signify a poet. But that in itself proves nothing: there were hundreds of poets in England in the early seventeenth century, many of them from wealthy backgrounds and with sufficient income to commission a portrait. An inflated sense of self-importance has always been a common occupational hazard for writers. But as far as we can tell, Shakespeare was a man notable for his reticence. He did not stand out in a crowd. He kept his opinions to himself. He made no effort to ensure that those of his writings published in his lifetime carried an image of the author. Would he really have commissioned a portrait of himself? And if he had done, wouldn't it have ended up at his house in Stratford?

Schoenbaum bluntly sums up the problem with the Chandos painting: its early history 'consists mainly of shadowy and contradictory traditions'. No one knows who the painter was, who the sitter was, or when the portrait was painted.

Interpretations of the Chandos painting are wildly subjective.

One Victorian commentator sneered that it could hardly be Shakespeare because the figure in the painting 'exhibits the complexion of a Jew, or rather that of a chimney-sweeper in the jaundice'. But in his book *Tudor and Jacobean Portraits* (1969), Sir Roy Strong asserted that Chandos had much in common with the effigy and the engraving: 'The main features tally; only the hair, beard and moustache are differently arranged.'

The coolly sceptical Schoenbaum disagrees. He thinks the painting differs significantly from the engraving: 'the forehead recedes rather than rising perpendicularly, the upper lip is short rather than long, and the chin pointed rather than round'.

You can see in Chandos whatever you want to see.

But there is another major problem with this oil painting. Schoenbaum mentions that 'It has been more than once retouched over the years.' To learn what retouching can imply you need only compare the famous Corpus Christi College portrait believed to be of Christopher Marlowe with its condition before it was restored. The painting is reproduced in glorious colour at the front of the paperback edition of Charles Nicholl's *The Reckoning: The Murder of Christopher Marlowe*. And it's gorgeous. Fabulously fresh and full of colour. It's full of life. Those eyes! Then take a look at p. 114 of Park Honan's *Christopher Marlowe: Poet & Spy* (OUP, 2005). It shows the painting before it was restored. Unfortunately it was only photographed in black and white. Nevertheless, the difference between the two versions is shocking.

In my view the Chandos portrait simply meets a psychological need for an image of Shakespeare that matches a romantic conception of genius. Genius is darkly handsome and sticks a gold earring in its ear. Genius doesn't put on weight, develop two chins and go bald.

Shakespeare's Portrait Again

So, the National Portrait Gallery has decided that the so-called Grafton Portrait of Shakespeare (in the collection of the John Rylands Library at Manchester University) isn't Shakespeare after all. This conclusion is based on the hugely expensive clothes which the young man in the painting, dated 1588, is wearing. Shakespeare at 24 couldn't have afforded clothes like that. It's a perfectly sound conclusion. In reality there was never anything to connect the painting to Shakespeare, apart from wishful thinking and the letters 'WS' on the back. These turned out to have been put there in the nineteenth century.

The Gallery is still researching its own so-called Chandos Portrait 'under the microscope'. 'While we haven't found any evidence that this is Shakespeare, we haven't found any evidence that it isn't,' says Dr Tanya Cooper, the Gallery's sixteenth-century curator. How true! And while I haven't found any evidence that Shakespeare ever pissed in my garden I haven't found any evidence that he didn't, so let's face it – *he might have done.*

The Grafton Portrait and the Chandos Portrait and the theory that at age seventeen Shakespeare joined the household of Alexander Hoghton of Lancashire all have one thing in common – a snobbish desire to link Shakespeare to the aristocracy or the landed gentry. The same goes for all the crackpot authors who assert that Shakespeare's works were secretly written by someone else – someone of greater social status and learning. They also express a desire to fill in a blank that can't ever be filled in. In a visual age we demand to know what Shakespeare looked like, as if it would help in some way in understanding his writing. Today's *Guardian* refers to 'the Martin Droeshout engraving, authenticated by Ben Jonson'.

Jonson's ten-line poem about the engraving is a double-edged thing, however. On the one hand he implies that the engraving brilliantly reproduces what Shakespeare really looked like and admires the way Droeshout 'hath hit / His face'. But Jonson also says that the engraver 'had a strife / with Nature, to out doo the life'. The poem could, in fact, be a piss-take ('oooh – it looks SO like him' – meaning 'what a crap portrait!'). When Jonson concludes with the words 'Reader, looke / Not on his Picture, but his Booke' he might be making the straightforward point that it's the writings that matter, not the man. Or he could be saying: ignore this truly awful image of the author and get stuck into the plays.

The Amazing Truth about William Shakespeare

Nobody knows on what day Shakespeare was born.

Shakespeare's preferred spelling of his name was 'Shakspere'. In Tudor printing the 'k' and the 's' overlapped, tending to cause part of one letter to snap off. A hyphen was substituted to prevent this. An 'e' was subsequently substituted for the hyphen and an 'a' added after the second 'e' to make the name appear more 'natural'. Hence *Shakespeare*.

Nobody knows what made a glover's son from a Warwickshire market town want to become an actor and nobody knows how he became an actor and playwright in London.

Shakespeare was not interested in projecting himself as a fascinating personality whose life and activities would be of inherent interest to other people.

Nor did he regard the writing of plays as an activity of enduring cultural interest and importance.

In his lifetime he was not regarded as a particularly interesting or unusual individual. His plays were not regarded as the greatest drama of the age.

The First Folio was slow to sell.

Nobody knows what the significance was of Shakespeare bequeathing his wife the second best bed.

These are just a few of the truths I've learned from the saner books about Shakespeare. I have 11 volumes of what I'd call conventional literary criticism, plus 3 books from the perspective of actors or directors (James Earl Jones's monograph on Othello, Tirzah Lowen's book *Peter Hall Directs 'Antony and Cleopatra'* and Michael Bogdanov and Michael Pennington's *The English Shakespeare Company*). I have 3 biographies – S. Schoenbaum's admirably factual and non-speculative *William Shakespeare, A Compact Documentary Life*, Park Honan's authoritative *Shakespeare: A Life* and Katherine Duncan-Jones's provocative and intelligent *Ungentle Shakespeare*. I also possess a copy of E. A. J. Honigman's controversial *Shakespeare: The 'Lost Years'*. I used to be a true Honigman believer but, influenced by the arguments of Schoenbaum and Duncan-Jones, I have now lost my faith – though I see that from time to time the debate still acrimoniously rumbles on between splenetic academics in the letters page of the *Times Literary Supplement*. I also have a copy of Anthony Burgess's large format Penguin coffee table book on the bard (it's a potboiler job like the new Ackroyd biography and I've only ever looked at the pictures). Add to this Eric Partridge's *Shakespeare's Bawdy* plus the more scholarly and comprehensive *The Dramatic Use of Bawdy in Shakespeare* by E. A. M. Colman.

And now we come on to my favourite books. I've always had a lot of respect for Anne Righter's low-key study *Shakespeare and the Idea of the Play*, with its central emphasis on Shakespeare's attitude to theatre and theatricality. She analyzes the way in which acting and illusion are prized in the plays up to about 1600 and then 'underwent a strange and precipitous reversal. At that point, the theatre and even the idea of imitation inexplicably went dark for Shakespeare, and the actor, all his splendour gone, became a symbol of disorder, of futility and pride.'

In a remainder shop I snapped up the handsome American hardback edition of *Berryman's Shakespeare*, edited by John Haffenden. This is a fabulously stimulating, ramshackle collection of essays by the poet John Berryman – the ruins of a full-length study which he never completed because of his alcoholism and because his poetry came first. It's a dipping-into book, rather than a read-in-one-go study.

I also have volume one of a vast Shakespeare lexicon, originally published in Berlin in 1902. I am still searching secondhand shops for volume two. If you want to know how often Shakespeare used a particular word, where he used it, and what its meanings were in the sixteenth century, this is a very valuable compilation. The lexicon was clearly produced by a madman and was written for those of us who have, like that character in *The Adventures of Augie March*, 'a weakness for complete information'.

And while on the topic of derangement, I forgot to say in my last post that I also own an edition of the sonnets produced by a crazy Baconian named Alfred Dodd. I came across it in a second hand bookshop and bought it for a laugh. Bacon conspiracy theorists are basically snobs who combine their paranoid delusions with a crass ignorance of sixteenth century society and culture, and assert that no one from a backward market town like Stratford could possibly have produced those wonderful plays, least of all a mere tradesman's son. No, it takes *fine breeding* and *class* to write stuff like *Hamlet*. And whereas you and I might think the sonnets are about love, death, sex, yearning, anger, jealousy, sadness and the stuff of human lives, Baconians know otherwise. The Dodd edition hilariously claims that the sonnets were just coded messages, in which Sir Francis Bacon was attempting to get the truth out to a wider world. The basic message being *I-am-bastard-son-of-Queen-Elizabeth-Please-help!* Among Dodd's many whacky proofs of his theory is that the ruff in the famous engraving of Shakespeare is deliberately shaped to look like a 'B'. (Look closely. It isn't.)

'Ideology works to efface contradiction,' remarks Terence Hawkes in *That Shakespeherian Rag*, and goes on to observe that 'The ideological mode of the Shakespeare industry can be said to be centripetal, integrating.' In this book and its sequel, *Meaning by Shakespeare*, Hawkes develops these insights in relation both to the cult of Shakespeare and to the plays. Hawkes is a hugely provocative and interesting cultural critic. I think he's right about the cultural uses to which Shakespeare has been put but often wrong about the drama. Reducing any art form to 'specific ideological strategies' is not in my view very helpful in determining why a particular play or a novel or a song is more compelling than another.

Lastly, what to my mind is one of the best books ever written about the man from Stratford. Gary Taylor's *Reinventing Shakespeare: A Cultural History from the Restoration to the Present*, is massive in its range and packed with interesting information and insights. But by the end of the book Taylor's lifelong marriage to Shakespeare is under severe strain, and he ends up explaining why he thinks Shakespeare isn't up there with the truly great writers.

That makes a grand total of 89 books by or about Shakespeare. (Time to chuck some out, I think. Those 11 volumes of academic lit. crit. can go for a start.)

But I'm also interested in the society in which Shakespeare lived. So for £1.80 in a charity shop I recently snapped up John Dover Wilson's *Life in Shakespeare's England*, a miscellany of writing from the age on topics as various as drunkenness, bear gardens, furniture and health. One of the best books I've ever come across in understanding Elizabethan England is *Elizabethan Life: Disorder* by F. G. Emmison, which is a record of trials and punishments in Essex in the second half of the sixteenth century (arson, riot, murder, 'immorality', 'assaults on officers' – it's very comprehensive). In the basement of Stamfords map shop in Covent Garden I bought their last copy of *The A-Z of Elizabethan London*, an obscure but lavish publication (£23) which presents an enlarged and annotated reproduction of the so-called 'Agas' map, chopping it up and turning it into the equivalent of the modern A-Z of London. And right now I'm slowly working my way through Peter Edwards's *The Horse Trade of Tudor and Stuart England*. Compulsive reading it isn't, but as a study of one aspect of the material conditions of the age it's interesting. I've learned that horse dealers were regarded as subversive and a threat to the stability of the Tudor state. Why? Because they were highly mobile, and moved around the country to do their business, spending time in inns and alehouses, 'spreading news and perhaps unorthodox views as they went'. To those in authority there was a conventional assumption that people who travelled around spread sedition. Hence the need to control and licence *common players*.

Kill Bill

This is becoming a trend. *Shakespeare trash.*

In the basement of Waterstone's, Covent Garden, I encountered in their Shakespeare section no less than three new titles on the theme of who-really-wrote-Shakespeare's-plays?

Firstly they had several copies of the paperback edition of a crackpot book about the 'real' Shakespeare, *The Truth Will Out*. They also had a gleaming hardback copy of the latest book to assert that the true author of the Shakespeare canon was Edward de Vere, the seventeenth Earl of Oxford. This theory was first promulgated by an ignoramus in 1920 and today, incredibly, it still thrives.

It's a stupid theory for many reasons, not least because the Earl died in 1604 and many of Shakespeare's greatest works were first published/performed after that year. *King Lear, Macbeth, Antony and Cleopatra*, etcetera. But the Oxfordians have an answer to that (they have an answer to everything). The plays have been misdated. Or de Vere left them almost finished and a few final touches were added by other hands at a later date. Or the plays were not by 'Shakespeare'/Oxford at all. You can invent any explanation you like. As none of them is rooted in documentation or historical knowledge and scholarship, it doesn't matter. You can fantasize to your heart's content. Once inside the asylum no one is going to criticise you for anything you say. Any nut can assure fellow nuts that the identity of the author of Shakespeare's plays is *an age-old mystery.*

One bizarre aspect of the alternative authorship underworld is that it often attains celebrity endorsement. Thus *The Truth Will Out* gets the imprimatur of the actor Mark Rylance. But the Oxfordians can do better than a small-timer like Rylance. They can cite no less a Renaissance scholar than Orson Welles.

Sigmund Freud was also an enthusiast. Even Henry James was wobbly on the authorship question. The gravitational pull of snobbery is, well, *awesome.* How could a shopkeeper's child from a dreary little market town have produced writing which has such *sheer class*?

The third book I came across was *Players* by Bertram Fields.

Who he?

BERTRAM FIELDS *is a prominent entertainment lawyer in America and the author of* **Royal Blood***.*

In short, another top Tudor scholar.

For centuries scholars have debated the true identity of the author of the works attributed to William Shakespeare. Sigmund Freud, Charles Dickens and John Gielgud, among others, have cast irresolvable doubt on the Stratford man and proposed alternatives from Christopher Marlowe to Queen Elizabeth I. **Players** *looks for the truth behind what is possibly the greatest conspiracy in literary history.*

In reality scholars have for centuries devoted enormous attention to the transmission and meaning of Shakespeare's texts and none at all to the notion that someone other than 'William Shakespeare' was their author. If you think someone other than Shakespeare wrote his plays you have a slight problem to deal with: the First Folio. It was compiled and published by John Heminges and Henry Condell, who were centrally involved in the Globe as shareholders, managers and actors. They both knew William Shakespeare.

Fields has the answer! The First Folio is a hoax! The plays were actually the work of Francis Bacon in collaboration with Edward de Vere. But Stratford landowner William Shakespeare obligingly agreed to be part of the conspiracy. Quite *why* I couldn't be bothered to find out, as my patience with books of this sort runs out after about two minutes.

Mart's Misquote

Today's feast of fun is supplied by effervescent Martin Amis, who answers *Independent* readers' questions.

To one questioner, he retorts:

> Islamism has received a great boost from its rejection of reason and its embrace of death, both of which are hugely energising, as Lenin and Hitler well understood. But Islamism is simply too poisonous to survive for very long.

Well, that's one major world religion out of the way, is it not?

Apparently Tibor Fischer wrote a bad review of Amis's novel *Yellow Dog*.

'Tibor Fischer is a creep and a wretch. Oh yeah: and a fat-arse,' quips Mart, who brings a new maturity to contemporary literary criticism.

My attention was particularly drawn to Mart's response to this question: 'Now that Saul Bellow has passed away, who do you regard as the greatest living American novelist(s)? PHILIP EAST, by email'.

> John Updike, and then your namesake, Mr Roth. With Don De Lillo coming up on the flank. That's just my opinion. One of the extraordinary things about Bellow was that his pre-eminence stared you in the face. As someone or other said of Shakespeare, 'Others abide our judgment. Thou art free.'

That 'someone or other' was Matthew Arnold. And I am sorry to say that Martin is misquoting his sonnet 'Shakespeare' (1849), which begins:

> Others abide our question. Thou art free.

Mart has also evidently failed to understand Matthew Arnold's point. The sonnet continues, 'We ask and ask – Thou smilest and art still, / Out-topping knowledge.'

Arnold is not arguing that Shakespeare was pre-eminent. Nobody for a moment thought that he wasn't. What concerns Arnold is Shakespeare's elusiveness as an artist and as a man. Other artists you can pin down in their art and their lives and in the connections you can make between the two. Not Shakespeare. To Matthew Arnold, Shakespeare was an enigma – a smiling Mona Lisa figure, impenetrable to understanding.

Mart has no more understanding of the poetry he cites than of, well, just about *anything* these days.

Will in the World

Is Stephen Greenblatt's biography of Shakespeare, *Will in the World*, worth reading? On the whole, yes. But cautiously.

Greenblatt has nothing at all new to divulge about Shakespeare's life. But he's a fluent, very readable author as well as being a major Shakespeare scholar, and his insights into the plays are worth knowing.

The drawbacks to the book are the inevitable vice of Shakespeare biographers: wild speculation. Greenblatt subscribes to the view that Shakespeare's father was a zealous Catholic and Shakespeare himself was That Way Inclined. This leads Greenblatt to pile speculation upon speculation until we get to a truly preposterous moment, when Shakespeare's destiny crosses that of the Jesuit martyr Edmund Campion: 'Let us imagine the two of them sitting together then, the sixteen year-old fledgling poet and actor and the forty-year-old Jesuit.'

No, let's not. The scenario is, to put it mildly, implausible.

'Shakespeare would have found Campion fascinating – even his mortal enemies conceded that he had charisma – and might even have recognised in him something of a kindred spirit,' Greenblatt asserts.

On the other hand Shakespeare might not have been a fledgling actor at sixteen, almost certainly never met Campion, and was, just possibly, thinking more about sex and girls than theology at that age.

'Not surprisingly, Shakespeare never referred openly to Campion.'

Now, Professor, that's a very dodgy line of reasoning. (I myself I am convinced that Shakespeare was abducted by Martians and not returned to earth until two years later. But not surprisingly Shakespeare never referred openly to his time on board the Martian flying saucer.)

The sonnets are a trap into which Greenblatt plummets like so many before him: 'It is possible that someone ... might well have had the clever idea of commissioning the poet to try his hand at persuading the narcissistic, effeminate young earl [of Southampton] to marry.'

Yes, and it's possible that the sonnets were written as coded messages by Francis Bacon, desperate to alert the world to the fact that he was Queen Elizabeth's bastard son – but on the whole I think not. On the whole I think that Park Honan's notion of Shakespeare's sonnets as a new twist on an old tradition, deliberately marketed as teasing mysteries, makes more sense than a banal, reductive reading which seeks to connect someone very low down in the social scale to the aristocracy.

Greenblatt heaps speculation upon speculation, until he is able to speak confidently of 'the vain young recipient of these poems'. But we don't know that there was a recipient. The sonnets are mental theatre. They are just as likely to be five finger exercises as mirrors of Shakespeare's soul. If you read Shakespeare's work reductively you are likely to end up with the view that he was frequently shipwrecked and often encountered beautiful young women dressed up as men.

Still, there's lots of good stuff in among the crazy guesswork. Where did Shakespeare get his reading material from? It's a good question. Books were, after all, a very expensive commodity in the sixteenth century. A book could cost the equivalent of a teacher's annual salary. In his early years, Shakespeare probably didn't have much money. Absorbing stuff in bookshops is certainly a possibility – actors, after all, had to have very good memories, and memorising words was a skill much more common in the sixteenth century than today. Greenblatt interestingly suggests that Shakespeare was able to get hold of books from the printer Richard Field: 'He was a hugely valuable resource for his young playwright friend from Stratford.'

Greenblatt's account of how and why Shakespeare came to depart from Stratford is the best and most convincing version of the Sir Thomas Lucy story that I've read. It's far from proven, but it's certainly plausible.

Greenblatt also subscribes to the modern view that Shakespeare's relationship with his wife Anne was not a happy one. This, too, I find very convincing.

His speculative instincts get the better of him when he moves on to the trial and public execution of Elizabeth's physician Dr Lopez. 'Was Shakespeare in the crowd?' he asks, and his answer, needless to say, is: *yes!*

Lopez was laughed at by the crowd: 'This laughter, welling up from the crowd at the foot of the scaffold, could well have triggered Shakespeare's achievement in *The Merchant of Venice*.'

On the other hand Shakespeare might have spent that day at his lodgings reading a good book.

The itch to connect Shakespeare to great people and great events, to my mind, is fundamentally misconceived. (By page 308 the Earl of Southampton has become Shakespeare's 'possible lover'.)

Greenblatt is very good on *Hamlet* and the late plays. As a dramatic critic he is much more interesting than he is as a biographer. His account of how Shakespeare developed soliloquy and interior monologue is brilliant.

Ultimately it's a racy read and worth a look. But if you have time for only one Shakespeare biography in your life then the one to go for is Park Honan's more sober and reliable account.

I spotted one howler. The leader of the English troops who carried out a notorious massacre in Ireland on 10 November 1580 was not, as Greenbatt says, Walter Ralegh (though he was present, as was Edmund Spenser). It was Arthur, Lord Grey of Wilton, K.G.

I say this with some confidence, having driven out to Milton Keynes – it's true what they say about the roundabouts there – to visit Lord Grey's much decayed tomb. He is one of the great English war criminals. Credit where credit is due.

A Coat of Arms

Shakespeare's artistry was, at times, rooted in his background and material interests. One example is the coat of arms which Shakespeare craved. Possession of a family coat of arms was a terrific sign of status in an age obsessed with the social pecking order. In Chapter Twelve of his book *1599*, James Shapiro very convincingly situates *As You Like It* in the context of the playwright's initial success in securing a coat of arms and his later efforts to improve upon it by establishing a connection with a branch of the Arden family whose own coat of arms derived (Oh. My. God.) from that of *the Beauchamps.*

Stephen Greenblatt also attends to this matter in his biography *Will in the World*. Greenblatt made me see *Twelfth Night* in a whole new way in his analysis of Malvolio. He argues, brilliantly I think, that 'Malvolio serves as the shadow side of Shakespeare's own fascination with achieving the status of a gentleman.'

Malvolio yearns to be something more than just a servant. He wants to join the elite. What Malvolio fantasizes, Shakespeare achieved – but through business acumen rather than marriage. And as Greenblatt notes, Malvolio very much resembles an actor in the way in which, fooled by Maria's fake letter, he begins to rehearse his new role as Olivia's prospective lover and husband. He dresses up in a costume. He practises speeches. He puts on a different facial expression in an effort to impress. Malvolio is Shakespeare – or rather, Shakespeare's ironic representation of his own professional life and social ambition, rendered into dark, bleak comedy.

There was another brilliant literary innovator in sixteenth century England – a pioneering writer who made the basic metre of Shakespeare's lines possible – and he also wanted to improve on his coat of arms. But that ambition *rather went to his head.* And now there's a new biography, which I can't wait to get my hands on: Jessie Childs, *Henry VIII's Last Victim: The Life and Times of Henry Howard, Earl of Surrey.*

Playing with Shakespeare's Shadow

In Borders on Oxford Street the new paperbacks display includes *Shadowplay*, by Clare Asquith. The cover quotes words of praise from Tom Paulin, who has thereby slumped considerably in my estimation.

Let's consider Asquith's contribution to contemporary Shakespeare scholarship.

She argues that the plays and poems are a network of crossword puzzle-like clues to his strong Catholic beliefs and his fears for England's future. Aside from being the first to spot this daring

Shakespearean code, Asquith also claims to be the first to have cracked it. 'You do get new insights into his life if you look at the code,' she says. 'He must have gone up to Oxford, as many Catholics did at the time, by finding a sympathetic college, such as Hertford, but not officially signing on.'

Such a relief to discover that Shakespeare went to Oxford, is it not? Somehow one always knew in one's bones he could not possibly have been a Cambridge man.

You may have thought that the characters in Shakespeare's plays were imaginary. Foolish you. Hamlet, for example, is *a thinly disguised portrait of Sir Philip Sidney*. And the plays aren't about ambition, jealousy, lust, self-delusion. Goodness, no. They are, in reality, secretly coded messages to the Catholic faithful.

'Is now the right time to overthrow Elizabeth and return ye nation to ye true religion?'

'I dunno. I reckon we need to get down to the Globe and pick up a few tips from Bill's new play.'

Such is the substance of *Shadowplay*. And with a title like that it's not hard to see that the author has an inadequate grasp of the concept of irony.

Let's consider just one of those proofs of Asquith's:

Sunburn
The sun represented divinity, and so sunburn denotes closeness to God. Shakespeare described himself as 'tanned' in Sonnet 62.

Now in the first place there are no grounds whatsoever for assuming that Sonnet 62 is autobiographical. You can concoct an historical context if you wish, but you can never prove it because the hard evidence just isn't there.

All you get in Sonnet 62 is a voice. And to conflate the voice of the poem with the voice of the poet is always a risky undertaking. A classic instance is supplied by Derek Walcott, who naïvely assumed that 'Naturally the Foundation will Bear Your Expenses' (i) accurately described a day in the life of Philip Larkin; and (ii) expressed Philip Larkin's fierce contempt for Remembrance Day. Unfortunately, Walcott's piece in the *New York Review of Books* (1 June 1989) is not available online. There, Walcott was cleverly alert to the troubling inconsistency between Larkin's crazed left-wing views and his acceptance of the Queen's Medal for Poetry.

The voice in Sonnet 62 confesses to being consumed by self-love, a sin for which there is no remedy. He thinks he is entirely beautiful. But when he looks in the mirror he sees his lined old face. He recognises that the beauty he describes is that of the young man he is addressing, superimposed on to his own aged body.

Or as the eminent Shakespeare scholar Katherine Duncan-Jones puts it in her edition of the Sonnets (Arden Shakespeare, 2001):

> In the first of the two sonnets on his own decrepitude, the speaker first rejoices in his own merit and beauty, then acknowledges that the beauties he boasts of belong to the young man whom he loves, and only vicariously to himself.

It's a dramatic situation. The sonnet belongs to that long sequence which explores the vexed relationship between an older man and a physically attractive younger man.

The speaker's face in the mirror is described as being 'Beated and chopt with tand antiquitie'.

In other words, it is battered ('beated') and lined ('chopt') with brown age ('tand antiquitie'). Tanned has two distinct associations. Partly it refers to exposure to sunlight. In this sense the word 'tand' may very well have been generated in the compositional process by the word 'chopt'. This survives in modern English as 'chapped', referring to skin cracking from exposure to frost or a low temperature. QV Petrarch. QV a popular contemporary songwriter: 'Yet she's true, like ice, like fire' (Bob Dylan, 'Love Minus Zero/No Limit').

The speaker, in short, is quite literally weather-beaten ('beated') by frost ('chopt'), sunlight ('tand') and the passage of time ('antiquitie'). Comprehensively smashed by winter and summer and the passing years.

But 'tand' also alludes to tanning. In his Penguin Classics edition of the Sonnets, John Kerrigan glosses it as 'leathery tanned Old Age which tans skin to leather'. In other words, the speaker represents himself as having brown, leathery skin. In his edition of the Sonnets (Yale, 2000), Stephen Booth suggests that 'beated' and 'chopt' may be, or pun on, 'now-forgotten tanner's terms'. Tanning was something Shakespeare had personal experience of, as his father prepared leather for glove-making.

We can therefore be reasonably confident about one aspect of Sonnet 62. This is that when Shakespeare introduced the word 'tand' *he was not making a concealed theological point.*

(In)corrupting Shakspere's Text

Re-reading *Twelfth Night* in my Arden edition (ed. J.M. Lothian and T.W. Craik), I became very suspicious of the stage direction in this passage:

> MALVOLIO: Seven of my people, with an obedient start, make out for him. I frown the while, and perchance wind up my watch, or play with my *[Touching his chain]* – some rich jewel. Toby approaches; curtsies there to me – (2.5.58-62)

In this passage, Malvolio is daydreaming that his employer, the countess Olivia, has married him. He deludes himself that she rather fancies him, and takes comfort from the knowledge that there are cases in which a wealthy aristocratic woman has married a servant. Malvolio is blissfully unaware that Olivia harbours no romantic affection for him whatsoever and has already become infatuated with Cesario, who only the audience knows is actually Viola disguised as a young man.

The comic absurdity of Malvolio's daydreams is made funnier still by the presence of Sir Toby Belch and Sir Andrew Aguecheek, who, unseen by Malvolio, have to listen to his disdain and contempt for them and his fantasies about how he will treat Sir Toby once he is master of the household. The comedy is deepened by their obligation to remain silent in the face of Malvolio's insolence. If they were to respond to his unflattering words they would ruin the plan to fool Malvolio with Maria's bogus letter (which purports to be a declaration of love from Olivia). Seething with fury, they remain in hiding. The audience roars with laughter at the multiple comic dimensions of this scene.

The passage in question unfolds Malvolio's fantasy that he has just ordered the servants to go and find 'my kinsman Toby'. While he waits for Sir Toby to be brought to him (in order, as we later learn, to tell him to cut down on his drinking), he kills time. And how does he imagine himself killing it?

Firstly, he frowns. Frowning is a fundamental aspect of Malvolio's character and his role. He is a humourless Puritan, who disapproves of drinking and high spirits and fun. The comic sub-plot involving Maria's fake letter exposes Malvolio's vanity and hypocrisy. He is a moralist who exempts himself from his own moral standards. (The name, I suppose, contains a pun on 'malevolence'.) Maria plays on his weaknesses and later tricks him into smiling. And the audience laughs.

Secondly, Malvolio imagines himself winding up his watch. The watch may be imaginary – a symbol of his raised status as Olivia's new husband. But it is a symbol perfectly in keeping with his morality, which is concerned with order and power. A timepiece allows an artificial structure to be imposed on the day. Malvolio, we can imagine, is someone who would be obsessed with punctuality.

Thirdly, he imagines himself playing with something. But what is it he plays with? The text doesn't tell us. Or rather, the Arden Shakspere text does: *Touching his chain*. Would that be a watch chain? Perhaps not. The Cambridge University Press edition of the play (1930; 1970) states in parentheses *touches his steward's chain an instant*. My Penguin edition (1973), ed. M. M. Mahood, states in parentheses *fingering his steward's chain of office*.

Now it seems to me fairly obvious that if Malvolio's hand strays anywhere at this point it isn't to his chest. For confirmation of my lewd suspicion I reached for my facsimile copy of the First Folio to check. There, the passage reads as follows:

Seauen of my people with an obedient ftart, make out for him. I frowne the while, and perchance winde vp my watch, or play with my fome rich Iewell: *Toby* approaches; curtfies there to me.

The only authoritative text that we have for *Twelfth Night* is the one published in the First Folio – a text which Mahood describes as 'very accurate and carefully punctuated'. She concludes that it is based on the original promptbook: 'This is evident from the theatrical practicality of the text as it stands. Actors' entrances are given at the point where they must begin to move on to the stage.'

Therefore modern editors are wrong to add interpolations of the sort I have identified. They have no authority to do so. Worse, in my opinion they have wilfully misunderstood the text at this point and then superimposed their own misreading of the text on to it, in turn misleading generations of readers as to the meaning of this passage.

Shakspere's text reads 'or play with my fome rich Iewell'. The actors didn't need a hyphen or a prompt between 'my' and 'some' to understand what is happening here. The joke is a simple one. Shakspeare is indicating to his audience that *Malvolio is a wanker*. Both in a literal and a figurative sense.

The textual extract in question is preceded by Malvolio's fantasy that he is a wearing a 'branched velvet gown, having come from a day-bed, where I have left Olivia sleeping'. In other words, Malvolio fantasizes that he has fucked Olivia to the point of exhaustion. Naked, he then slips on a sensuous, lavishly embroidered velvet gown. His imagination is pornographic – or at any rate, masturbatory. But after sexual pleasure comes a different sort of thrill – the power of dominance and punishment. Having dominated his mistress, Malvolio looks forward to chastising Sir Toby, whom he imagines having to curtsy to him. And he is no longer *Sir* Toby but merely *Toby*. And in making a knight curtsy, Malvolio removes his masculinity and feminizes him. Malvolio isn't just a wanker; he's also a proto-fascist. Susan Sontag's brilliant essay on Leni Riefenstahl is pertinent here: fascist aesthetics, argues Sontag, is preoccupied, among other things, with situations of *control* and *submissive behaviour*.

In this extract Shakspere indicates that Malvolio is a wanker in three ways. Firstly, Malvolio dreams that he will 'perchance wind up my watch'. To wind up an old-fashioned watch was to cup it in your hand and twist a knob. It meant clutching it, manipulating it. It involved friction and the use of a hand. In short, it was the perfect symbol of male masturbation. Malvolio's mind is running wild with dreams of sex and power and it seems reasonable to suppose that, as the actor playing the part spoke these words about winding up a watch, he would begin to make motions with his hands, probably in the region of his groin, which would set the audience sniggering.

The analogy between winding up a watch and masturbating is then reinforced by the words 'or play with my'. Malvolio's thoughts unconsciously turn to his penis and the actor's hands, whether or not they have done so before, now move to his crotch. Aware of where his thoughts have led him, Malvolio then gasps 'some rich jewel'. He is anxious to shift his train of thought away from the uncomfortable reality that he is none of the things he has imagined but just a lonely, repressed sexual fantasist. But the audience's laughter now reaches, so to speak, a climax – because what else is a man's penis but 'some rich jewel'?

It makes no sense to suggest that the passage requires Malvolio to imagine himself fiddling with his chain of office, because in his fantasy he is Olivia's husband, not her steward. As her husband he would no longer be wearing a chain.

The Cambridge edition blandly asserts that *'Twelfth Night* remains the politest of Shakespeare's Comedies'. This interpretation rests on ignoring or *not understanding* all the play's jokes about cunts, wankers, pricks, fucking and Olivia's prodigious pissings.

Part Six: At the Movies

Ryan's Daughter: Romanticising British Imperialism

Ryan's Daughter is the cinematic equivalent of gorging on a bucket of strawberry ice cream. The director David Lean had a great eye for exquisitely framed shots of beautiful landscapes and the scenery in the movie is fabulous. Vast empty sands, enormous cliffs, boiling seas, cloud pouring over the mountains like smoke. The movie, not surprisingly, seems to have done wonders for the tourist trade in the Dingle peninsula. *Ryan's Daughter* perfectly fits the thesis developed by Colin McArthur in his British Film Institute monograph, *Television and History*, about film makers who operate 'within certain autonomous conceptions of drama, rather than within a conception of form within which history is signified; i.e. they are more interested in arresting visual effects than historical knowledge'.

The performances in *Ryan's Daughter* are excellent. Trevor Howard is on top form as a salty Catholic priest. Robert Mitchum, though hideously miscast as an undersexed schoolteacher, turns in a dignified, impressively low key performance. John Mills hams it up as the village idiot. Sarah Miles rolls her eyes and emotes as a romantic heroine should do. And Christopher Jones, tormented by memories of the horrors of warfare, appears to be in throes of acute constipation. He also does a marvellous limp.

And those are about the kindest things you can say about the movie. On the negative side, it's preposterously long-winded, humourless, simplistic, crudely manipulative, and a blatant, dismal attempt to repeat the commercially successful *Dr Zhivago* formula. The soundtrack even at times sounds almost identical to some of the music from *Dr Zhivago*.

The plot, apparently inspired by (gasp) *Madame Bovary*, is rendered as melodrama. The lovers meet by a waterfall and a lonely tower. They consummate their passion in a wood covered in bluebells. They meet and embrace on a rocky skyline. They wander along the empty sands. All that's missing is the message, 'Ireland – for that romantic break you'll never forget'. When the affair ends the hero kills himself, as they do in romantic concoctions. (QV *Elvira Madigan*, with its risible ending and relentless Mozart soundtrack.) Alas, blowing yourself up with explosives as a splendid romantic gesture has rather been spoiled as a narrative device by certain realities of contemporary history.

Lean has a fondness for creaky symbolism (white for innocence, red for blood and sexuality, plus various phallic props). Economy and subtlety are alien to his movie-making style. The clumsiest moment in *Ryan's Daughter* is surely the bit where Trevor Howard speaks sternly to Sarah Miles. 'Child, what are you after?' he asks. Lean then cuts to a shot of seagulls in the sky overhead. Then back to Howard, who says, 'Wings, is it?' I mean, *come on*.

In *Dr Zhivago*, Lean conflated Bolshevism and Stalinism, but gave us a nice revolutionary (Alec Guinness) to balance all the nasty ones. Having travestied Russian history, Lean moved on to simplify Irish history. In *Ryan's Daughter* the British occupying forces are decent men doing a good job under difficult circumstances. The soldier in the pub says he's just obeying orders and doing what anyone in his position would do. This unanswerable cracker barrel wisdom silences the uppity Irish patriots. But this is a liberal film, so we get the usual sleight of hand about giving both points of view. 'Get out of my country!' shouts the leader of the resistance at the British soldiers. But the thrust of the movie is to marginalise that moment and perspective.

One genial senior British officer confides at some length that he's a coward. These are not the violent representatives of empire but loveable ordinary blokes with *feelings*. And the film's tragic hero is a brave Brit, who does the decent thing, whereas the Irish resistance to occupation is represented by Tim O'Leary, played by Barry Foster. We first encounter O'Leary shooting a fat old policeman in the back and then moving in close to finish him off. A cold-blooded killer. But he gets his just deserts when he is himself shot in the back in a scene which replicates him shooting the policeman. Gosh, there's a message for us all there, isn't there?

Perhaps of most interest is the representation of the ordinary Irish people. What they are basically is *a mob* – a bullying, turbulent mass constantly threatening to get out of control. There's a big, coarse girl who represents crude animal sexuality (as opposed to Sarah Miles, who represents refined romantic sexuality); the girl, significantly, is a passionate admirer of Tim O'Leary. The ordinary people are easily manipulated. They need to be controlled by ideological authority (the Catholic Church, in the form of wise, salty Trevor Howard) and by state force (British occupation). *When there is nothing restraining them, they turn ugly.* The villagers try Sarah Miles in her absence and, mistakenly, find her guilty of betraying O'Leary to the Brits. So they strip her naked and chop her hair off.

An Irish village is no place for a woman of refinement or a decent schoolteacher who represents cultural aspiration and the middle ground of politics. They are forced out by the brutish, hysterical mob. In short, the victims of occupation and British imperialism and those who resist it are the problem. Those who remain aloof from the resistance and those who repress it – they are the truly noble ones.

Terror-dactyls

The franchise wears very thin in *Jurassic Park III*. Too many chases through the forest; too many preposterously unlikely narrow escapes; too many moments when even the cast have trouble summoning up more than a vaguely bored, half-anxious expression as they stare at an emptiness which will later be filled with a computer generated image.

The sub-text of the movie is that an attractive younger woman who leaves her ugly little storekeeper husband for another man, a handsome athletic hunk, and takes their kid, will pay a heavy price for her faithlessness. The hunk flies high – literally – attached literally – to the couple's child. But uncontrollable forces bring the hunk crashing down and destroy those who are accomplices in his bonding. He becomes the man who fell to earth. He dies.

Later, the faithless wife is forced to embrace her lover's monstrously decayed corpse. What drew the fresh-faced blonde young wife away from her ugly middle-aged husband was, we can intuit, sex. For a few disturbing seconds her punishment is a medieval one. Screaming with disgust and terror, she is bonded to her dead lover while standing. Beneath sinful carnality lies worms and hellish punishment! This is a knee-trembler in hell. This is literally a dance of death.

No coincidence that the little ugly guy is a storekeeper, a repository of the values of trade, commerce and the American capitalist dream. Plus he deals in bathrooms (QV. 'cleansing' below). The same uncontrollable force that liquidated his sexual competitor – dinosaurs – permits him to show his hidden reserves of masculinity. He wins back the cool attractive young blonde and the kid, aided at the end, cosmetically, by a bravura display of US military force. In terms of the plot the military display is pointless, but it seems to function as a re-play of D-Day, reminding us of the historically seamless nature of the US army's commitment to protecting 'us' all from terror.

The most frightening dinosaurs are the pterodactyls. They are mean. They are even more disturbing than raptors. A pterodactyl seizes the American child and takes him off to be fed to a nest of hungry baby pterodactyls. He is saved by the hero's assistant, who happens to be an ace hang-glider. He, too, is a handsome hunk. But he displays no sexual interest in the wife, so he is permitted to live.

The movie ends with a final shot of three pterodactyls flying through the clouds. The wife nervously laughs and says that next they'll be nesting in Oklahoma. A hugely resonant line this. It taps deep reserves of affluent white American anxiety. This is racism incarnate. Black sinister aliens are troubling our way of life! They are heading our way! They might even move in – *nest* – next door!

No coincidence that 'Oklahoma' is a name with the word 'home' lodged inside it. The nuclear family is under threat both from feminism (wives who depart for more handsome, sexier men) and from dark alien immigrants. The three pterodactyls are the Blacks! The Hispanics!

No coincidence, either, that the pterodactyls threaten to nest in Oklahoma. The pterodactyls are subhuman. They are vermin, really. They require eradicating. The house – the home – the nation – must be cleansed. No coincidence, either, I think, that the first two syllables of the word 'pterodactyl' are the same as those of the word 'terrorist'. At a sub-textual level, the pterodactyls are Arabs, heading the way of the USA with violent intent. This anxiety has long been dramatised in Hollywood movies – *Reel Bad Arabs*.

Robert Mitchum in *The Locket*

Her monstrous secret wrecked three men's lives.

I've seen two brilliant movies starring Robert Mitchum – *Night of the Hunter* (1955) and *Cape Fear* (1962). If you've never seen either of those classic movies, you should. In both movies Mitchum plays a terrifying killer who is coming to get you (or rather, coming to get characters with whom you, the viewer, identify totally). *Night of the Hunter* is a strange, poetic movie, quite unlike your average Hollywood potboiler. Looking it up in my copy of Mick Martin and Marsha Porter's movie guide, I see they advise 'watch for the graceful, haunting shot of the children's freshly killed mother'. Quite.

Cape Fear is more conventional in format but raises the crime/revenge movie to the level of art. Lots of darkness and shadows and atmosphere and suggestiveness. And equally as frightening to watch as *Night of the Hunter*. Mitchum also pops up briefly in a cameo role in Martin Scorsese's 1991 re-make of *Cape Fear*, which, though it has its moments, isn't a patch on the original.

And now I've just discovered a third Robert Mitchum masterpiece – *The Locket* (1946). But before discussing it, let me briefly pay homage to one other Robert Mitchum movie. The actor occupies centre stage at the end of the D-Day blockbuster *The Longest Day* (1963). The bit where the Omaha beach defences finally fall. There's jaunty military music, the vehicles pour by through the sand dunes into France, Mitchum grins and chomps on a fat cigar, and there's a glow in your heart as you realise the Second World War is basically won. God bless America.

The Longest Day is a much better and more accurate D-Day movie than *Saving Private Ryan*. Spielberg might do a better job at recreating the reality of the initial assault at Omaha beach, but there's an underlying nastiness to his movie, one of the sub-texts of which is that it's right to murder prisoners of war. Spielberg is the ideologist of American imperialism. *The Longest Day*, though Hollywood to the core, is a far more humane and intelligent movie. That may have been because a lot of the people involved in making it had personal experience of war.

And now to my Mitchum list I add *The Locket*. I was attracted to it by the fact that it starred Mitchum and also that it was briefly mentioned in my TV guide as having been unpopular on first release because of its complicated flashbacks.

By my rigorous postmodernist standards, the flashbacks in *The Locket* turned out to be not all that complicated. But I suppose by Hollywood standards, especially for the time, they were revolutionary.

The film starts on a wedding day. A wealthy man is about to marry his beautiful, vivacious young fiancée. But he is called away from the pre-wedding reception because a stranger has called with an urgent message. The message being: *Don't marry this crazy woman! She may seem cute but she's dangerous!* The stranger, who is a psychiatrist, claims he is the bride's former husband. And he says he knows how her prospective new husband must feel, because he was once in a similar situation ...

Flashback to the previous marriage. Not long after the wedding day a stranger calls at the psychiatrist's office. He tells him that only his new wife can save the life of an innocent man, who is due to be executed for murder the next day. The stranger in the psychiatrist's office is Robert Mitchum. And he tells the story of his own involvement with the heroine.

Flashback to the relationship with Mitchum. In the course of which he discovers something shocking and disturbing about the girl. And the reason for it is contained in a traumatic episode in her childhood ...

Flashback to the traumatic episode ...

I was immediately reminded of *Marnie* (1964). There are some striking parallels between *The Locket* and Hitchcock's late movie. (On a Hitchcock trivia note, according to one website I consulted, the set used in *The Locket* for the house of Mrs. Willis is the same one used for the house of Alex Sebastian [Claude Rains] in Hitchcock's *Notorious* [1946].)

The Locket has a Russian doll structure. But in the end the multiple flashbacks all fold together and revert to the present. There's a clever twist at the end.

It's an interesting movie for more than just its fractured narrative form, or its film noir cinematography. It's about class differences. It's also about gender. The engine of the movie is transgression by two women. *The Locket* also belongs to that period in which Freudian psychology was taken immensely seriously by Hollywood. At one point the authority of the psychiatrist, who regards Robert Mitchum as delusional, is challenged by the audience's knowledge that Mitchum is right in what he says. It's a hugely ironic and entertaining scene, in which Mitchum is flattened by smug Freudian certainty:

> 'You have a tendency to doubt other people's motives ... Doubt is a symbol. When we're prone to doubt others it's a sign that we're unsure of ourselves ... You show an abnormal and obsessive concern in this matter. Isn't it possible, Mr Clyde, that you're really trying to save your ego, your self-esteem as a man?'

And having crushed Mitchum with science, the psychiatrist hands him some pills, saying: 'Here. Take one of these every hour. Try to rest.'

Afterwards, Mitchum is described by the psychiatrist as 'a paranoiac with guilt fantasies'.

Thus, someone who is rightly concerned with justice and truth, is authoritatively identified as a bit of a nutter and in need of sedation.

In portraying transgression, *The Locket* itself transgresses. It explodes conventional chronology and narrative form. It challenges the authority of Freudian psychiatry. It questions all kinds of knowledge and authority. On what do we base our knowledge of anything? And how well do we really know another person, even the person closest to us?

But, in the end, *The Locket* was a commercial mainstream product. Ultimately the movie damps down and extinguishes its own radicalism. The past unfolds back into the present. Transgression is punished. Freudian psychiatry has the final, authoritative word. (Incidentally, the psychiatrist's name is, er, Blair.) The class structure remains intact. The movie's ultimate message is: *don't get upset. Don't try to be different. Don't get ideas above your station. Don't attempt to change how things were meant to be.*

Now try to get some rest.

The play of *Daisies*

Daisies (1966) is a Czech movie directed by Věra Chytilová. I first saw it on BBC2, I think probably some time in the mid-1980s.

I had never seen a movie like it before and haven't since. It's an extraordinary piece of film-making and I watch it every couple of years.

It's a difficult movie to describe. It consists of a sequence of scenes which centre on two young women. The scenes which they occupy are naturalistic – an outdoor swimming pool, a restaurant, the women's toilet at the restaurant, their apartment, a railway station, a town street at dawn, a river, a large building which contains a symphony orchestra and a table set for a banquet.

But the women themselves are represented in a largely non-naturalistic fashion. They are forever putting on large quantities of eye-shadow, which give them a doll-like appearance. Their behaviour is infantile. They disturb and destroy things, and for much of the movie they are seen eating or drinking. All through the movie they keep snickering in a shrill, childish way.

Their behaviour is also overtly non-naturalistic. At times they break into dance routines. Sometimes they walk stiffly, like robots. At times they dress up in outlandish ways. Their dialogue is deadpan and disconnected. In so far as the movie has an organising principle it is repetition: it keeps returning to the same settings. But the return does not enlighten.

If there is a central impulse here it's play. The women are, as one of them says, 'spoiled girls'. They produce nothing. All they do is consume and destroy. There is a quiet joy in this consumption and destruction. And their destruction is of the minor, harmless sort.

At the start and end of *Daisies* we get authentic war footage. Perhaps the point is that the behaviour of grownups is much worse than that of spoiled infants. Yet the film resists that kind of easy deduction. Its form expresses its content. The medium is the message. *Daisies* annihilates the normal conventions of film grammar. It has no sequential or coherent narrative. Some scenes are grey, most are brightly lit and lush with colour. The grain of the image switches abruptly: the colouration changes without explanation. At times the image is speeded up. When the women begin to cut things up with scissors, the image itself is shredded.

Most of all *Daisies* is a film which exploits to the full the possibilities of soundtrack. Often the soundtrack works against the grain of the image. It's an unnerving effect when set against the naturalistic conventions of almost all cinema.

The play of *Daisies* is one of comedy and joy. It is not a movie for miserabilists. What *Tristram Shandy* did for the genre of the novel,

Daisies does for cinema. Like *Tristram Shandy* it rides on a wave of exuberance; it is not for those who require a narrative that unfolds a story, in which elegantly manufactured characters move towards a terminus that is simultaneously enlightening and heartwarming and uplifting and sad and satisfying and wise.

Everyone and everything is being laughed at in *Daisies*, including any viewer who seeks to domesticate it with explanation. At times the narrative becomes pure collage – a blur of images impossible to pin down or retrieve or make sense of. Bourgeois couples are mocked. Lecherous old men are mocked. Romantic young men are mocked. The workers are mocked. Decency and good manners are mocked. The machinery of order is mocked.

Daisies is a movie which refuses to participate in society.

Padenie Berlina

This Russian movie (1949) is simultaneously both risible and weirdly compelling. The developing love between a steel worker and a teacher is interrupted by war. She is captured and ends up in a concentration camp, he resists the Nazi invader, fights his way to Berlin, and is reunited with her. Their love story is counterpointed with the historic role played by a lovely old gentleman named Stalin – a keen gardener, a shrewd military strategist and a genial, good-humoured all-round nice guy.

This restored, rarely seen Soviet epic directed by Mikhail Chiaureli is Soviet cinema's definitive Stalinist recreation of World War II and serves as the crowning moment in Stalin's postwar deification. Stalin himself worked on the screenplay for this blockbuster epic, fine-tuning its portrayal of the dictator as father-hero to his people. The film's remarkable recreations of the battle for Berlin, climaxing in the bitter struggle over the Reichstag, impressed even the film's Western critics with their gritty realism and sheer spectacle. Equally memorable is the film's depiction of Hitler and his inner circle, whose folly and intrigues play out on sets that recreate the grandiosity of the Fueher's Chancellory and the claustrophobia of his bunker with surrealistic intensity.

It says in a DVD catalogue, and I wouldn't disagree.

The start of the movie is oddly reminiscent both of Monty Python and *The Sound of Music*, as a bunch of kids make their way through a vast sunlit field of flowers accompanied by a jaunty folk song. 'Let's go to the steel plant!' says their beaming teacher. And with great enthusiasm they go. The love interest that subsequently develops between Natasha and stout number-one steel worker Aliosha is of the adolescent, broad-brushstroke sort – a matter of lingering looks, sulks and emotional simplicity. One moment they are embracing in a field, the next planes are whizzing overhead, explosions erupt all around them and troops come pouring through the corn. Luckily for everyone, Stalin is there to organise the fightback.

One of the highlights of the movie is the portrayal of Hitler and his entourage – wildly over the top but curiously persuasive. This Hitler is barking mad, though the scenes with Eva Braun have a comic realism – she fusses over his dandruff – entirely lacking in the po-faced Soviet romance. The irony deployed has all the subtlety of a sledgehammer but visually the shrinking and disintegration of Hitler's world is very well done.

Some of the war scenes are oddly amateurish – hand to hand fighting is rendered as a matter of pushing and shoving and the violence of war is sanitised. But the great set piece battle scenes are impressive, especially the climax in Berlin. Though I am afraid a modern non-Russian audience is likely to snigger cruelly at the scene in which a commanding officer plants a full, passionate lips-on-lips kiss on each of his brave soldiers.

In the background, directing victory, is Stalin. His mission, we learn, is not just to win the war but to bring peace to the Polish, Ukrainian and Belorussian people. Awfully sweet of him. And once the red flag has been raised on the roof of the Reichstag, some of the troops start dancing in the street, while everyone cheers and sings, 'Glory to Stalin, glory, glory!'

> *Glory to Stalin!*
> *He is forever true to the vow that he made to Lenin.*
> *Our friend and teacher has confidence in the people.*
> *Together with the people*
> *He has always prevailed.*
> *Great Leader,*
> *We wish you health and strength for many years.*

Apparently Stalin liked the movie.

Stir of Echoes

In every mind there is a door that has never been opened.

Stir of Echoes is a haunted house movie set in contemporary Chicago. As a ghost story, it's additionally scary because it's set in a small, pretty average kind of American urban home, among a pleasant, ordinary young working class couple with a small child.

The small child is psychically gifted and communes with the ghost of a murdered teenage girl. Mom and Paw don't take too much notice; the kid's just chattering to himself. But then the husband is hypnotised by his witchy, drug-taking sister-in-law, who inadvertently opens a door in his mind, which lets him see the ghost too. And the ghost has a simple message: *DIG*. So he starts to dig up the back garden. He's convinced there are human remains there somewhere.

His sceptical wife becomes concerned by his weird behaviour and mood swings but it's no use. He's obsessed. But he can't find the body. There's nothing in the garden. Then the wife is called away with the child to her mother's funeral.

As a psychic thriller it's pretty good. I'm with those who prefer it to *The Sixth Sense*, with which it has various features in common.

The sub-text is interesting. The small child obviously represents the radical American historian Howard Zinn. He perceives the atrocious reality of which other eyes are ignorant. He speaks – but his voice is marginalised. But in time others come to appreciate the truth of his subversive insights. The drug taking radical sister-in-law opens up the mind of the husband, who represents the working class. He begins to seek out the truth of the society in which he lives (which is symbolised by the house). He begins *a radical interrogation of the structure*, using ever more powerful tools. The words 'Marxism-Leninism' are never mentioned, yet this is surely what powers *the deconstruction of the existing order*.

And when at last praxis and theory fuse – when an accurate analysis is confirmed by reality – the ruling class intervenes with violence to suppress the threat to the established order. The younger generation represents the US army, licensed to commit atrocities; the older generation represents their protectors, the administration. At this point the wife is forced into solidarity with the husband and obliged to use revolutionary violence to defend the fruits of the radical demolition of the social foundations.

In an interview in April 2001, the American crime novelist James Ellroy remarked:

> America itself as an entity was founded on a bedrock of racism, slavery, land-grabs and the slaughter of the indigenous people. That's it.

Stir of Echoes is about the radical recovery of that history by an enlightened proletariat.

Part Seven: Giving Up

Rimbaud

Very few writers give up. The trajectory of a literary career commonly involves discovery, success, the writing of the work for which the writer is remembered, and then a tailing off. Writers soldier on to the bitter end. Joseph Conrad went on turning out novels long after he'd lost the ability to create the sort of fiction for which he is nowadays remembered. Hemingway, after those impressive early works, went on to write excruciating tosh like *Across the River and into the Trees*.

Shakespeare gave up. But then he wrote for money. Having made enough for a comfortable retirement, he quit. He had no interest in writing as self-expression. The final part of his life was not devoted to *Shakespeare's Sonnets Reloaded*. If he'd needed the money he might have done it, but he didn't. Besides, *Shakespeare's Sonnets* were not a commercial success. There were no further editions in his lifetime. What the reading public preferred was raunchy stuff like *Venus and Adonis* and *Lucrece*. In his retirement, gardening and hawking would quite possibly have seemed a lot more interesting to Shakespeare than writing.

Rimbaud provides the exemplary case of a writer who packs it all in. What is even more astonishing than this case of a writer who quits is how early, in his case, it happened. Before his twenty-first birthday he had changed the course of French literary history. As Arthur Symons put it in his pioneering monograph *The Symbolist Movement in Literature* (1899):

> He catches at verse, at prose, invents a sort of *vers libre* before anyone else, not quite knowing what to do with it, invents a quite new way of writing prose, which Laforgue will turn to account later on; and having suggested, with some impatience, half the things that his own and the next generation are to busy themselves with developing, he gives up writing, as an inadequate form, to which he is also inadequate.

Rimbaud: modernist. His poetry finds a new space for literary attention: the commonplace and the everyday. Ham sandwiches. Beer. Farting. Head lice. But he also finds a new poetic language, with a place for everyday slang, everyday obscenity. His education taught him how to write Latin verse; his earliest poems mimic the famous (and now forgotten) French poets of his teenage years. Mysteriously, single-handedly, he becomes the originator of the modernist lyric.

But, as a modernist, he also doubts the enterprise. The solidity and linearity of conventional literatures seem fraudulent and false. The fragmentary beckons. In the prose poems, as Graham Hough once remarked, 'the firm outlines of pictorial presentation or narrative or logical sequence all disappear, and meaning arises uncertainly, through a film of unanalysable suggestion'. Or as Symons put it, 'he kneaded prose as he kneaded verse, making it a disarticulated, abstract, mathematically lyrical thing'.

In T. S. Eliot's 'East Coker' a voice, announcing that twenty years have passed ('largely wasted'), reflects on a difficult encounter with language:

Trying to learn to use words, and every attempt
Is a wholly new start, and a different kind of failure
Because one has only learnt to get the better of words
For the thing one no longer has to say, or the way in which
One is no longer disposed to say it.

The inner logic of modernism is silence. But whereas almost all modernists attempt to write about their engagement with that logic, seeking out 'a different kind of failure', Rimbaud accepted it. He gave up on literature. From the age of twenty-one he abandoned poetry and literary prose. From that time he neither wrote it nor read it. That vertiginous awareness seems to have required another kind of rejection, of both France and European society generally.

Rimbaud ended up in Africa. And the book to read about that is Charles Nicholl's *Somebody Else*. As an account of life after literature, it is far more compelling than a yarn-spinning novel. Rimbaud pared away everything from his past, including politics:

You send me the latest political news. If only you knew how little I care: for over two years now I haven't touched a newspaper. All those debates are incomprehensible to me now.

He spent years in Harar, in Somalia (or Somaliland), which Nicholls, who followed the Rimbaud trail, describes as 'a long way from anywhere'.

Rimbaud learned to speak fluent Arabic. He read the Koran. He reinvented himself as a trader – a man of practicalities. When an associate who had been back to France discovered that Rimbaud had once been a poet and had a growing reputation, he was astonished. When he confronted Rimbaud with the news, the ex-poet furiously replied, 'absurd, ridiculous, disgusting'. His writing was a thing of the distant past, an unpleasant memory.

The only writing that mattered to him now was concerned with specifics: data, geographical information, inventories. A portable theodolyte. A pocket-sized aneroid barometer. A surveyor's line. Purchase and retail prices, potential profit. The transport of 1,755 rifles and 750,000 rounds of ammunition.

Seizing the goods of a debtor, Rimbaud discovered that the man's widow had already disposed of the valuables. All that was left was worthless. It included 34 notebooks in which the man had written his memoirs. Rimbaud burned the lot. This he later regretted, having then learned that 'certain property deeds were shuffled in among these confessions'.

Illness forced Rimbaud back to France and a dismal ending. There were just two mourners at his graveside: his sister Isabelle and his mother. A fiction would end the narrative earlier than that, at the moment when Rimbaud crossed the lunar landscape of the obscure and remote salt lake of Assal, 500 feet below sea level. In the words of Nicholls,

> if Rimbaud's years in Africa seem like a flight from what he was – from Europe, from poetry, from himself – then it is surely here, on this desolate desert trek, that he reaches the furthest point of that arrow-flight, arriving at this utter privation, at this landscape of nothingness ...

Human lives are ragged and repetitious and lack the neat trajectories of those consoling fictions which, lacking novelty, involve dramatic climaxes and heart-warming resolutions.

To the End of Everything: Ann Quin's *Tripticks*

Ann Quin's final novel *Tripticks* (1972) hasn't attracted much in the way of attention, but then neither has the novelist herself. Currently, the available critical commentary is very small and the life is elusive. Quin died in the month of August 1973 but the specific day of her death is not identified in any published material that I've seen.

Her fiction, by the easygoing standards of today's corporate literary fiction, is 'difficult' and is now only available in American editions. On the face of it Ann Quin seems an attractive figure for a biography – the disturbed young female artist who commits suicide – but presumably poor sales and critical neglect have made a biography commercially unattractive, especially in the era of celebrity publishing. How could a Quin biography ever hope to sell as many copies as that of such an awesome cultural giant as Billie Piper?

This is unfortunate, as with every year that passes the chances of finding witnesses to Quin's life diminish. The absence of a biography is particularly frustrating as her writing seems to have been energised by themes of sexuality and power which were rooted in personal experience.

Although not a Catholic, Quin was educated at the Convent of the Blessed Sacrament in Brighton – an experience which she hated and which evidently marked her for life. In a rare interview she described its impact:

> A ritualistic culture that gave me a conscience. A death wish and a sense of sin. Also a great lust to find out, experience what evil really was.

No coincidence that the last two words of *Tripticks* are 'The Inquisition'. Authority and language, for Quin, are always entangled with religion, sexuality, punishment and power.

Quin's continuing neglect indicts not just corporate publishing but British literary culture as a whole. No contemporary British writers apart from Stewart Home and Lee Rourke seem ever to have shown any enthusiasm for her work, and I'm not aware of any British academic interest, even though there are hundreds of people out there employed to teach modern fiction, publishing innumerable articles and books on the topic. The situation is not helped by the fact that the major Quin manuscript collection (papers, manuscripts and publishers' correspondence) is held at the University of Indiana.

One of the very few critics to respond to Quin's work is the American critic Philip Stevick, in his essay 'Voices in the Head: Style and Consciousness in the Fiction of Ann Quin' in *Breaking the Sequence: Women's Experimental Fiction* (ed. Ellen G. Friedman and Miriam Fuchs, Princeton University Press, 1989). Stevick usefully draws attention to three aspects of Quin's writing which doubtless account for resistance to her work: the instability of the narrative voice/s, a narrow, ahistorical focus on the inner turbulence of a self in conflict with others, and indifference to storytelling and the manipulated patterns of a plot.

The lengthiest essay on Quin that I've managed to find is the one by Judith Mackrell in Jay L. Halio (ed.), *Dictionary of Literary Biography, Vol. 14, British Novelists Since 1960*, Part 2 (Detroit, 1983), which I went to the British Library to read. *Tripticks* describes the narrator protagonist's trip across the USA, which occurs ostensibly while being followed by the first of his three ex-wives and her young lover. Mackrell says

> During his journey, the series of bizarre incidents that occur and fantasies he experiences are juxtaposed with flashbacks from the past, all of which have a dual purpose. On the one hand, they reveal the hero's erotic obsessions and paranoia; on the other hand, they satirize, either through style or theme, some aspect of American culture.

These are the two polarities of the novel – a fractured sensibility engaging with – or overwhelmed by – American reality.

The cover of the first edition (Calder and Boyars, 1972) privileges some aspects of this narrative friction. It consists of three partitioned vertical panels beneath the title *TRIPTICKS*, printed in red inside a wavy frame, in a font suggesting a blur of speed. At the top of the first panel on the left is the sketch (in black and white in a black frame with a shadow effect suggesting depth) of the back of a man's head – that of the mysterious narrator, presumably. Below it is a drawing of what looks like a falling raindrop, in scarlet, on a white background. Beneath that, forming the base of the panel, are the words *Nipples completely bitten off* above another raindrop.

The central panel is split in two. The top panel consists of three scarlet falling drops. The shorter base panel contains the words *She* undid her leather bikini.

The final panel begins with a single falling drop, beneath which is the sketch of the upper torso of a woman with her face blanked out by a white rectangle. This, presumably, is the narrator's 'Number 1 X-wife'. The sketch is contained within a thin frame above which are the words *Lashed together with rawhide*. The base panel is blank, apart from the words *a novel by ANN QUIN drawings by C. ANNAND*

The three quotations indicate that this is a novel which is interested in sexuality. The first one suggests extreme violence with a sexual dimension, the second one a prelude to consensual sex, and the third bondage. But these teasing fragments also evoke the language of sensation. 'Nipples completely bitten off' might come from a newspaper report of a shocking crime. 'She undid her leather bikini' could be found in pornography or the sex scene in a popular novel. 'Lashed together with rawhide' evokes tying someone up, either in a western or in sadomasochistic activity. *Tripticks* is not simply interested in these subjects. It is also interested in how they are represented.

As for those red drops of falling rain. They could be so much else. Tears of grief or rage. Dripping blood, perhaps. Drops of lysergic acid or LSD – an hallucinogen used to take people on trips through inner space. (Drugs are a theme in *Tripticks* and we hear of 'amphetamine trips'.) And inside each identical drop is an identical tick. 'Tick' in the sense of 'small mark'.

Tripticks is an inventory, every item duly noted. And the opposite of a tick is an 'X'. And this is a novel of three ex-wives (or X-wives). A tick is also a parasite or, figuratively, 'an unpleasant or despicable person'. *Tripticks* is over-populated with such types. We ask what makes a person tick. A trip into the mind supplies possible answers. But to trip is also, sometimes, to fall.

Most obviously, *Tripticks* puns on the word 'triptych', a painting done on three panels. Alluding to the narrator's memories of three X-wives. Although Quin, whose second novel is *Three* and whose third novel *Passages* includes three narratives, was always obsessed with clusters of three. At its simplest: three characters. Three competing perspectives.

Tripticks is not so much an anti-novel as what I'd call counter-fiction. Anti-novels can often be hugely entertaining and readable (*The Life and Opinions of Tristram Shandy, Gentleman*, say, or *The*

French Lieutenant's Woman). But *Tripticks* declines to entertain. It refuses to conform at every level to orthodox readerly expectation of what a novel should be or might be. Its form offends the eye. Most obviously, as a novel with illustrations. But in other ways as well.

John Calder's cheapskate production values serve a useful aesthetic function in *Tripticks*. The book has a crude, coarse appearance. The font is ugly. The text is ragged and shapeless – the technical term for which is 'unjustified'. And Quin is not interested in supplying justification for her characters and what they do. The text is fractured, short blocks of prose which end in lists, or turn into verse, or snap shut in the face of a void, a gap, a fissure.

As for those illustrations, some seem to have been photocopied out of books or newspapers. Most are original line-drawings. But they are fairly crude and not particularly original. Some are reminiscent of the work of pop artist Roy Lichenstein. One or two seem to have their origins in Magritte's work. They have a second-hand, second-rate quality. They show figures, faces, American scenes. But they are either cropped or incomplete. They flaunt their inadequacy as illustrations. They do and do not illustrate.

The first sentence of *Berg* throws down the gauntlet to *Brighton Rock*. The first sentence of *Tripticks* nods in the direction of *Moby-Dick*: 'I have many names. Many faces.' Identity fractures, overwhelmed by memory, fantasy, the lurid, *ersatz* quality of American reality. It's the narrative style Joan Schuman in *Tucson Weekly* (21 February 2002) calls 'multi-voice staging; sentences begin and end indeterminately, making the reading a delicious, slow, confounding process'.

Tripticks has sometimes been hailed as satire, but true satire is informed by rage and a sense of something better. *Tripticks* mocks, but the mockery has an exhausted, apathetic feel. Depletion is the word that comes most often to mind reading the book. An epic journey begins – but it ends nowhere. The human drama fizzles out, catches fire, then fizzles out again. Repeatedly.

The narrator anticipates his end in cinematic terms:

> I saw their car off to the right. But I could see no sign of either my X-wife or her lover. Hiding perhaps in the back, the gun loaded, waiting, ready to leap out. The bloody ending as inevitable as the climax of a Greek tragedy.
>
> A cinematic ending.

But though the narrator visualizes high drama, the narrative invests no energy in recreating one. It is animated by flickering images without depth – some 'real', some surreal, some cinematic or theatrical. The entire book is 'A hotbed of unrest'. It's hard to pin down. The reader is overwhelmed by narrative possibilities which raise themselves, then fizzle out.

Whoever wrote the explanatory blurb at the start of the book seems overwhelmed too. The reader is informed that *Tripticks* is about a 'strange network of convoluted interpersonal relationships' involving the narrator, his in-laws, 'plus an assortment of three pepped-up, freaked-out culturally-confused X-wives, the weird, zonked Nightripper and a retinue of bizarre aunts, mothers, retainers etc.'.

That terminal 'etc.' attempts to put a stopper on a narrative that won't stop flowing in all directions. It submits to every reader's instinct to make sense of narrative by explaining it with a short description. It's what readers, reviewers and blurb writers all do: they say what a novel is 'about', before going on to evaluate its merits. But attempting to summarise *Tripticks* is like attempting to summarise *Tristram Shandy* or *Finnegans Wake*. The text wriggles free of any attempt at confinement.

This blurb is reproduced on the dustjacket, with additional material:

> This, her fourth novel, is a riotous spoof on the evasive, hypocritical and maladjusted inter-familial relationships engendered by a society which has been overtaken by the mechanisms of its own development. The staccato superimposition of image upon image recreates, with the flickering fascination of a home movie, a society gone mad – a society in which cars are more important than legs, drugs than peace of mind, and success more important than anything. Read this and you'll never be able to look at America with a straight face again!

But that final tired sentence replicates the kind of text which *Tripticks* confronts. It's a novel of image and information overload, but the images and the information lack depth or meaning. It replicates a condition of modernity which hasn't dated. When I look around me I see people sealed in one-ton metal bubbles. I see bipeds in the street with white wire emerging from their ears. I watch others shouting into plastic wafers. There's teevee, games consoles, the internet, newspapers, CDs, DVDs, the news, music, interviews with celebrities, cookery programmes, charity events, festivals. *Information overload.*

But where does this all end?

In *Tripticks* it ends with the narrator retreating into a church. But the calm of that place allows only 'a space before the scream inside' – an explosive Munch-like scream combining alienation, revulsion and an acute, claustrophobic sense of oppression.

> I opened my mouth. But no words. Only the words of others I saw, like ads, texts, psalms, from those who had attempted to persuade me into their systems. A power I did not want to possess. The Inquisition.

The narrator gives up and becomes mute. Words and writing are associated with power and persuasion. The systems which are rejected are capitalism and religion but also writing. Persuasion is somehow bound up with oppression: language is a device for interrogation but interrogation can also result in punishment. Language is itself punishing and oppressive. So, by implication, is literature.

Tripticks not only confronts and resists the dominant discourse – the texts of America – it also resists the condition of modern fiction. It declines to offer consolations and satisfactions. As *a good read* it doesn't work. It ends in obscurity and silence.

Ann Quin seems to renounce fiction in her final published novel. She gave up on the aspiration to fail again, fail better. Her suicide the year after *Tripticks* was published seems humanly consistent with the last page of the novel.

Tripticks ends not with language but with drawings. On the last page, after the final words, are six small framed sketches. One shows a hilly rural landscape, five show a mysterious exotic building with a balcony. Two of these sketches include a tower like a phallus. These landscapes are empty. They could almost be storyboards for a strange surreal movie.

In one, the sky is scored with four vertical lines, as if marking the descending passage of someone who has just jumped from the balcony to the ground far below.

The End.

www.ingramcontent.com/pod-product-compliance
Lightning Source LLC
Chambersburg PA
CBHW051754040426
42446CB00007B/363